Herbert Wright

INSTANT CITIES

black dog
publishing
london uk

06
INTRODUCTION

INTRODUCTION

Ever since the Archigram group took on the notion of the instant city in the 1960s the concept has been reinterpreted by architects, developers, artists, designers and filmmakers alike; producing results that are both inspiring and disparaging in equal measure. Archigram conceived of their project, *Instant City*, as a technological event, whose mobility would allow it to travel to underdeveloped towns and cities, as an attempt to 'advance' such places. The project embraced the aesthetics of advertising and popular culture and deliberately intended to overstimulate the user of the *Instant City* with the imagery and iconography of the media. Since then the term "instant city" has often come to signify those cities that bring dramatic change in the wake of their construction or evolution. However, the instant city began to emerge long before Archigram conceived of their project in the 1960s.

Nowadays, we commonly understand a city to be an urban settlement with a large population. Uruk, the first settlement generally considered to be a city, and established only 6,000 years ago, shares a lot of the characteristics associated with more recent cities—it become a walled administrative, trading and religious capital with a complex cosmopolitan culture, and its population may have reached 80,000. The Tokyo-Yokohama conurbation, currently the world's largest city, comprises over 34 million—almost three times the entire world population in Uruk's time.

In practical terms anything referred to as 'instant' comes about very quickly. It may take just a few minutes to make an instant coffee, for example. Cities, of course, do not emerge in minutes, even theoretical ones, although they can be encountered instantly (arriving on Midtown's Eighth Avenue after taking the New York subway A train from JFK is a dramatic example). Nevertheless, minutes serve as a measure for how fast cities are growing. Using figures from Demographia's list of urban populations and growth, the average time it takes for Delhi or Lagos to gain one new inhabitant is just over a minute, while Jakarta's is only 55 seconds.[1]

But the term "instant city" should not be taken too literally. In *Instant Cities*, it is an umbrella for diverse urban phenomena, coming at a unique time in the city's development. Over half of the world's six billion inhabitants live in cities, and by mid-century, three-quarters of the projected world population nine billion will. Humanity at the start of the third millennium is immersed in three phenomena that define our lives: urban environment, globalisation and immediacy. The Canadian media theorist, Marshall McLuhan, predicted that electronic communications would create a "global village", a term he used in his 1962 book *The Gutenberg Galaxy*. He spelt out what this means to the city in his most famous book, *The Medium is the Message*: "The circuited city of the future will not be the huge hunk of concentrated real estate created by the railway. It will take on a totally new meaning under conditions of very rapid movement. It will be an information megalopolis."[2] In 2007, 550 mobile phones, and an estimated 1.24 billion internet users, accelerate the spread of this information megalopolis. Many predicted that electronic media would disperse the city via the mechanism of home-working, but the trend is the opposite—cities are growing in size and density. McLuhan's global village is not just instantaneously connected across the planet, it has turned out to be urban. Even in the remotest areas and the most traditional societies, ideas and products forged in the city drive social and material change in people's lives.

To assess the 'instant city', we need to range from the exploding megacities of developing countries to the constant re-engineering of wealthy cityscapes, from concepts of cities in design and fiction to the realities of the built environment, and from socialist ideas about the city of a century ago to today's sustainable aspirations for this century. *Instant Cities* explores these issues by considering the play of opposites—how cities develop by organic growth or conscious planning; the concepts of ideal urbanisms or utopias, as opposed to the dystopias that have existed and exist in many modern and contemporary cities; the city of the imagination and its interaction with reality; the morphology of the city, and the conflict between compact centres and urban sprawl; the role of movement in what is, essentially, a stationary built environment; the question of the city's 'character', where global forces interact with local identity; and finally, the conflict that plays itself out in the city, between humanity's activity and the well-being of the planet.

Of course, the city is more than just configurations of buildings and infrastructure—it is also the ways in which humanity occupies it. The exchange of ideas and goods underlies civilisation, and their marketplaces are the city. This makes the city not just the most compelling environment to live in, but essential to understand.

Instant Cities is divided into seven loosely themed sections, all of which explore the nature and characteristics of the instant city as it stands today. Each section is informed by selected case studies and previously published text, both of which are intended to reveal the complexities inherent in the city in more detail.

"Growth/Masterplan" traces those cities whose planning, and more recently whose construction, appears to take place very rapidly. It spans references to some of man's earliest settlements, whose plans are seemingly archaic by today's standards, to the new towns of the nineteenth to the twenty-first century whose very construction was perceived by their planners as a solution to the negative aspects of urban living. Similarly covered in this section are those cities whose growth is unprecendented—Shenzhen and other such cities in China and elsewhere—whose planners find it difficult to keep pace with the demand necessitated by rapid expansions in population, and the slums of the developing world where no 'planning' appears to have taken place (revealing some of them, however, to be complex sites of organisation in their own right). The case studies in this section discuss the cities of Abuja, Astana and Kinshasa in detail, while Alexander D'Hooghe's essay "Siberia as Analogous Territory" examines the acceleration of masterplanning in Siberia through two case studies, Akademgorodok and Bio-Akademgorodok and the ability evidenced by these of planners to reconcile the opposing paradigms of the Soviet coloniser and the scientific community already existing there.

"Utopia/Dystopia" explores those seemingly idealistic visions of the future city and the sad reality of many such visions as they moved to becoming more 'dystopia' than 'utopia' in their evolution, citing such references as Marx, the Situationists, the Industrial Towns as proposed by Cadbury, WH Lever, in towns such as Pullman, Chicago, the New Urbanist vision of communities like Seaside, California—which would later be satirised in the film, *The Truman Show*—and works by Le Corbusier. The examples of Cumbernauld, Dhavari and Thames Town are discussed in detail here, while Shumon Basar's essay "12 Ultimate Critical Steps to Sudden Urban Success" appropriates the concept of 'self help' in relation to the country of Dubai, in an attempt to outline the key points a city must adhere to, to be utopian.

The next section, "Fantasy/Reality", also ties in with visions of utopia, but here fantastical and all-encompassing cities are perceived, as it were, in an instant: the most iconic being those presented by the films *Metropolis*, *Bladerunner*, and *The Fifth Element*. This section also looks at how the city of fantasy has influenced real cities, as evidenced in the work of Archigram, the Metabolists and in Buckminster Fuller's geodesic domes. In this section "The Explosion of Space: Architecture and the Filmic Imaginary", by Anthony Vidler, explores the use of the city in films as a site of horror, for "psycho-spaces", the seduction of the street through the figure of the *flâneur* and more broadly the shifts in the relationship between architects, the architecture of the city and its representation on the screen. The case studies in this section pay particular attention to the fantastical cities to be found in the virtual world of Second Life and the work of the Metabolists.

"Nuclear/Distributed" addresses how rapid growth culminates in the cityscape, pointing toward the phenomena of the Central Business District as a major site of importance and the proliferation of 'culture' magnets, such as the Walt Disney Hall and the Guggenheim Museum in Bilbao, which become central focal points around which other new developments are rapidly built. It also examines how shopping malls can serve a similar purpose, encouraging not only the urban (or suburban) growth of larger developments in the vicinity, but also how similar developments occur along transport networks, which themselves become the focus of activity. This section also explores those cities that appear to grow on the periphery of other environments, such as Joel Garreau's 'Edge Cities', and the 'hyper-dense' cities informed by upward, rather than outward, expansion. Here, the case studies look at the examples of Atlanta, Moscow City and Stapleton. Edward Soja's essay "Exopolis: The Restructuring of the Urban Form" concentrates on Los Angeles as an example of urban sprawl that is, seemingly, without boundaries.

"Nomadic/Rooted" looks at shifting communities, such as the Bedouins in the Arabian Desert, refugee camps with their complex systems of organisation and hierarchy, and at that technological enabler of nomadism and movement—the car—as well as other modes of transport that have shaped the cities in which we live. The case studies in this section look at two of the most innovative enablers of transport today, Beijing's Terminal 3 Airport and the Dubai Metro, while Manuel Herz' essay "Somali Refugees in Eastleigh, Nairobi" takes as its subject the diaspora of refugees in the suburb of Eastleigh, Nairobi, an area whose structure and function has impacted greatly on its surrounding suburbs.

"Global/Local" explores how cities can operate both on global and local levels, and cites such examples as those cities in the developing world which appear to adopt a Western urban aesthetic. Looking at psychogeography and the way in which it focuses on particular, rather than generic, aspects of a city, this section further considers communities within communities, such as those that temporarily sprung up at Woodstock in the 1960s, or locales such as Chinatowns, where more-or-less self-sufficient communities are settled. We then move on to look at the phenomena of world or global cities and all that they have come to encompass, as well as how they have increasingly become defined by technology. The case studies in this section cite New Songdo City and Tokyo as exemplars of 'green' planning while, taking Hungary as a starting point, Laszló Rajk's "(De)construction in (Post) socialist Europe: Continuous and Variable Use of Spaces and Methods" examines how signifiers of 'local' architecture are incorporated into new structures that speak more 'globally' to their audience and users.

Finally, "Humanity/Environment" looks at the ever-increasing concern of architects and developers to create buildings, environments and entire cities that are both sustainable and may counteract some of the devastating consequences projected to come into effect as a result of climate change. In so doing, this section begins to set out what we can expect the cities of the future to look like. Here, iconic 'eco-buildings' are discussed along with one of the earliest proposals for an entire 'eco-city', Arcosanti, by Italian-American architect, Paolo Soleri, some of whose principles would later be made manifest in the zero-energy proposals for the city of Dongtan in China. The case studies in this section discuss Arcosanti and Rizhao in further detail. "Elevation Five and the Future of Green", by Peter Clegg, explores sustainable design by taking examples from revolutionary public transport and the urbanism and architecture of Curitiba, Brazil, and Freiburg, Germany, as well work by the architect John Miller.

In all of this *Instant Cities* documents the changing nature of the built environment in an effort to determine how today's rapidly-forming new settlements sit in relation to various ideas throughout history, from ancient civilisations to Renaissance 'ideal cities', through to the industrial and the modern cities of the nineteenth and twenty-first centuries. By looking at the phenomenal growth of the built environment from multiple perspectives, *Instant Cities* attempts to further contribute to our understanding of how today's city is changing, and what it might some day become.

1. Demographia World Urban Areas Projections 2007
and 2020, March 2007.
2. McLuhan, Marshall, and Quentin Fiore, *The Medium
is the Message*, New York: Random House, 1967.

GROWTH |

MASTERPLAN

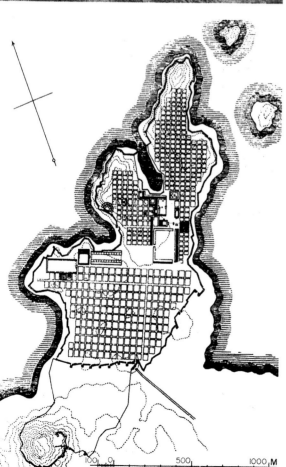

While an architectural design defines a building before it comes to fruition, a masterplan deals with a much wider built environment. Masterplans are employed to solve problems such as congestion or a perceived lack in allocated public space—problems that often result from the unstructured growth that occurs as such areas expand to accommodate a growing population. Masterplanning is a multi-disciplinary practice, drawing on fields as wide-ranging as town planning, architecture, landscape design or enviro-economics. Much of the history of the city has resulted from the rise of the urban masterplan and its endless struggles against spontaneous, unplanned growth.

This section offers a brief survey of urban growth, and how different approaches to its conception have been received. Taking up discussions current in architectural theory, it offers an analysis of three main types of urban settlement: the 'new town', so-called "megacities" and the informal settlements of the developing world.

One of the earliest settlements in existence is purported to be the ancient town of Çatalhöyük, Turkey, which was discovered by modern archaeologists in 1958 and dates from around 7500 BC. Consisting of predominantly domestic buildings, the site had no obvious public spaces to speak of, and while some dwellings housed elaborate murals typical of public buildings, the original function of such structures is not clear. With over 10,000 inhabitants, it is surprising that the maze-like configuration of Çatalhöyük's residential fabric had no pathways or streets to divide the settlement.

For millennia, such organic, unplanned characteristics defined the city's structure and location. As great civilisations arose, however, such formations came to be planned more stringently, with city planners seeking to tame chaotic growth in favour of military or socially inspired masterplans. Dinocrates of Rhodes devised the plan for Alexandria in the fourth century BC, which is perhaps the earliest known example of a 'planned city'. Conceived to rival Naucractis as the Hellenistic centre of Egypt and to serve as a link between the Nile and Greece, Alexandria became one of the largest cities in the world in just 100 years—no mean feat in the fourth century. Its 'planning' became manifest in the three sections into which it was divided; Brucheum (the Greek or Royal quarter, which was later expanded to include a fourth quarter), the Jewish quarter and Rhakotis (the Egyptian quarter). The city was made up of various parallel streets and there were two main promenades, lined with arcades, which led to the city centre where the Mausoleum of Alexander was located.

Alexandria's planning focused largely on the interconnection of important sites rather than the built environment as a whole. In time, however, architects would broaden their scope to encompass the wider urban environment. Christopher Wren's masterplan for London after the Great Fire of 1666 is one example, a proposal that would have seen London reconfigured into a rational grid that ignored all existing roads and land ownership. Unfortunately,

Engraved for Harrison's History of London.

S.ʳ Christopher Wren's Plan for Rebuilding the City of London after the dreadful Conflagration in 1666.

A Scale of 880 Yards or ½ a Mile.

* * *the part of the above Plan faintly shaded shews the extent of the Fire.*

perhaps, it was never realised, as the Corporation of London did not have the finances, nor the vision, to implement it (or any other plans that were put forward by Wren's contemporaries) and the old street pattern remained, with only minor improvements and rebuilding taking place. Other capital cities created or re-engineered in this manner include: Peter the Great's St Petersburg, 1703, the capital of Russia for more than 200 years and still one of the country's largest cities; Pierre Charles d'Enfant's Washington DC, 1791, comprising large, avenues and streets radiating out from key transport zones, public spaces and buildings, as well as a diamond-shaped 'federal district' almost 16 square kilometres; Baron Georges-Eugène Haussmann's Paris, 1853, which saw Haussmann widely criticised for his aggressive removal of many of the city's Medieval streets and their replacement with large boulevards, and for his various restrictions on building facades and city facilities. More recently, Lucio Costa's Brasilia, 1964, which is widely accredited with following the principles of the Athens Charter of 1933 to the letter, created distinct zones for living, recreation, working and circulation.[1] Finally, the Nigerian government's 1970s Abuja, developed by International Planning Associates (the American consultantancy firm established by Vally Koveryand), was also divided into separate districts for living and working. All these cities are examples of political regimes made geographically manifest. However, when such regimes end, so can the cities they have engendered. Such was Albert Speer's Welthauptstadt Germania Berlin, 1936, the 'world city' envisioned by Adolf Hitler for Berlin, of which only a small proportion was realised before the end of the Second World War. Contemporary masterplans now rarely preserve political authority and, generally, focus more on creating better living conditions for the inhabitants of a city. In recent years, the private sector has come to the fore as the largest producer of masterplans; more of which are being proposed and built than ever before. However, when compared to the spread of unplanned urban growth, they cover only a tiny fraction of the Earth's surface.

Opposite top: Çatalhöyük, Turkey, thought to be one of the oldest known settlements. The entire site comprises mostly domestic buildings, with little evidence of any public spaces or structures. As there were no streets or alleys to speak of it is thought that Çatalhöyük's inhabitants used the roofs of their homes to navigate the city.

Opposite bottom: Miletus, an ancient city in Western Anatolia. It is renowned for its grid-like layout which would later form the basis of town planning in a large number of Roman cities.

Above: Christopher Wren's Plan for rebuilding the city of London after the Great Fire of London in 1666.

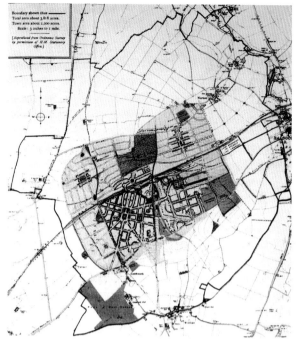

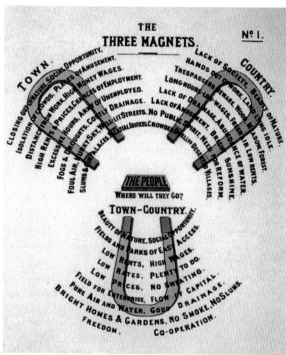

Top: Barry Parker and Raymond Unwin's First Plan for Letchworth, 1904. Founded in 1903, Letchworth was the world's first Garden City and had a profound impact on the planning of future New Towns. Located in Hertfordshire, England, it was projected to have a population of approximatively 34,000.

Bottom: The Three Magnets diagram, in Ebenezer Howard, *To-Morrow: a Peaceful Path to Real Reform,* 1898. Howard's book called for the creation of towns that would unite the advantages of city life with the pleasures of the countryside.

Opposite: Patrick Abercrombie, *The County of London Plan,* 1943. Here the plan of London has been divided into marked residential areas, the purpose of which was to identify those areas with a "high proportion of obscolescent property", in relation to others that were used with more regularity.

NEW TOWNS

While Wren, d'Enfant, Haussman and Costa focused on masterplans of more epic proportions, there were others who took it upon themselves to address the structure of these cities' outlying towns and villages, and their relationship to one another, in what would eventually become known as the development of 'New Towns'. While many associate the concept of the New Town with the Garden Cities of Ebenezer Howard, some of the earliest examples of such planning date back as far as the Medieval period. A result of the growth in population in the years between 1000 and 1350 AD, many 'new towns' arose whose constituent parts were carefully planned streets and public spaces (such as markets) all of which served to strengthen the links between the centre and outlying domestic areas. While this growth was often perceived as organic, the organisation of such towns can still be discerned in their present incarnation, particularly in the structure of such English church towns as Canterbury, York and Bath. Similar principles were put into practice in North America, within such colonial settlements as Savannah, Georgia. One of the last British capitals to be established in America, city plans at the time of its inception (in the early 1700s) clearly show a pattern of connected streets, and municipal squares as devised by its architect, General James Edward Oglethorpe.

Back on British soil, the appalling conditions of the poor in London in the nineteenth century gave rise to early plans for idealistic, self-sufficient towns, notably Ebenezer Howard's Garden Cities, which sought to integrate the best elements of the city and countryside. Howard's concept of the Garden City first came to attention in the publication *ToMorrow: A Peaceful Path to Real Reform,* 1898 (which would later be republished as *Garden Cities of To-Morrow,* 1902), in which he offered a possible solution to the problems of city living. Howard posited a new kind of planned town, one that offered its inhabitants all the advantages of city living (such as employment and entertainment) as well as the benefits proferred by the country (fresh air, natural beauty and the like). Howard founded the Garden Cities Association in 1899 and, shortly after, his Garden Cities began to proliferate in Britain, notably Letchworth Garden City and Welwyn Garden City. Howard's ideas were to influence the work of many architects, including Hermann Muthesius and Bruno Taut during the Weimar period, along with many subsequent garden cities; notably Hampstead Garden Suburb and Brentham Garden Suburb in Britain and Virginia's Hilton Village and Pittsburgh's Chatham Village in America. Howard's vision of the Garden City is epitomised by the 'three magnets' diagram, which shows 'the people' (followed by the question "where will they go?") in the centre of three magnets; 'town', 'country' and 'town-country'. Town-country is an amalgamation of the pros of both town and city—low rents, high wages, plenty to do—while dispensing with the cons—excessive hours, fogs, droughts, isolation from crowds, lack of society or lack of amusement. After the Second World War, Howard's vision was appropriated by the British government, who were seeking to address the ever-growing population in London (which had peaked at 8.6 million in 1939) and in other British cities (which were still characterised by large families occupying small living spaces with shared sanitation and kitchens). A possible resolution

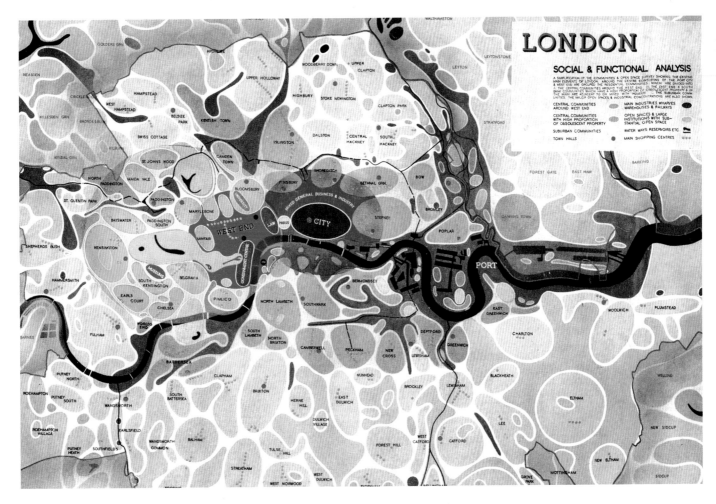

was produced in 1944 by urban planner, Patrick Abercrombie, in the form of the *County of London Plan*, 1943, and the *Greater London Regional Plan*, 1944. The plans were prepared for the London County Council and proposed to address such issues as traffic congestion, urban sprawl and inadequate housing by constructing a number of ring roads around the city to preserve the surrounding countryside and to avoid the sub-urbanisation of the New Towns beyond.

Elsewhere in Britain, towns such as East Kilbride and Cumbernauld would foster the ethos of Howard's Garden Cities. Located in the southeastern suburbs of Glasgow, East Kilbride was one of the first of such towns to rise to prominence in the 1940s. Initially a small settlement in the Lanarkshire countryside, East Kilbride was allocated as one of five sites for the Scottish New Towns proposed by the Greater Glasgow Regional Plan in 1946. The Plan intended to house many of those working in the city of Glasgow, where bomb damage had greatly limited the amount of living space, into nearby towns and villages. East Kilbride is divided into several precincts, each with local shops, schools and community facilities, all of which are divided from the town 'centre' by a ring road. As evidence of its success, East Kilbride is one of the largest towns in Scotland, and continues to grow: further additions to the town centre include a new arts centre, theatre, museum and town square. Where East Kilbride has been heralded as a success, Cumbernauld's reception has been somewhat disparaging and it is largely derided by the inhabitants of its outlying precincts for not providing easy access to the commercial centre or suitable facilities for its residents

The second wave of New Towns in Britain offer less monotonous built environments. The best example is Milton Keynes, which was formally designated a New Town in 1967, encompassing Wolverton, Stoney Stratford and Bletchley as well as many small villages in-between. The town's architects incorporated variety into the town centre with crisp, steel-and-glass architecture, and into neighbourhood housing through the use of differing styles for domestic buildings.

Plan of Savannah, 1734, General James Edward Oglethorpe. Located in Georgia, America, the city was founded in 1733. Its repeated geometric patterns and unparalleld open spaces make it one of the most significant achievements in the history of town planning.

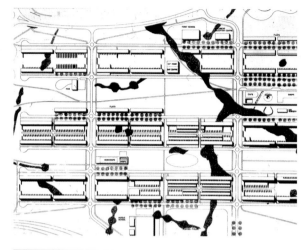

The diversification of architecture in the centre continues, with examples ranging from the 'neo classical' Ecumenical Church to the modern Milton Keynes Gallery.

New Towns certainly contributed to the post-war decline of city populations. However, the economies of these towns, as well as older country towns, are still dependent on such cities, evidenced by the volume of people who still commute from the former to the latter. In Britain, the new towns in the Southeast were, effectively, another wave of London's suburban expansion, rather than being decentralised populations that bypassed the greenbelt into commuter towns. (Tony Travers labelled this extension of London as the "Greater Southeast"; an integrated urban economic unit, which now has a population of approximately 20 million).[2] Meanwhile, London's population has bounced back since 1988s low of 6.7 million, and is expected to reach eight million by 2016. Areas beyond London's greenbelt have also consistently expanded, and of the British government's three million new homes target, set in 2007 for 2020, the majority will be situated in the Greater Southeast. The largest government-sponsored plan in Britain is the Thames Gateway, whose redevelopment will take place along the eastern section of the Thames Estuary. As recently as 2008, no less than four of 15 proposals for new British towns (of which ten will be approved) were in counties adjacent to London. Planned decentralisation can be seen, then, as merely perpetuating unplanned urban spread.

TOO BUSY TO PLAN

While Milton Keynes may be Europe's largest post-war New Town, having grown from a population of 40,000 in 1967, to approximately 220,000 in 2006, this hardly compares to the world's largest city, Shenzhen. Shenzhen is a city that has become synonymous with the term "megacity". Commonly used to describe metropolitan areas whose total population exceeds ten million, megacities are distinguishable (from global cities) by rapid growth, spatial density, informal economics and social fragmentation, often composed of more than one metropolitan area conflated into a connected built environment.

Shenzhen certainly epitomises all these qualities. Once a meagre fishing village, its official population peaked at eight million in 2005. This figure did not account for its unregistered inhabitants, and is now reckoned to be a conurbation of about 12 million 'residents'.

Such growth is symptomatic of China's ever-expanding economy as a whole. Deng Xiaoping, the late leader of the Communist Party of China, kick-started the country's economic boom in the 1970s and 80s by establishing Special Economic Zones (SEZs), that lifted restraints on development and aimed to attract foreign investment. The first SEZs were established in Guangdong Province. Shenzhen was officially made a SEZ in 1980. Its meteoric rise finds parallels in the growth of Tokyo during Japan's post-war industrial boom, when it expanded in population—at five per cent annually—from six million in 1949 to 10.2 million by 1962. In contrast, Shenzhen's population started from a rural

base and grew at over 12 per cent annually in the 1980s and 90s. Shenzhen's growth is intractably linked to Hong Kong, which is just across the Sham Chun and Sha Tau Kok Rivers. Much of its built environment has been developed by Hong Kong investors, who exploit the lower labour and land costs to effectively make it—and the wider Pearl River Delta region beyond—an extension of itself. As such, Hong Kong-Shenzhen can be considered an integrated urban economic unit, with a combined population of almost 20 million—putting it on a par with the most economically dynamic cities of the world.

In 1996, Shenzhen's showcase Shun Hing Square development, designed by Hong Kong-based Thomas KY Cheung, became the world's fourth tallest skyscraper project at 384 metres and 69 storeys. According to Nancy Lin, in *The Great Leap Forward*, the incredible pace of building in Shenzhen is clearly demonstrated by the 41 per cent average annual rise in construction between 1979 and 1994.[3] In the 1990s, the whole Pearl River Delta had an accelerated programme of projects—bigger factories, more residential complexes and offices, airports, railway stations and roads—than ever before seen in China, all planned and built at breakneck speed.

While Shenzhen thrived in the 1990s, much of what was built during this time was later designated as possessing at least one of 'The Five Lacks'—design, drawings, permits, construction supervision and reports. Housing and infrastructure were built as cheaply as possible, throwing up unauthorised and overcrowded residential blocks, inhabited by people that were not legally allowed to live there. In the public sector, funds for construction were limited, new hospitals were soon overwhelmed and electricity and sewage treatment demand constantly outpaced new plant capacity. Shenzhen, like much of urban China, continues to grow organically. However, because economic growth in this area is robust (and is currently expanding at a rate quicker than population growth) urban design and planning is now more viable, bringing the potential of a structured consolidation

of living and building standards within reach. This is not necessarily the case in the rapidly-expanding 'megacities' located in other parts of the world.

SLUM CITY

Traditional slums are commonly understood as high-density, unsanitised and polluted neighbourhoods where poverty is concentrated; exemplified by London's East End or Glasgow's Gorbals during the Victorian era. Today, slums abound like never before, both in the developed and developing world. The global urban population is due to reach five billion by 2030, four billion of whom will live in the developing world. As urban planning fails to keep up with such growth, this is where the large proportion of slums will arise. This does not bode well for the new megacities expected to emerge by 2020—Delhi, Jakarta, Lagos, Mumbai, Manilla, Mexico City and São Paulo. It is in these areas where 95 per cent of urban expansion is currently localised, according to the Nairobi-based UN Human Settlements Programme agency UN-HABITAT. The organisation has also calculated that, in 2005, 998 million people lived in slums, based on criteria such as durable housing, personal living area, access to clean water and sanitation and property tenure.[4] Most slum-dwellers were in South Asia (276 million) and East Asia (212 million), where slums are expanding at just over two per cent annually. However, it is in Sub-Saharan Africa, where 200 million slum-dwellers are increasing at a phenomenal rate of 4.5 per cent annually, that the most dramatic increases of such 'communities' are projected to take place.

Some of these slums such as Mumbai's Dharavi have roots deeply embedded in the urban fabric, but most are new, especially the shanty towns that materialise as the rural poor migrate to the city in huge numbers. Many of these new shanty towns proliferated in the 1970s and 80s as a result—as Mike Davis, in *Planet of Slums,* claims—of the policies imposed by the World Bank and IMF to address developing world debt; forcing a withdrawal of public services, privatisation and a drive to grow cash (rather than subsistence) crops.[5] The exodus from the countryside that drives slum expansion is not just a result of such schemes, but also due to the disenfranchisement of agriculture by persistent agricultural subsidies in the developed world, even as these are withdrawn in the developing world.

Quality of life is poor in the developing world slum. Child malnutrition rates fall substantially from slums, to rural spaces, to non-slum urban areas. Local pollution has a drastic effect on health, while sanitation is often non-existent, and few facilities—water supply, emergency services, waste collection—exist. Any terrain can be appropriated for housing, including rubbish tips, the edge of railway lines, and cemeteries. If natural forces don't threaten the livelihood of slum-dwellers (such as in Rio de Janeiro, where hillside favela dwellings are continually threatened by mudslides in severe weather), then slum clearance programmes do. Shelter is made from anything that is available; brick, plastic, blocks of cement and scrap wood.

Opposite top: Housing Project in Ecatepec, Mexico City. Despite the apparent organisation of the Project's archietcture (as evidenced by its immense grid-like formation) the inhabitants of Ecatepec are not necessarily better off than those that live in the 'organically' formed slums found elsewhere in Latin America. Most of those living in the Project receive the minimum working wage and have to compete for such resources as water and electricity. Photograph by Scott Peterman.

Opposite bottom: Rocinha favela, Rio de Janeiro, Brazil. Rocinha, the largest and most urbanised favela in Brazil, is located in the South Zone of Rio de Janeiro. Compared to other slums, Rocinha has a more developed structure, and most buildings are made of concrete and have basic sanitation, electricity and plumbing. Rocinha is often cited as an example of a greatly improved area of squatter housing and has been given a certain legitimacy by the government.

Top: A dwelling in the slum of Kibera, Nairobi, demonstrating the use of recycled materials in its construction.

AD HOC AND NON-PLAN

Informal or illegal structures are not confined to the slums of the developing world. Conflict zones are an example of another type of environment where unplanned urban areas develop. Cities like Grozny and Beirut are full of rapidly made infill structures that recycle the remaining debris from damaged and destroyed buildings in their construction.

In the cities of the developed world, architects themselves have entered into the ad hoc. In 2002, the Rotterdam-based practice MVRDV planned a temporary *Container City* using 3,500 containers stacked 15 high, to create a vast hall with exhibition, eating and sleeping facilities. Architect Frank Gehry's own house in Los Angeles—aesthetically at least—hints at the ad hoc constructions in the developing world's slums; colliding wood and metal sections into bizarre angles and configurations. These are examples of, following postmodernism in America, of what is labelled 'deconstructivist' architecture. The concept of deconstruction was first entertained by French philosopher, Jaques Derrida, in the 1960s, but he insisted that it was impossible to define it succinctly. Derrida was interested in identifying—in text or language—not the meaning such forms of communication intend to confer, but rather the contradictions offered by their constituent parts. More explicitly, Derrida claimed that deconstruction was 'anti-structuralist', aiming to decompose the structure of texts, while at the same time concerned with how its myriad elements come together in an 'ensemble'. This metaphor can easily be applied to deconstructivist architecture, which is characterised by its eclectic use of diverse architectural elements, stripped away from their original setting (or 'meaning'), to form a new ensemble (with a different architectural 'language'). In this century, deconstructivist architecture can be seen from the trophy buildings of Gehry or Zaha Hadid to the works of the Hungarian, Laszló Rajk, which combine local and global iconography in their construction. In America, entire cities are dominated by the eclectic and unplanned. The competing, colliding fashions of architecture and myriad sub-cultures in built-up Manhattan, or the rise and fall of neighbourhood

Top: Contemporary Beirut's urban fabric is noted for its complexities and contradictions. From the 1950s onwards the city experienced sudden widespread urbanisation and largely unplanned construction of high-rise towers, while, more recently, civil war, Israeli attacks and Syrian occupation obliterated much of the city's landscape. In many areas destroyed or ruined historic buildings lie next to Western skyscrapers.

Opposite top: Night view of the Las Vegas Strip, a 6.4 kilometre section of the Las Vegas Boulevard.

Opposite bottom: The iconic gateway building by Norwegian architecture firm, Snøhetta Architects.

social identities in sprawled-out Los Angeles, are examples of dynamic urban deconstruction at play. Las Vegas, with its unfettered, exuberant abandoning of aesthetics and planning, is perhaps the most obvious example of this trend.

In 1969, Peter Hall and architect Cedric Price, along with architectural historian Reyner Banham (editor of *New Society* and known for his enthusiasm for the neon-lit strip of Las Vegas), published an article called "Non-Plan: An Experiment in Freedom". They concluded that nothing exciting ever happens when there is a plan in place, and that personal choice was better than the imposed aesthetics of any plan, ultimately advocating the abandonment of town planning altogether.

PLAN B

Since the 1980s, urban planning has found a new place in the market economy, through the commissioning by developers of high-specification office and luxury residential buildings. In Britain, Margaret Thatcher's government by-passed local authority planning organisations by establishing the London Docklands Development Corporation (LDDC), and offered developers tax breaks as an incentive for speculative building ventures. This resulted in the fast-track development of a new financial quarter at Canary Wharf, based on an original plan by American architects, Skidmore, Owings and Merril, which marked the start of luxury residential redevelopment in the moribund docklands specified in the LDDC's own plan. In the 1990s, Shanghai's Pudong proliferated on an even bigger scale when it was made a SEZ (similar in many ways to the LDDC), and current plans continue to guide its expansion. The Gulf States have virtually no planning constraints and are enthusiastic consumers of masterplans—including those that map out entire new cities. In 2006, the emirate of Ras al Khameih commissioned Rem Koolhaas' practice, OMA, to plan an entire desert city (designed for at least 150,000 inhabitants) called the RAK Gateway. The city is entirely contained within a structure that draws upon traditional Arabian town planning, but also contains high-rise buildings and a spectacular convention centre. Taking a lead from this development, the emirate then commissioned a further complex from Norwegian architects, Snøhetta, who are planning a lugubriously curving complex on the desert highway adjacent to the new city. These are some of the planned cities that appear to promise a new future.

A further focus for such urban planning is that of environmental sustainability and, more recently, there is also a desire for social sustainability too—that is, providing an environment in which social 'harmony', and the 'social' needs of inhabitants are met. Here, the model city may well be Curitiba, a city of 1.8 million, 400 kilometres south of São Paulo in Brazil. In 1964, at the same time that the city of Brasilia was being planned as a modernist showcase on a greenfield site, the visionary architect, Jaime Lerner, started work on a masterplan that adapted Howard's Garden City idea to an expanding, but historic, town which had already reached a population of 430,000 four years earlier. Lerner's plan avoided recourse to major redevelopment and grand civil engineering projects. It proposed a protected greenbelt, the preservation of the historic centre, traffic reduction and

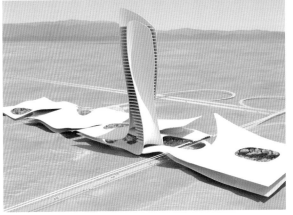

improved public transport. After 1968, when the plan was adopted, it grew to become an environmental, social and development blueprint for the city. From the 1980s, self-financing city-wide recycling was introduced and the city government devolved locally to special arcades where citizens were served on a more direct and approachable level. Favelas had emerged by the river, which resulted in their waste being discharged into the water supply with the run-off from winter rain. The favela dwellers were re-housed in permanent buildings and riverside parks replaced their old dwellings. Much else of Curitiba's planning has a social dimension beyond housing and social services. An example is the celebration of the city's rich ethnic roots—after Chicago, Curitiba claims to have the largest Polish population in the world—and has large communities descended from Japanese, Italian and other nationalities.

Curitiba is not an instant city—founded in 1693 its development has spanned centuries—but its planning serves to make it the ideal to which other cities might subscribe. The recipe is holistic—catering to social and environmental credentials that many market-based masterplans now aim for. Compared to the megacity pretensions held by many cities in the Gulf States, Russia, and elsewhere, it may only offer a 'Plan B' future by comparison—a future not based on gleaming office districts, cultural quarters or waterside residential developments. However, in the 'megacities' of the developing world, there are scant prospects for investment in such grandiose plans. But Curitiba, rather promisingly, suggests there are realistic solutions to the problems of unplanned growth.

1. The Athens Charter was established after
the fourth meeting of the *Congrès International
d'Architecture Moderne* (CIAM) in 1933. Counting Le
Corbusier and Sigfried Gideon as two of it members,
CIAM's core philosophy was to formalise modernist
principles in architecture, and it heralded the belief
that architecture could be utilised, both politically
and economically, to improve the world we live in.
After a meeting in 1933, in which the idea of the
'Functional City' was discussed, the Athens Charter
was published.

2. This compares with the conurbations of the other
two world cities, Tokyo-Yokohama (34 million)
and New York with its adjacent urban regions
and 'exurbs' in New Jersey and Connecticut (21
million). Tokyo, too, sought to decentralise into new
developments such as Tama New Town, which is now
just part of the greater conurbation.

3. Chuihua Chung, Jeffrey Inaba, Rem Koolhaas, Sze
Tsung Leong eds., *The Great Leap Forward* Harvard
Design School, 2001.

4. UN-HABITAT 2005 Global Urban Observatory,
Urban Indicators Programme, Phase III.

5. Davis, Mike, *Planet of Slums*, London: Verso, 2006.

Opposite top: Aerial
view of Brasilia circa
1960s. Brasilia was
planned and developed
between 1956 and
1960 by urban planner
Lúcio Costa, architect
Oscar Niemeyer and
landscape designer
Roberto Burle Marx.
Since its inauguration
in 1960, it has become
one of the most widely
cited landmarks
in the history of
urban planning.

Opposite bottom: View
of Curitiba, Brasil.
Curitiba is considered
one of the best
examples of urban
planning and
aligned to a model
for sustainable
development. It has
been particularly
praised for its eco-
efficient transportation
system and its
environmental and
social programmes.
Image courtesy of
Vinícius Dittrich.

Top: Brazil National
Congress, Brasilia,
Brazil. Most of
Brasilia's official
buildings, such as the
National Congress
pictured opposite,
were designed by
Niemeyer and were
intended to be
harmonious with the
city's overall design.
Image Courtesy of
Steven Wright.

ABUJA

Visitors to Abuja, Nigeria's official capital since 1991, often come away praising its beauty and orderliness; with its wide, tree-lined boulevards, elegant and well-appointed office buildings and free-flowing traffic system, it is something of an oasis of calm and serenity. Far less often, however, are these same visitors to be heard proselytising on the city's charm, character and romance.

Abuja is a modern, planned, purpose-built Federal Capital Territory (FCT), and was pieced together in 1976 from borrowed sections of other central Nigerian territories; Nassarawa, Kogi and Niger. The location was chosen for its central position (a gesture of unity and harmony in a multi-ethnic polyglot country like Nigeria) and for its potential for allowing effective growth in the future. The 250 square kilometres that now make up the city of Abuja was designated as the area for planning and development that would eventually replace overcrowded, congested and chaotic Lagos as the country's capital. The Federal Capital Development Authority (FCDA) was established with the mandate to execute, implement and oversee the development of this new FCT.

The FCDA engaged American-based planning consultants, International Planning Associates (IPA) to submit a masterplan for the development of the new capital city and its surrounding area. The IPA plan was approved for implementation in February 1979, and was widely praised for its elegance and strength of design; (many of the city's vistas are modelled on Washington, DC). It divided the city into sectors to be developed over four construction phases, and the city's projected capacity at the end of phases one and two was to be around approximately 3.1 million people. Its population was estimated to exceed 1.4 million in the greater metropolitan area in 2005.

The buildings of the downtown area are undoubtedly impressive. An enormous mosque—complete with a golden dome nestling amid four minarets—represents Nigeria's population of 65 million Muslims, while an, equally huge, non-denominational church sits less than one kilometre away, representing a similar number of Christians. Each of Nigeria's 36 states has its own office building in the city centre, with a lively spirit of one-upmanship governing their expensive fit-outs.

If the IPA city plan had been implemented rigidly by the FCDA over the years, perhaps Abuja would not find itself in the position it does today. However, as the city's development inevitably prompted huge population growth—without the housing stock or infrastructure to sustain it—successive administrations turned a blind eye to the plan for a number of years, allowing a huge amount of unofficial and spontaneous building to take place both in the city centre and in its suburban districts. The planners' provision of villa-style homes and luxury apartment complexes for diplomats and civil servants didn't quite cater to the needs of the general population in Abuja, and so they built more suitable accommodation for themselves away from the sweeping boulevards and towering apartment buildings of the city centre.

Not until the city's high-profile minister, Nasir el'Rufa'i—nicknamed "Mr Demolition"—began his 'masterplan restoration' project in 2003 had the IPA plan been consulted in earnest for a long time, despite being hung on all government office walls. Starting with knocking down several illegally built houses in the city centre, el'Rufa'i's project gradually rolled out across the largely spontaneously-built suburban districts. "By the time I was

ABUJA, ASTANA AND KINSHASA

appointed minister of the Federal Capital Territory", he argued,

> Abuja was going the way of Lagos. There was disorder; there was no respect for the masterplan for the development of Abuja; people were building structures all over the place, in places reserved for parks and recreational facilities; religious institutions' plots were being converted for other uses.[1]

The restoration plan sought to correct this uncontrolled development in the most direct of ways.

El'Rufa'i was famously quoted during the clearances as saying that Abuja was "not a city for the poor", and later modified this (after international outcry) to "not a city for idlers".[2] Quite how the industrious populations of the suburban and satellite districts—who serve the city's government ministers as car park attendants and waiters and taxi drivers for a pittance—are "idlers" is not immediately apparent, nor explained. The Social and Economic Rights Action Centre (SERAC), in Lagos, estimates that 70 per cent of Abuja's population lives in slums or the poorer areas of towns, and that up to

24 distinct areas of the city have now been cleared. No adequate notice period was given by the government before demolition began, and no provision for resettlement or compensation was made. Communities, markets, shops, places of worship, commercial and private buildings have all been demolished, along with the most vulnerable areas—the satellite communities along the Abuja Airport Road—including Chika, Aleita, Galadimawa, Lugbe, Kuchigoro, Piwoyi, Pyakasa, Gosa and Karamajigi.

The city authorities have begun a systematic eradication of those amenities—housing, street trades, okada (motorcycle taxis)—that serve the ordinary citizens of the city. In a representative illustration of the city fathers' logic, water sellers have recently been banned; the government argued, quite sensibly, that their presence was contributing to health problems, as they were selling unclean water. They stated that safe water provision was the responsibility of the government, but they then did not increase the numbers of stand pipes serving the areas in which the water sellers had worked. This incident is present-day Abuja all over: it sounds eminently sensible in the abstract, but, in

practise, it is the ordinary citizens of the city that come off worse.

The city's commitment to a modern and luxury experience has created a dependence on service industries, but the infrastructure to support this was never planned for. Even civil servants—who make up much of Abuja's workforce and for whom the city was purportedly designed—struggle to pay rent on city centre apartments; they earn around 30,000 naira (about £125 per month, while a room in the city centre costs at least twice that and rent must be paid up front one or two years in advance). Many live the bizarre dichotomy of working in plush air conditioned offices, and returning home in the evening to an illegal one-room shack. The chances of those scraping a living from the service industries finding an officially sanctioned home within their budget are virtually nil. El'Rufa'i claimed that Abuja can support those who busy themselves with the important professions—government services, the law, even construction—but ignored those who serve them. The motorway cloverleaves speak of a society where the car is king, but beyond the diplomatic limos and 4x4s, the roads are empty.

In attempting to eliminate Abuja's social diversity, the government could be accused of removing all the 'life', energy and character from the city. It is very much an administrative place; quiet, orderly, and often very empty. Abuja aims to be a world city, but world cities generally have a vibrant life outside their administrative and governmental function. There is nowhere to buy hot snacks or cold drinks on the streets, it is increasingly difficult to find a street newspaper vendors, while musicians and buskers are outlawed. In order to maintain the peace and tranquillity of the city the FCDA despatches the Environmental Task

Force to round up and arrest the people eeking out a living on Abuja's streets, returning the city to peace and tranquillity. While the government's responsibility in providing an orderly and functional administrative centre has not diminished, the negative prior experience of Lagos's problems has resulted in designing and legislating out the possibility for any sort of natural or organic development. In creating a modern city—with its widespread wireless internet capability, well-planned and pedestrian-friendly traffic systems and good security—the FDCA have gone too far. In its bid to be viewed as a world

city, Abuja was in contention to host the 2014 Commonwealth Games. Had it been successful (it was beaten by the city of Glasgow), it would have been the first African city to hold the event. In 2005, Minister El'Rufa'i announced plans for the construction of a 'Technology Village' modelled on America's Silicon Valley in a bid to allow the Nigerian capital to be a player in the global 'information revolution'. If built, it could provide facilities for over 150,000 IT graduates.[3]

Artist's rendering of the Millenium Park in Abuja by Manfredi Nicoletti Architects, 2003–2005.

1. Nasir el'Rufa'i cited in "Nigeria: 'Mr Demolition' Talks of Changing a City and a Country", allAfrica. com, 14 March 2007. See: http://allafrica.com/ stories/200703140731.html

2. Nasir el'Rufa'i quoted in "Life of Poverty in Abuja's Wealth", BBC News Online, 13 February 2007. See: http://news.bbc.co.uk/1/hi/world/africa/6355269.stm

3. "'Technology Village expected to absorb 150,000 Graduates' says el-Rufa'i'", official Nigerian government press release, 4 February 2005. See: http://www.fct.gov.ng/NR/rdonlyres/9FDDBF1E-771A-4A16-B3BB-1374837768D6/0/ MicrosoftWordRELEASEONATVPROJECT.pdf

32

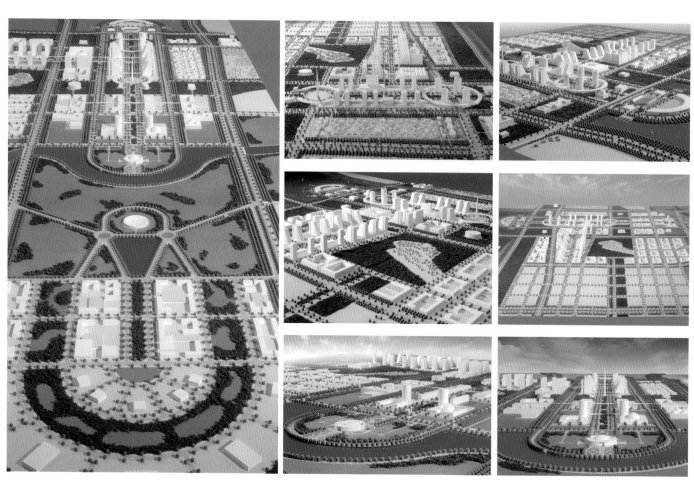

Kisho Kurokawa's
proposal for the Astana
masterplan, 1998,
eventually chosen for
implementation by the
Kazakh government.

ASTANA

When the Republic of Kazakhstan was created after the collapse of the Soviet Union, the decision was taken by the president, Nursultan Nazarbayev, to move the capital from the traditional regional centre of Almaty to Akmola—shortly after renamed Astana—on the vast and windblown Central Asian steppe, and the city was declared official capital of the ninth largest country in the world in 1997. The decision was not a popular one. The inhospitable northern territory of Kazakhstan suffers winters that can hit minus 40˚C, and the provincial outpost that is now Astana—with a population of less than 300,000 in 1997—was felt to be lacking in infrastructure, cultural vibrancy and a sense of place; the weekend flights back to Almaty, still full of commuting civil servants, demonstrates as much.

Astana is a city well used to having new identities imposed upon it according to the needs and whims of different regimes: historically it has been a provincial centre with perennially-shifting titles and uses, having been renamed frequently over the years. Its first incarnation was as Akmola, then Akmolinsk, then Tselinograd ("Virgin Lands City"—it was the key town

in Krushchev's mass grain cultivation programme of the 1950s), then Akmola again, and finally Astana (literally "capital city" in Kazakh). Its latest incarnation sees it as the seat of administrative and political power in a newly independent and oil-rich republic, rapidly developing an aesthetic fit for Kazakhstan's burgeoning nationhood and desired international status with an ambitious, aspirational—and, according to many commentators, monomaniacal—programme of works under the guidance of a prestigious group of masterplanners and architects (and, of course, under Nazarbayev himself).

Astana's immediate redevelopment consisted of an almost pathological programme of renaming streets and re-facing Soviet-era buildings (the flimsy aluminium facia and new glazing of the current Ministry of Foreign Affairs, for example, veils the former Hotel Moscow) in an attempt to overwrite all trace of the Soviet era with an aspirational, specifically Kazakh, identity. However, these superficial changes didn't quite do it for Nazarbayev. If Astana was to become a world city, construction was key and Nazarbayev's idiosyncratic architectural

imagination is unchecked—Astana's skyline began to change rapidly as huge building programmes were implemented at a dizzying speed.

In April 1998, the Kazakh government had issued a tender invitation for the development of a masterplan for the development of a new city centre in Astana. 40 applicants from 19 different nations were courted, and 27 proposals were eventually received. The proposal put forward by Japanese architect, Kisho Kurokawa, best known as one of the founders of the Metabolist Movement of the 1960s, eventually won the tender. It focused on three key aspects of Kurokawa's architectural thought: symbiosis, metabolism and abstract symbolism. Symbiosis was to be achieved through the fusion of the existing 'old city', on the right bank of the river Ishim, with an entirely new administrative centre on the left bank (many of the other plans put forward proposed completely demolishing the older town centre and housing). A further symbiosis of manmade and natural environments was embodied in the proposed 'River City', new residential areas shaped, evocatively, "like potatoes", which followed the course of the river.[1] Metabolism was to be represented by the linear zoning of the new city centre into seven distinct areas (with a view to effective future development, including green 'buffer' zones to protect the city from the harsh climate of the steppe), and abstract symbolism was to be applied through the physical expression of a distillation of traditional Kazakh cultural symbols (the conical shape of a nomad's traditional hat, for example) into something universal and platonic, creating in architecture a suitable mythology for the new capital.

Kurokawa's plan was adopted formally in 2001, but its implementation was not without conflict. New development on the left bank of the Ishim had already begun to another plan submitted by a Saudi practice (Nazarbayev is not one for hanging around) and the Kurokawa masterplan had to then accommodate those things which had already been built. Its adoption, in retrospect, seems largely nominal; key features of the plan have never been realised, such as the planting of a forest around the perimeter of the city, and Kurokawa's Japanese office do not keep records of how the plan has been implemented. Perhaps the potato-shaped

residential districts didn't offer a grand enough 'new mythology' for Nazarbayev's liking. Despite the official importance placed on Kurokawa's masterplan, many of the city's buildings seem to have been designed and constructed to Nazarbayev's own personal specifications, he has been widely quoted as saying: "I am the architect of Astana and I am not ashamed to say that."[2]

It is statements like this that have fuelled concerns that the construction of the new city has more to do with the creation of a personal mythology than a new Kazakh, along the symbolic lines proposed by Kurokawa. One such example is Astana's new landmark building, the Tree of Life (or Baiterek), completed in 2002. The Tree of Life is a 97 metre high observation tower which reifies in steel latticework and gold mirror glass the Kazakh fable of the Samruk bird, which lays its golden egg in the Baiterek, or poplar tree. When the Samruk flies away, a snake eats the egg. The bird returns the following year and lays another egg, and the same happens again; this goes on , year after year. Along with the slightly odd comment this bleak fable of constant renewal seems to pass on the city the building surveys, the most remarkable feature of the Tree of Life

is the imprint of Nazarbayev's own hand set in a huge triangular gold ingot at the observation tower (it is said that newlyweds touch it for luck).

The Kazakh government claims it has spent £7.7 billion so far on construction, although some believe this figure is actually much higher. The other new architectural gems studding the new Astana skyline are just as grandiose, if similarly surreal: a national archive shaped in the form of a golden egg, the Ministry of Transport shaped like a giant cigarette lighter, two 30-storey cones in gold mirror glass. But by far the most striking of all the strategies employed in the creation of the new capital, however, is Nazarbayev's commissioning of signature buildings from international 'starchitects'. Astana has now built up quite a collection in the left bank New City area, with Nazarbayev adding to his roster of internationally acclaimed names continually (in addition to Kisho Kurokawa's stewardship of the masterplan, Manfredi Nicoletti of Italy has designed a boat-like concert hall, and of course, the British practice Foster+Partners has famously been developing an impressive presence in the city).

A rendering of the Abu Dhabi Plaza complex designed by Foster+Partners. The cluster of towers of varying heights will form a mixed-use development, incorporating energy-efficient strategies that are based around its self-insulating properties.

Khan Shatyry
entertainment centre,
Astana, designed by
Foster+Partners. This
tent-like structure
will house a multi-use
leisure complex.

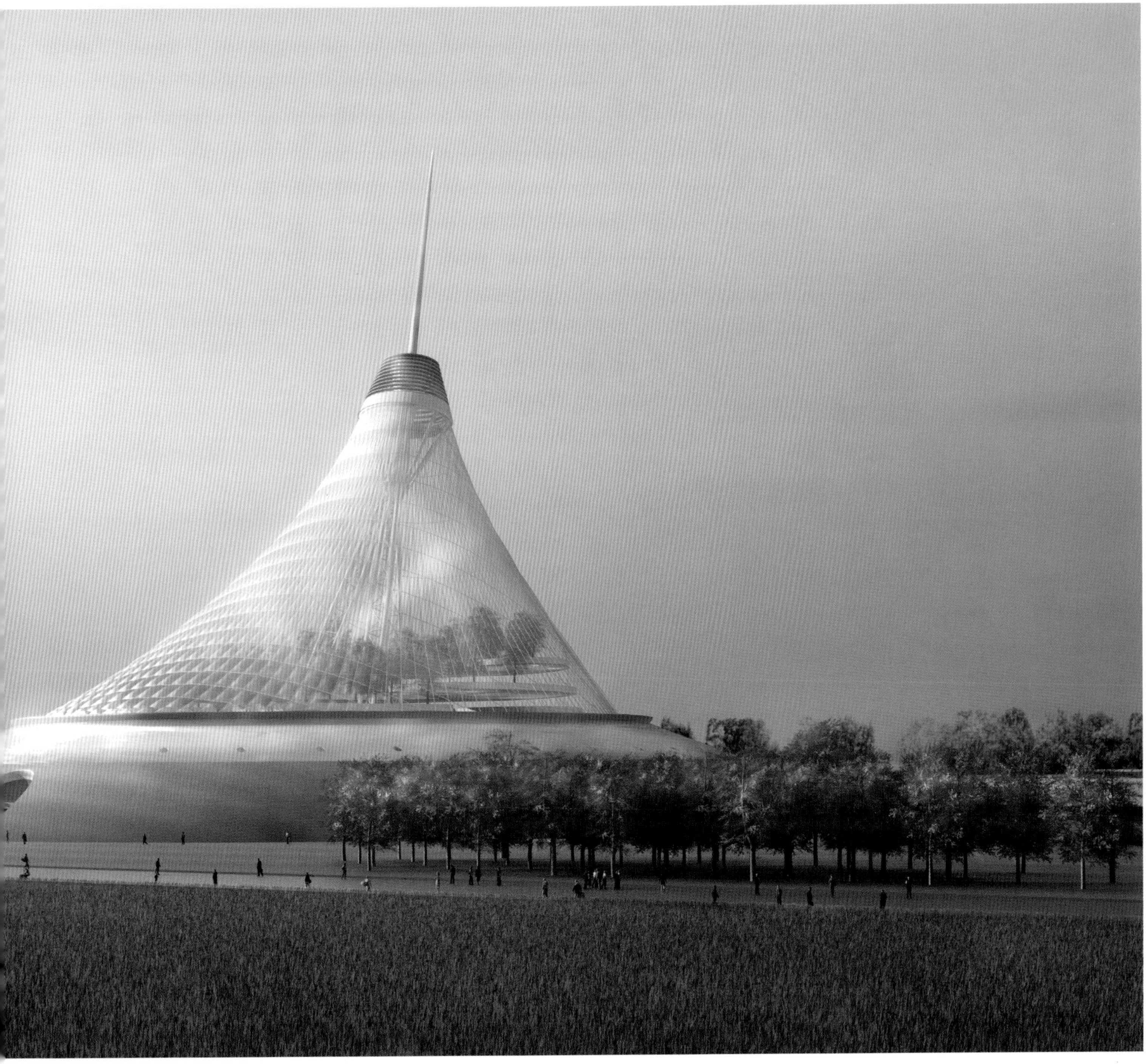

Foster+Partners is by far the biggest coup in Nazarbayev's name game. After Astana hosted 2003's inaugural Congress of Leaders of World and Traditional Religions in 2003, Nazarbayev proposed that this would become a triennial event in the city with an appropriate permanent structure to house it. He approached the practice with a proposal for a giant pyramid-shaped structure, asking whether they would like to take the project on given that it must be ready in time for the next Congress in 2006. Nazarbayev's proposal was to become Foster+Partners' Palace of Peace and Reconciliation, an enormous 62 metres wide by 62 metres high object going from briefing to completion in just 21 months. Foster+Partners' first scheme for the building was modelled on the Great Pyramid of Cheops (230 metres wide by 146 metres high) and formed entirely out of stained glass. This scale was considered too epic even for Astana, however, and. the final design was comparatively modest, faced in granite and with stained glass by artist, Brian Clarke, confined to the very apex of the building (although it still had room to accommodate a late request from the President; a 1,500-seat opera house). Foster+Partners' next commission in Astana

was the Khan Shatyry Entertainment Centre, a self-contained, temperature-controlled leisure complex rising 200 metres from an elliptical base in a transparent tent-like structure (echoing the form of a traditional nomadic yurt). Held by a mast, the huge structure is clad in ETFE, a material that transfers heat and light into the building's interior spaces while sheltering them from extreme weather conditions. In an area larger than that of ten football stadiums, the building includes green spaces along with commercial and retail spaces; a terraced indoor park steps up the whole height of the building, and a tropical water park includes wave pools, a river and a waterfall. A central multi-purpose space will accommodate a programme of leisure events forming the cultural hub of the building. At completion, in 2007, the peak of the Khan Shatyry was the highest in Astana, but this record isn't expected to last very long. Foster+Partners' work on these two projects has gone down well on the steppe, and the practice is currently overseeing construction of another major, mixed-use development, Abu Dhabi Plaza. A 'city within a city', it takes the form of a staggered matrix of buildings, with its highest elevations to the north expected to form a barrier against the harsh winds

that Astana is subject to. Its base is formed by a retail and leisure podium and a hotel, which then rises to form a series of office and residential towers. Again, thermo-efficiency is an important aspect of the design, with the matrix of blocks forming a compact and effective means of insulation, and the spaces between the towers providing areas for a winter garden and a network of sheltered pedestrian routes through the development. Many have expressed surprise that Foster+Partners should work so enthusiastically with a client that has such clearly-defined tastes and a patchy democratic record. In defence, Norman Foster claims: "If somebody says, 'hey there is this congress meeting point/public space/university/exhibition space and we need it in two years', you know, that makes your pulse quicken and slightly takes your breath away."[3] Astana offers a rare chance to experiment, to work quickly, and with relatively few regulations. As critic, Hugh Pearman, puts it, Foster+Partners, and others like them, "can use Astana as a testing ground."[4]

It is an experiment that shows no signs of slowing. The population has more than doubled (to 600,200) since the capital was doubled (to 600,200) since the capital was moved in late 2007, and the designation of the left bank New City area as a Special Economic Zone in 2001, with its favourable tax conditions for foreign and domestic investment, has precipitated a wave of similarly ambitious projects. Great tracts of undeveloped land are being hoarded with blown-up CGI images of that which is still to come. As we move towards Astana's nominal 2030 'completion' date with its accompanying one million plus projected population, it is becoming increasingly difficult to keep track of what is still at proposal stage and what has already been topped out and signed off. Other buildings in the pipeline are Kinori Kikutake's 49-storey 'Republic' business centre; the 'Continent-Bravo' business centre designed to resemble a rhythmic gymnast's ribbons; the 'Batygai' complex, a covered 'city within a city' featuring a school, hospital, retail units and office premises surrounded by towers of apartments and hotel accommodation; and Astana Stadium, pencilled in for completion before the end of 2008. There are also rumblings regarding a proposed underground metro system. The centrepiece of the city, is thought to be yet another tower; envisioned as a bullet-shaped, blue glass structure that refers to the pointed hats of Kazakh national dress. It would be the tallest building in Central Asia, at nearly 400 metres.

It hasn't taken long for the national pastime of renaming to catch up with President Nazarbayev's vision. Each of his new buildings has quickly generated an unflattering local nickname: the Baiterek 'Tree of Life' has become the 'Chupa Chups', after the lollipop. The Ministry of Transport is now known as the 'Lighter' (unfortunately positioned near the semicircular KazMunaiGaz building so that, together, the complex has gained the moniker the 'Ashtray'). These murmurings of internal dissent at least suggest—while Astana's latest reinvention goes on apace around them—that there is something afoot in the city to temper Nazarbayev's architectural fervour. The city's renaming programme is now distinctly bottom-up, and certainly less than aspirational.

1. Takashi, Tsubokura, "Astana as the New Capital—Masterplan by a Japanese Architect Kisho Kurokawa". See: http://www.astanamp.kepter.kz/sub4.html

2. Nursultan Nazarbayev quoted in Woodman, Ellis, "Palace of Peace and Accord, Kazakhstan by Foster+Partners", *Building Design*, 22 September 2006.

3. Norman Foster quoted in Steen, Michael, "Astana—British Architect Builds First Kazakh Pyramid", *Moscow Times*, 17 October 2006.

4. Hugh Pearman quoted in Steen, Michael, "Astana—British Architect Builds First Kazakh Pyramid".

View of Kinshasa with
the Congo River in
the background.

KINSHASA

On the banks of the Congo River, 3.2 kilometres across the water from Brazzaville, lies Kinshasa, capital of the Democratic Republic of the Congo (DRC). Approximately 20 kilometres along its north-south axis, and more than 30 kilometres east to west, Kinshasa is the most populous city in the Central African region. The city's 2007 population is estimated at somewhere between five and eight million people, but exact figures are not known.

Kinshasa has been the seat of many regimes, and has suffered the consequences of colonial rule, decolonisation, postcolonial dictatorship and war for over a century. It has been the capital of the DRC, of Zaire, and of Belgian Congo, and has operated under many monikers both official and unofficial: Léopoldville, Kinshasa, Kin la Belle (Kinshasa the Beautiful) and, latterly, Kin la Poubelle (Kinshasa the Dustbin).

Kinshasa is a city on the cusp of becoming a megacity, but its urban provenance is incredibly recent. According to the UN World Urbanisation Report, by 2015 Kinshasa will be the most populous French-speaking city in the world, and will be the twenty-ninth most populous in the world, with a projected 8.68 million inhabitants.

However, when the DRC (often called Congo-Kinshasa, to distinguish it from Congo-Brazzaville across the river) gained its independence from Belgium in 1960, Kinshasa had a population of just 400,000. The colonial authorities had only upped its classification from a 'district urbain' to a city in 1941 and, until independence, the city's population growth was strictly controlled. Kinshasa is a nascent megacity without an urban tradition, and this brings its own problems; its exponential population increase has left its already fragile infrastructure's capacity to cope far behind.

Kinshasa is a city of stark juxtapositions. There is a sharp distinction to be drawn between the *Ville* (the urban downtown area, laid out in the colonial period) and the *Cité* (the suburban residential areas of the city, much of which can be classified as slums). The main artery of the *Ville*, the tree-lined Boulevard 30 Juin, is often referred to as a tropical Champs Élysées with its designer shops and high-rise buildings (like the 22-storey SOZACOM headquarters, for example). In the *Cité*, there are an estimated 30,000 children living on the streets, many having been accused of witchcraft by their families and abandoned. As a country, the DRC has immense mineral wealth but Kinshasa has the dubious distinction of being home to the poorest slum area in the world, according to a 2003 UN report.

The area now occupied by Kinshasa was named Léopoldville by Henry Morton Stanley in 1881 after his benefactor, King Léopold II of Belgium. It originally operated as a minor trading post, but the completion of the Matadi-Kinshasa Railway in 1898 sparked development in the area and created the early infrastructure that allowed the efficient and ruthless exploitation of the Congo's natural resources. In 1920 Léopoldville was promoted to the status of capital of Belgian Congo; in 1965 the city was renamed Kinshasa by president Mobutu Sese Seko as part of his 'Africanisation' drive, after a village which had once stood on the site.

Colonial Léopoldville was subject to strict architectural and zoning restrictions, racial segregation legislation and a work-permit system limiting the movement of Africans

to the cities. The area of the city still known as the *Ville*—or sometimes the *Ville Blanche*—is a remnant of this period, and still houses the economic, political and commercial centres of the city. The *cités planifiées* (planned suburbs), built for the African population of colonial Léopoldville by the *Office des Cités Africaines*, are still considered desirable places to live, despite their age and current state of disrepair. Major changes in the patterns of the city's urbanisation occurred immediately after independence. When restrictions on movement and ownership were lifted, Africans were urged to reclaim the land previously denied to them by the colonial regime and a wave of spontaneous, and largely unplanned, building began. The population exploded when women and children could settle in the city from rural areas, forbidden under the colonial regime. The dense slum areas of the *Cité* really began to come into their own, and now occupy more than 75 per cent of the city. The city swelled further outwards— encompassing previously European-owned farmland and beginning an ongoing process of ex-urbanisation—encroaching further and further every year upon the land surrounding the city. Very little urban planning took (or still takes) place, and those state planning

schemes that were drawn up have been largely ignored, with tribal elders often handling land transfer deals. (The Kinshasa Hôtel de Ville's website currently features images of the municipal clearing of *constructions anarchiques* [unauthorised buildings], but these are incredibly small-scale programmes in comparison to the vast areas of the city made up of such unauthorised constructions.)

The different periods in Kinshasa's history have all left their mark on the physical fabric of the city. From the colonial period it retains a marooned planned city centre with abandoned municipal buildings, grand libraries that house no books, and a zoo with no animals. From the postcolonial Mobutist regime, there are public buildings replete with names redolent of his nepotistic tendencies. The city is strewn with evidence of the regime's centralisation drive, which over-invested in Kinshasa's development only to withdraw support a few years later, leaving its public works projects to crumble. The vast Inga Dam hydroelectric power project, completed by the Mobutu government, for example, has the capacity to reduce Kinshasa's (and much of the DRC's) dependence on scarce fuel wood, but has never been properly

managed; it still operates at a negligible proportion of its capacity.

This civic mismanagement—when coupled with the imposition of the punitive Structural Adjustment Programmes in the 1980s by the World Bank and the International Monetary Fund (widely accredited with worsening and hastening the collapse of urban services, increasing poverty, disease and unemployment in developing world cities) was disastrous for Kinshasa and, as Mike Davis puts it in *Planet of Slums*, an "inevitable recipe for the mass production of slums".[1]

In addition to this, the city is still recovering from the effects of a period of civil war between 1996 and 2003. Mobutu's 32 year regime was forcibly ended, and a war involving nine nations, seven years and an estimated 5.4 million fatalities, began. Although most actual combat took place in the east of the country, Kinshasa—as the seat of government—changed hands numerous times and lost control of tracts of the country. By 2003, the DRC's output—via Kinshasa— had reached an all-time low, its external debt had rocketed, and foreign investment had all but dwindled away. The war had intensified Kinshasa's already chronic problems: lack

Above: A bustling city street in Kinshasa.

Opposite: An apartment block in Kinshasa, DRC.

of infrastructure, unstable legal system, corruption and uncontrollable inflation; displaced populations from all over the country poured into the city.

As a city largely operating without an official infrastructure, Kinshasa has become a model of that omnipresent developing world survival strategy: the development advance of an informal sector. In Kinshasa, this has evolved into a complex parallel economy, whose services range from the operation of privatised 'public' transport running alongside expensive and overcrowded municipal bus services, to the more traditional one-man operations: khadaffis (petrol traffickers), *cambistes* (illegal money-changers) and the ubiquitous *ligablos* (street vendors). The informal sector is all-pervasive; even wage earners supplement their income with an additional informal role (various studies have found that employed workers derive more than half of their income from such additional jobs in the 'informal economy').

These flexible and innovative strategies for survival have prompted a call for a re-orientation of the way Kinshasa is appraised in Western analyses. Theorists such as Filip De Boek have recently argued that Kinshasa, and its urban identity, cannot be understood

through conventional architectural, urban planning and top-down policy-based discourses. Instead, he claims, the city should rather be approached as a "flexible and adaptive urban landscape" where the Kinois generate new urban forms out of their material circumstances. De Boek argues that "the infrastructure and architecture that function best in Kinshasa are almost totally invisible on a material level", citing the innumerable commercial enterprises which take place outside built structures. Similarly, René Devisch locates Kinshasa's true heart in the vibrant bar and live music culture of the *Cité*, which provides, he argues, a locus for reconstructing a sense of agency and personal fulfilment.

However, these qualitative modes of analysis can't disguise the privations suffered by Kinshasa's urban dwellers. The public health crisis, for example, shows no sign of abating. Kinshasa was the site of the first documented case of HIV infection in 1959, and now an estimated 20 per cent of the population are HIV positive. Treatable and preventable diseases like polio, cholera, malaria and diarrhoea are killers in Kinshasa, where 75 per cent of the population can't afford formal healthcare, such as it is, and many resort to

Pentecostal faith healing or local witchcraft for treatment. The average annual income in Kinshasa is around £50, and 50 per cent of the population have just one meal a day (25 per cent have just one meal every two days). On the UN's Human Development Index—which takes into account factors like life expectancy, literacy and school enrolment levels—the DRC comes in 168th place. In the index compiled specifically for developing countries, the HDI-1, the DRC comes 88th out of 108.

1. Davis, Mike, Planet of Slums, London: Verso, 2006.

SIBERIA AS ANALOGOUS TERRITORY

Alexander D'Hooghe

"City air makes free." This old saying (from the Low Countries) dates from the time when groups of craftsmen first liberated themselves from church and state by declaring their cities to be outside the totality of feudal rule. Fast-forward, then, to the second half of the twentieth century, a time when, if anything, belief in the saying had grown stronger. Faced with the accelerating disintegration of Western cities after the Second World War, a great many architects placed the pursuit of urbanity, metropolitanism—cityness—at the centre of their endeavours. Its emancipatory potential as a place where conventions were systematically broken down and created anew became ever more attractive, and consequently, the recreation of this condition has been a major purpose of post-war architecture: Archigram's Beehives, Robert Venturi's density of signs and Rem Koolhaas's Culture of Congestion are architectural propositions steered by a belief in metropolitanism.

Siberia, incredibly large, flat and snow-ridden, is the least dense, most expansive territory in the world. It is the extreme opposite of metropolitanism, a total periphery so vast and inhospitable that here, too, possibilities for freedom arise.

The following is a description of the almost conquest of Siberia in the 1950s and 60s by the development of an apparatus of secret scientific complexes. Two such complexes, Akademgorodok and Bio-Akademgorodok, established around Siberia's capital, Novosibirsk, exemplify the territory's ability to reconcile contradictory agendas: the control and colonisation strategies of the regime, and the resistance and emancipation tactics of the scientific community.

Here the Soviet mindset of constructivity—aiming for collective statements of identity as victories over the totalising frameworks of history, culture or nature—was finally fulfilled. We can read the scientific complexes as examples of such collective statements caught in architecture, where contradictions within the Soviet society were superimposed and brought to a point of synthesis.

Siberia's relevance for the West is therefore double. On the one hand, its giant territory—a system without a horizon—crystallises and radicalises key conditions of our own post-urban realm, that nebulous haze of post-, ex-, sub- and dis-urban sequences which together establish the sprawling territory. On the other hand, the Soviet strategy of deploying a series of 'complexes' as civilising devices in the midst of this canvas gives the West a template for intervention in its own sprawling territories which is at least worth debating.

AWAKING A SLEEPING GIANT

It is already May and in Russia the woods are green and filled with the song of nightingales, while in the south the acacias and lilacs are in bloom. But here, on the road from Tyumen to Tomsk, the earth is brown, the forests are bare, there is leaden-coloured ice on the lakes and snow is still lying on the banks and in the gullies… a little later we overtake a party of convicts. Fetters ring as 30 or 40 men walk along the road, flanked by armed soldiers, with two carts bringing up the rear…. The convicts and soldiers are worn out; the road is bad and they haven't the strength to walk…. All across from Tyumen to Tomsk there are no hamlets or farmsteads but only large villages, which lie at a distance of 20, 25 to 40 versts from each other. You meet no estates on the way, for there are no landowners here. You will see no factories, mills or inns. The only objects reminding you of man as you travel along the road are the telegraph wires humming in the wind, and the verst posts along the road. The Siberian highway is the longest and, I think, the most hideous in the entire world… at every station we… cry indignantly: 'What a miserable, appalling road!' And the station clerk tells us: 'This is nothing yet, wait until you get to Kozulka!'…. It is along such an artery that civilisation is said to flow into Siberia![1]

Such was the despair Siberia inflicted on its visitors, according to Anton Chekhov in his 1890 travelogue, "Across Siberia". Siberia has been called 'the failed ocean'—a flat, barely sea-level plain, an alternately swampy or frozen land spanning 11 time zones: God's uncompleted task. But the name Siberia, derived from the Mongolian 'Sibir', or 'sleeping land', hints at its promise, too. An inventory of its sleeping wealth reveals huge deposits of coal, petroleum, natural gas, diamonds, iron ore and gold; epic stands of first-growth timber; and massive freshwater rivers rich in wildlife and hydro-electric capacity.

Siberia's wealth was not lost on Lenin:

If a bourgeois government supported by outside help should establish itself in power in Siberia, and Eastern Russia becomes lost to the Soviet Union, then in Western Russia the Soviet Power would become weakened to the point that it could hardly hold out for long…. The development of those natural resources by methods of modern technology will provide unprecedented progress of the productive forces.[2]

After the 1917 October Revolution, Soviet Moscow turned away from its ports and borders, and set out on a project of inward expansion based upon the unlocking of its own space, about three quarters of which was Siberia. This development of strategic resources was also wrapped in ideology. Point nine of Karl Marx' Communist Manifesto—the "gradual abolition of all the distinction between town and country by a more equable distribution of the populace over the country"—was translated into the planning concept of the 'unified territory'. This stated purpose coloured the successive stages of Soviet development, from the electrification plan 1920–1921 through the agricultural, industrial and scientific movements of the 1930s, 40s, 50s and 60s, to the terra-forming ambitions of the 70s and 80s.

Nonetheless, Siberia's historical sense of otherness, as a vast, otherworldly territory populated by criminals, outcasts and former serfs, continued to exist in the Soviet era. Here exiled dissidents were able to operate with relative freedom within an otherwise authoritarian regime. Siberia functioned as an internal escape valve, providing a place where all the repressed and unfit could be parked out of sight. But this outlet also had revolutionary potential. In fact, as Sibera was made more accessible after the Second World War, its otherness began to capture and influence the imagination and form of mainstream Soviet Communism.

EARLY TEMPLATES FOR THE COLONISATION OF SIBERIA
STAGE ONE: ANTENNAE OF A NEW CULTURE
The town of Novonikolayevsk, as Siberia's capital was originally called, was founded in 1893 where the Trans-Siberian Railway met the river Ob, somewhere close to the geographical heart of what would later become the Soviet Union. The city grew quickly and, by 1917, had the look of a Wild West town: A Lunacharsky, commissar for education and enlightenment under Lenin, called it the "Chicago of the East". In 1926 it was renamed simply Novosibirsk—'New Siberia'. By 1989 Novosibirsk had become Siberia's major industrial and scientific centre, and the third largest city in the USSR, counting more than 1.4 million inhabitants. The development of Novosibirsk, as recorded in its urbanism, reflects the successive colonisation waves of Siberia: culture, industry and science.

In the years following Stalin's 1926 ascension to the party leadership, Novosibirsk was redefined by a series of architecture projects which served to transmit the ideology of the regime from the centre to the periphery. For example, in the late 1920s, the architects C Greenberg and ML Kurilko were commissioned

to design the Mass Action House of Culture and Science, a constructivist palace whose typology, like that of the Moscow Soviet Palace, provided for the staging of mass performances and parades.[3] Construction began in 1930, but technical problems and, more important, a change of course in Moscow, soon brought it to a halt. In a speech to the Party Plenum in 1931, Party Commissioner, L Kaganovich, had announced that "the debate over what constitutes a Communist city is irrelevant. Our cities are Communist by virtue of their position within the boundaries of the Soviet Union." His words signalled the end of constructivism and the arrival of socialist realism and left the builders of the Mass Action House of Culture and Science in a quandary. As NG Chernyshevsky might have said, what is to be done? To abandon the half-finished project would have been a repudiation of Lenin's reign, so instead the building was completed as an oversize, heavily ornamented neo classical meeting hall and opera house with remarkable similarities to the first layers of Boris Iofan's wedding cake Soviet Palace.

The use of architectural objects as antennae for broadcasting the regime's rhetoric throughout Siberia confirms Hannah Arendt's thesis about the structure of totalitarian systems: that they rely on the replication, proliferation and diffusion of a central idea in all the veins and nodes of the territory. This phenomenon was at work in the architectural symbolism of Novosibirsk, as a summary copy of the form of Moscow power, but as the shifts in Moscow were transmitted into peripheral architectures, its successive positions were recorded and frozen into the urban morphology, as markers of the internal contradictions at play in the centre. The history of this and other buildings point to a central characteristic of Siberian 'otherness': what could not have happened in the centre of Moscow, where it was feared that any appearance of contradiction might lead to a destabilisation of the entire empire (representation and official discourse were too important to allow for architectural deviance), was apparently allowed in Novosibirsk.[4] From the mid-1950s on, precisely this characteristic would permit the scientific complexes to develop semi-independently, with displays of an architectural monumentality speaking in a tongue that was foreign to the dogmas of Moscow.

STAGE TWO: THE PRODUCTIVE COMPLEX
Stalin's reordering of Soviet production under a succession of Five Year Plans challenged existing models of spatial and urban organisation, and created a set of conditions which would heavily influence the later development of the scientific complex. The first plan, introduced in 1928, called for the shock-development of both

Left: Aerial view of the scientific research and education centre Akademgorodok, Novosibirsk, Russia.

Right: Artist's rendering of the Moscow Soviet Palace.

agriculture (collectivisation) and industry, and set the heartbeat of Soviet development on a five year rhythm of increasingly unattainable production quotas followed by frantic attempts to fill them.[5] Henceforth, planning would be organised by sectors of production output: raw steel, machinery, vehicles, shoes, cloth, food. The result was a series of vertical structures leading from the assembly line all the way to the central ministry in Moscow, competing corporations in which capitalist production incentives were replaced with threats to the very survival of the collective.

The most tangible territorial footprint of this new logic was the typology of the productive complex, which signalled that the organisation of space would be subordinated completely to the purpose of increasing production. The Soviet corollary to the capitalist factory town, it centred on a production line but also included housing and amenities for the workers. The linearity of production often forced its logic onto the other structures, resulting in a generally linear unit of development. As a result of this singular obsession with mass production, every aspect of reality had to be redrawn to fit the new generic type, no matter how outlandish. The Urals-Kuznetsk Combine is a good example: this complex combined the iron ore deposits of the Urals with the coal basins of West Siberia (Novokuznetsk, Altai) into a 1,500 kilometre long factory, with a railway line for transporting the goods from one basin to the other.[6]

The very notion of 'city' had been blown up, exposed as a bourgeois artefact and replaced by the purely functional and output-orientated unit of the productive complex. Similarly, the territorial planning for Siberia designated its regional identities wholly on the basis of their productive capacities. The Soviets were not going to be dominated by nature, geography and history in their quest for a new culture of production. The productive complex is thus as much an expression of Soviet constructivity in urban planning as was the earlier aesthetic of constructivism in architecture. Both manifestations share the assumption that form, organisation and identity are the result of conscious choices made by or on behalf of the collective.

THE FOUNDATIONS FOR SCIENTIFIC URBANISM
A REVOLUTIONARY MOMENT
After Stalin's death, in 1953, Kruschev, as the new party secretary, was anxious to emphasise his regime's greater enlightenment and efficiency, not least for reasons of stark necessity. As the geographers J Pallot and DJB Shaw have shown in their study of Soviet planning, the systemic-emergency condition called up by successive Five Year Plans had contributed to a severe housing crisis.[7] Production lines were built and workers relocated with few provisions made for such necessities as housing, schools and markets. Kruschev attributed this crisis to the rigidity of Stalin's sectorial model and embarked on a re-organisation of the bureaucratic structure by region (space) rather than by function (sector), installing a series of economic departments (Sovnarkhozy) which gave each region unprecedented autonomy. In doing so, he helped legitimise a post-war hype in the USSR, namely the paradigm of cybernetics.

First posited by Norbert Wiener in 1949 at MIT, this new systems theory promised to bridge the divide between technology, sociology and nature. Cybernetics' premise was that systems possess a self-organising capability through which they evolve more or less autonomously. Crucial in this systems theory is

Top: Aerial of a large linear boulevard in Akademgorodok.

Bottom:
An image depicting the relationship between 'centre' (European Russia) and 'periphery' (Siberia).

feedback flows of information, which steer and correct the system. Cybernetics enjoyed an extremely awkward position in the USSR. As the philosopher of science, Loren Graham, has written: "The subject matter of cybernetics—the control of dynamic processes and the prevention of increasing disorder within them—was exactly the concern of Soviet administrators."[8] But while control fed into the strategies of central power (the hope for more efficiency), the autonomy implicit in cybernetics appealed to the resistance tactics of the intelligentsia, particularly scientists eager to regain freedom of thought after the Stalin era. Like Siberia itself, cybernetics resonated with conflicting agendas and interests which, if transcended, would raise hopes for the progress of the collective. Although it never lived up to its full promise in the Soviet Union, cybernetics was the final, crucial ingredient in the optimism that inspired the creation of Akademgorodok, Bio-Akademgorodok and the entire network of scientific complexes by which the colonisation of Siberia would be organised from 1957 onwards.

THE FIRST AKADEMGORODOK
Akademgorodok's form is a record of the two contrasting projections that brought it into existence: the utopian vision of the scientist Mikhail Lavrentev, and the power of Kruschev. Lavrentev and Kruschev met in the military academy at Ufa (Siberia) during the Second World War, after which Lavrentev went on to make a career in the Soviet Academy of Sciences. When Kruschev was appointed as Stalin's successor, Lavrentev saw his opportunity and travelled to Moscow to make an ambitious proposal: to build a science town far from the Moscow bureaucracy which would have the twin purposes of developing Siberian resources and testing the relevance of cybernetics. On 18 May 1957 the Council of Ministers announced the decision:

[t]o create in Siberia a powerful centre; to organise the Siberian division of the Academy of Sciences of the USSR and build for it a city of science not far from Novosibirsk with premises for scientific institutes and well-designed housing for the staff…. [And] to consider [as] the fundamental problem of the Siberian division the broad problem of theoretical and experimental research […] toward […] the successful development of the productive forces of Siberia and the Far East.[9]

Moscow thought it was sponsoring a colonisation project, but for Lavrentev, Akademgorodok was, above all, about freedom of thought, a scientific Arcadia surrounded by the forest and dotted with vernacular brick housing. Here is how Dimitry Belayev, later vice-president of the Siberian Branch of the Academy of Sciences, described the place:

When I arrived here in 1957, there was absolutely nothing. Just the forest and a cottage in the woods where Lavrentev and his wife lived. His closest colleagues had come with him, some with their families, some alone. Since there was nowhere for them to live they had built a hut and organised a commune. Those were marvellous, unforgettable times[10]

The contrasting agendas underlying Akademgorodok's existence would continue to push and pull its form in two directions. Kruschev admired techniques of mass production and Taylorisation and, in order to speed up the lagging construction, he insisted on using prefabricated units in the place of Lavrentev's brick. The

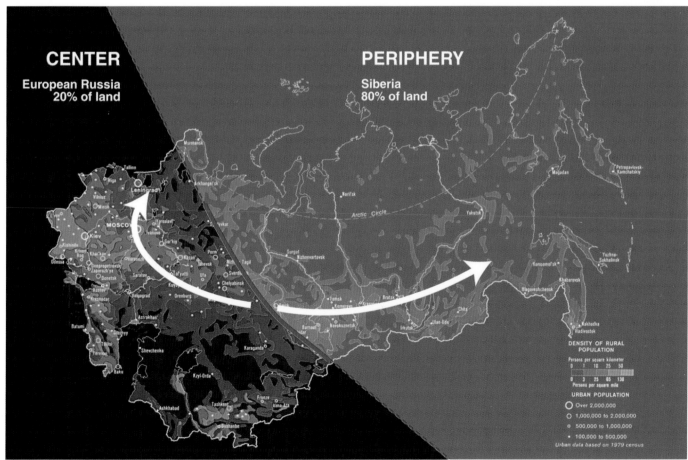

CENTER

European Russia
20% of land

PERIPHERY

Siberia
80% of land

DENSITY OF RURAL
POPULATION

Persons per square kilometer
0   1   10   25   50

0   3   25   65   130
Persons per square mile

URBAN POPULATION

○ Over 2,000,000

○ 1,000,000 to 2,000,000

○ 500,000 to 1,000,000

• 100,000 to 500,000

Urban data based on 1979 census

Today one enters Akademgorodok by a large linear boulevard. On the right the pine forest is largely untouched; on the left, wooden barracks and small shops emerge between the forest. This was temporary housing built for the construction workers. After a while, the boulevard turns sharply to the right, and a strange monumental-modernist building appears: the presidium of the Siberian branch of the Academy of Sciences. The boulevard continues in a straight line, offering glimpses of various monumental research institutes between the pine trees on each side. Pedestrians and cars crowd this forest on the 'Boulevard of Science', recently renamed Lavrentev Boulevard. Finally, the boulevard again curves to the right. Repetitive residential blocks appear here, denser and closer to the road. The streets are becoming increasingly crowded, which is strange because the boulevard is about to end in a solid mass of pine trees. Apparently, the plan foresaw the continuation of the boulevard through the forest, because a couple of hundred metres down the road it would reach the beaches of the Ob Sea. Instead, the boulevard takes a sharp turn to the right, dead-ending in the town centre with shopping, a cinema, a hotel and the club of scientists.

BIO-AKADEMGORODOK

If Akademgorodok established the precedent for freedom of scientific thought in Siberia, in Bio-Akademgorodok, to the southwest of Novosibirsk, the scientific complex developed its own clear formal template as a discrete unit of development. This settlement, in which architecture, urbanism and construction were folded into one act of creation, consists of two geometrical figures. One is the kilometre-long skywalk along which the scientific laboratories were arrayed. The other is even bigger: a series of circles with diameters of one kilometre. The living quarters, called Microrayons ('small districts'), were built to house 20,000 and contain amenities such as shopping and schools.

THE SCIENTIFIC COMPLEX: A PROTOTYPE
MONUMENTAL STRINGS

The template for the scientific complex features a double linear band, the first structured on the production line and the second placed adjacent to the first. If Western Europe patented the radially expanding city, and the American West staged the grid city, it appears that Siberia put forward another model, banded urbanism, and not just as a theoretical concept, but as a massively implemented reality. It is almost as if the government planner NA Miliutin's 1930 concept of linear development had become a reality over the following 60 years.

PLANNING DIAGRAMS

The Microrayon, built to house between 4,000 and 20,000 people, became the key concept in post-war residential urbanism under the rule of Kruschev's administration. It was developed into an absolute category for the planning of new towns all across the Soviet Union, but its particular combination with the monumental scientific component generated the template for several of the Siberian scientific complexes.

The Microrayon's documentation shows us an algorithm for the prefabrication of all aspects of life. This was a general consequence of the rigidities of Soviet planning, but it was also very useful for developments in far-outlying, hostile environments. Because the arctic climate made construction impossible,

production of these had just started, and Kruschev wanted to make Akademgorodok a showcase for the new technology. Early versions of the Kruschevka, as this housing typology came to be known, came without kitchens, plastering, doors or windows. "Build your home with your own hands" was a popular slogan on Soviet posters of the time. For that reason substantial architectural input by the inhabitants became necessary. They not only furnished interiors but also transformed balconies into indoor spaces. Using prefabricated construction elements for walls, openings, floors, windows, heating, Kruschev's design teams came up with a catalogue of variations on a prototype. Four to five storeys high, it was one section extruded into a beam with varying lengths. Every building had communal entrances and staircases, small living spaces and central heating.

In 1959, Kruschev made a stopover in Akademgorodok and set foot in what was, by then, a massive construction site, with workers and scientists surviving in wooden barracks in the forest as ten research institutes were erected. Upon seeing a model for a 12-storey hotel, Kruschev asked: "Why make all this fuss about 12 floors? Why are you trying to imitate New York skyscrapers?" Then, he leaned forward and, imitating scissors with his hands, snipped away the top four floors: "That is what I think about this skyscraper."[11] But there was also a strategic consideration at play. Apart from the hotel, none of complex's buildings surpassed five floors; appropriately for a secret city, the forest covered its tracks. Just like in the Western suburb, nature was used to hide civilisation; it served as a camouflage net, intent on obscuring the purposes that speak through the forms of civilisation.

Above: A cinema building in Akademgorodok, one of many community leisure facilities in the city.

Opposite: Plan of a 'Microrayon', the name given to the vast buildings designed as living quarters, and built to house 20,000 people and community facilities.

Scientists came to live in Akademgorodok in great numbers— 13,500 by 1964—and many brought their families as well. Olga Makarovoja, a resident of Novosibirsk, described these early years in an almost utopian fashion:

This town had the most amazing atmosphere. Everybody was more or less paid equally, and the hierarchical distinctions so typical for the bourgeois academy had evaporated. Faculty, students and workers would meet and discuss for hours, sometimes even for days. They would sit outside in the summer or by the fireplace in the winter. Discussion could emerge anywhere, anytime, and nobody would stop them. Drinking, dancing, inventing, calculating; it would all happen in the same place at the same moment. Yes, their families were not always so happy to be out here in the forest, but for the scientists it was as close to heaven as they could be. Here they had their own playground.[12]

several of the northern complexes were entirely prefabricated, transported in the summertime on wide-deck ships.

The rules for the planning, programming and production of Microrayons were published in the SnIP document "Planning and Construction in Cities and Urban Settlements". SnIP prescribed programme, surface and even form for new settlements. It dictated the ratios of open space per person, the size and forms of schools, the number of markets and the size of their inventories, the density in relation to the overall size of the settlement and the maximum distances between amenities. Above all, the Microrayon was planned as a self-sufficient entity. All facilities necessary for everyday survival had to be within a short walk's distance, preferably at the centre of the Microrayon.

The circular districts in Bio-Akademgorodok are a quasi-perfect materialisation of the SniP diagram. It is almost as if all mediations between the diagram and the settlement's form have been abolished. Here bureaucratic planning rules regained the utopian dimension so lacking in other prefabricated complexes in Soviet Russia.

An endless straight road leads us through empty, snow-covered fields. It is snowing again, and the horizon disappears as the sky blends with the earth. Through the haze we distinguish a series of silhouettes. To the left, monuments of varying heights appear in linear succession. A slender superstructure also appears: a kilometre long elevated skyway which connects the monuments. These are the research labs. Our car stops.

The skyway is now near us, hovering in mid-air at the third level on its slender legs. We enter the monumental Club of Scientists and find ourselves in an almost sacral space, four storeys high, covered with mosaics describing heroic scientists and soldiers on expeditions all over Siberia. There is a series of curving staircases and bridges crossing the space. Upon climbing them, we are led to a huge window looking out over the steppe. Then we find ourselves on the level of the almost endless walkway. We are alone as the perspective of corridor stretches out into infinity at both sides. We leave the building and float over the steppe into another majestic modernist building.

On the other side of the linear entry roadway, we see the contours of a long curving ten-storey high apartment superstructure—are we in Le Corbusier's Plan Obus? No, because the curve appears to be closing in on itself. It is a circular entity. Yet in the distance, a similar curve is already appearing. We are leaving the monuments, and cross the road for a closer inspection. The huge circles are constructed as a sequence of identical, slightly curved slabs: a Stonehenge of Kruschevkas. Inside, there is a white modernist village with two- to four-storey houses and slabs. The wind has calmed down thanks to the protection of the big blocks. After five to ten minutes we reach the centre of the settlement. There is a meeting club, a school and a market.

STRANDED SPACE SHIPS

By choosing to lift itself up from the plains, the Siberian scientific complex decided to no longer be defined by harsh winds, snow and ice, and frozen marshes. It had determined to emancipate itself from its own context. Thus, the scientific complex became a victory over emptiness, a sign of a society determined to construct its own figure. In a sense, we find its extreme speculation in

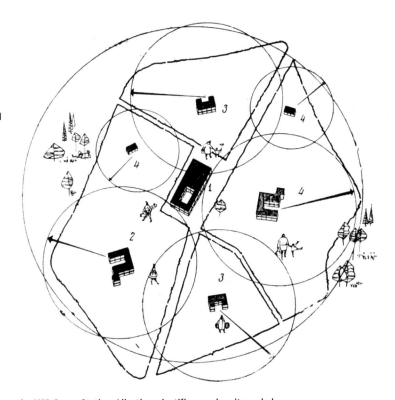

the MIR Space Station. Like the scientific complex, it needed to defend itself against the vast, hostile, endlessly surrounding emptiness. In order to succeed, a complete human habitat had to be offered in a capsular form. Its autonomy and self-sufficiency distinguished the form and organisation of these complexes from their capitalist counterparts in Greenland and Alaska, where corporations made up for the harsh if not impossible working conditions with cash. However, as we know, the Soviet economy was not based on the exchange of capital, and therefore another incentive was necessary to attract workers and scientists to these remote, hostile and isolated areas. The incentive here was urbanism and architecture. Great amounts of labour were spent on creating environments with a comparatively high standard of living. Especially in the Kruschev era, Siberia was prioritised and attention was paid to making its settlements showcases that would be capable of attracting scientists from other parts of the country. Gersh Budker, one such scientist, did not think twice: "It is great to have a place that the big wigs don't visit, and we don't permit the little ones to join us." With relative autonomy from the dogmas of Moscow and with an increased standard of living, the lure of Siberia became hard to resist.

THE FINAL PROJECT

The scientific complexes were both outposts of Moscow and refuges from it, a double agenda which was also apparent in the research undertaken there. At these complexes, radical plans were developed to unlock the Siberian territory to its fullest. With a project called the Siberian-Asian Balance, scientists proposed to correct a major 'irrationality' of Siberia's southern edge, which had fairly moderate temperatures but was too arid for development. For that reason they proposed to reverse the flow of the continent's main rivers, which were—and are still—flowing northward into the Arctic. If the Arctic ice deposits could be melted, they could be used for the irrigation of Southern Siberian and Central Asia. In order to dig these canals, the scientists proposed placing a sequence of nuclear explosives from the north to the south.

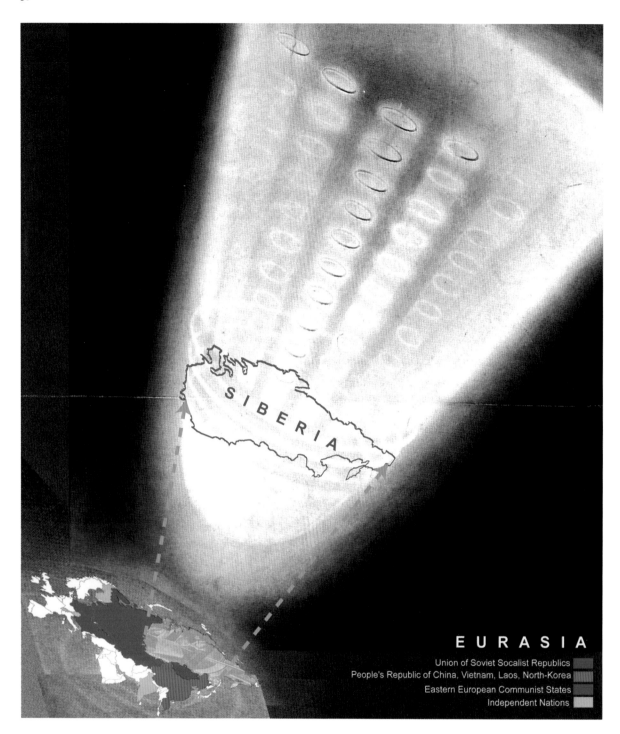

EURASIA

Union of Soviet Socialist Republics
People's Republic of China, Vietnam, Laos, North-Korea
Eastern European Communist States
Independent Nations

Futuristic diagram
situating Siberia in
Eurasia, the continent
composed of Europe
and Asia.

This 'solution' to the aridity problem of Siberia's southern
edge would have done nothing to improve the harsh cold of
the remaining territory. A plan was subsequently devised for the
warming up of Siberia. Led by the geographer, Pyotr Borisov, a
team of scientists proposed building a dam across the Bering Strait.
Deep under the water's surface, a number of pumps were to suck
water out of the Arctic and into the Pacific Ocean. The volume of
water that disappeared at the Arctic Ocean's eastern edge would
have to be balanced by a new inflow at its western edge. The Gulf
Stream, carrying warm equatorial waters to Scandinavia, would be
pulled all the way to the east and into the Arctic Ocean. This, it was
hypothesised, would heat up Siberia's northern edge. Instead of ice
and cold, there would suddenly be a giant continent with a moderate
climate. Though crude and exploitative, these propositions were also
possessed of a naive, even sincere desire to create a new Garden of

Eden, a contradiction which echoes the mutually exclusive agendas
on which the scientific complex was founded.

CONCLUSION: THE PROMISE OF THE PERIPHERY

With the collapse of the Soviet dream, the scientific assault on
this major landmass finally came to a halt, stuck in the mud, only
halfway there. Siberia, the ultimate Soviet periphery, served
as a white canvas, a space for phantasmagoric projections and
utopian desires, like a science fiction scenario. But while the
outer space of science fiction is defined in opposition to reality,
Siberian space operated simultaneously in both modes: reality
and fiction. The Soviets succumbed to its mirages and invested
real people and real goods into it. The apotheosis of the Soviet
assault never materialised, yet in the very moment of stalling
implementation, a new form emerged: the scientific complex.

In this form, Soviet planning abandoned its own totalising inclinations for a series of finite, concrete interventions. In these projects, planning, architecture, landscape and infrastructure design collapsed into one single, powerful gesture defining a moment of civilisational identity in the midst of boundless inhospitable fields.

The key concept here is constructivity. Russian Constructivism was only one moment in a pervasive mental habit which assumes that identity is a wilful act of construction. Constructivity is a collective mindset that believes civilisation can emancipate itself from the straitjackets of nature. Constructivity is about the pursuit of a choice made by or at least on behalf of the collective.

But this collective constructivity could only emerge in the ultimate periphery of Siberia, because there, two conflicting agendas were finally balancing each other: the strategic interests of the central bureaucracy, eager to expand its power, versus the tactical interests of scientists and other forces of resistance, which aimed to establish a degree of autonomy and independence from the centre. The peripheral geography of the new complexes liberated them from the continued hegemony of the empire elsewhere.

Thus, Siberia instructs us that the emancipatory promise of constructivity becomes most pregnant in its boundless peripheries. There it begins to abandon its own totalising ambitions, and focuses increasingly on discrete development fragments, uniting the contradictory agendas of central power and resistance.

Therein lies the fundamental promise of Siberia as an analogous territory for our own sprawling peripheries in the West. The notion of a civilisational complex in the midst of this inhospitable wilderness could be investigated as a strategy for our own totality, namely that of privatised sprawl. For indeed, the unifying condition of endless sprawl displays a striking analogy with the Siberian canvas. Imagine for a moment the Boston–Washington Corridor, the Seattle–Vancouver system or the Blue Banana in Europe (stretching from London via the Low Countries through the Rhône Valley into Marseille, ending in Barcelona). Siberia is almost like a generic but radicalised version of these sprawling territories. Both systems are without a horizon; both exhibit a lack of centrality; and both feature a capsular development logic. But Siberia, as an analogous territory, also shows us the promise contained within our own quagmire. It is here, more than in the global city centres, where an experiment based on the unification of contradictory agendas could give rise to a new set of operations. By allowing ourselves a mindset of constructivity, a constellation of complexes can emerge that is not transfixed by the territory as it is, but dares once more to stake out a claim about how we want to see our own civilisation: how it ought to be.

Finally, the Siberian analogy shows that the quasi-endless periphery, resulting from successive waves of sub-urbanisation, is a zone of tremendous promise. Its indeterminacy allows for a new constructivity. Here, experimentation with deviant architectures is much more likely than in the centres of power.[13]

1. Quoted in Sansone, Vittorio, *Siberia: Epic of the Century*, Moscow: Progress Publishers, 1980, pp. 98–99.

2. Lenin in "Interview with Arthur Ransome, Correspondent of the Daily News", *Collected Works*, Vol. 42, 1917–1923, Moscow: Progress Publishers, 1969, p. 67.

3. Plans to be found in the Novosibirsk State University Architecture Department.

4. For example, the Bauhaus architect Ernst May and his Brigades built a series of five housing blocks in the early 1930s, of which two were later refurbished in the manner of socialist realism.

5. The collectivisation of agriculture: the transformation of thousands of farms into 'agricultural productive complexes'.

6. After the Second World War large coal basins were found in the Urals, and the 1,500 kilometre 'factory' became redundant. The Kuznetsk is still a major basin.

7. Pallot, J, and DJB Shaw, *Planning in the Soviet Union*, London: Croom Helm, 1981.

8. Graham, Loren, *Science, Philosophy and Human Behaviour in the Soviet Union*, New York: Columbia University Press, 1987.

9. Quoted in Josephson, Paul, *New Atlantis Revisited*, New Jersey: Princeton University Press, 1997, pp. 9–25.

10. Josephson, *New Atlantis Revisited*, p. 14.

11. Author's interview, 10 April 2001.

12. Josephson, *New Atlantis Revisited*.

13. This text would never have been possible without the support of Bart Goldhoorn in Moscow and Alexander Lozhkin in Novosibirsk. The first researches into the development of Siberia were done within the framework of Rem Koolhaas's History of Communism project at the Harvard Design School, 2000–2002.

UTOPIA

| DYSTOPIA

Utopia without dystopia is like Heaven without Hell. When William Blake wrote about the "dark satanic mills" in 1804, he may not have been referring to the numerous factories, pollution, poverty and despair brought about by the Industrial Revolution, but these examples serve as shorthand for the urban dystopias that would begin to emerge in the nineteenth century. Such dystopias have been challenged by the idealistic and utopian proposals of architects and planners. Unfortunately, however, many of those utopias realised have themselves developed dystopic connotations (often originating from the very properties that gave rise to their utopian character in the first place). This phenomena might come about for any number of reasons—inequalities across communities may be magnified, or new communities with poor living conditions might develop to supply labour to the utopian settlement. Of course, in some sense, the idea of utopia is dependent on who imagines it. For millions of the rural poor, who migrate to the cities of the developing world, the swelling shanty towns they inhabit might appear wholly dystopic, but could also offer salvation from rural poverty and oppression. The modest dreams realised by such migrant workers might be just as valid a utopia as those conceived of by idealists and planners.

In 1339, Ambrogio Lorenzetti painted a great 14-metre long fresco, *The Effects of Good Governance*, depicting a detailed representation of a densely populated city, at work and play. This may be the first example of a European representation of an urban ideal that does not include metaphysical intervention (in the form of gods or goddesses) and instead depicts ordinary people undertaking ordinary tasks. The artist and critic Julian Bell notes that the commissioners of the work, the Sienna Council who "channelled banking profits into public works", were saying "this is how things should be in the republic".[1] Their utopia was a propaganda tool, evidence of the fact that, even before the word is coined, a built utopia serves a political purpose. The word "utopia" comes from Thomas More's 1515 book of the same name, in which he describes the imaginary island of Utopia. More's Utopia is the site of the fictional city of Amaurote, which prohibits private ownership and nationalises everything from property to governmental decision. This story sounds distinctly like a model for totalitarian socialism, and indeed More's tale is rife with socialist politics.

SITUATING UTOPIA PHILOSOPHICALLY

Many philosophers of the left have spun utopian tales in an effort to illustrate how an improved world might provide solutions for perceived injustices. Marx is the obvious example, projecting that the socialist ideal of a classless society was a historical inevitability, and elaborating what that society might look like in his utopian framework. It is, however, Marxist-influenced philosophers in France who bring urban philosophy more up to date. One such example is a whimsical 1953 essay by Giles Ivain, in which he laments how materialism has made leisure empty, and what was required was a new urbanism (not to be confused with the New Urbanism that arose three decades later in America). Ivain describes an imaginary city where districts "could correspond to the whole spectrum of diverse feelings that one encounters by chance in everyday life: Bizarre Quarter; Happy Quarter (specially reserved for habitation); Noble and Tragic Quarter (for good children); Historical Quarter (museums, schools); Useful Quarter (hospital, tool shops); Sinister Quarter, etc".[2] This is hardly a practical formula from which to start building a utopia, but oddly, it was taken on board as an urbanist position by the Lettrists, a collection of avant-garde artists who would evolve into the Situationists, a group of politically and artistically focused individuals, including Guy Debord and the Dutch painter Constant Nieuwenhuys, amongst others, who also had roots in the Marxist theory that would aspire to major social transformations in the period.

Like the Situationists, Henri Lefebvre was interested in a classless society, but had parted ways with the group in 1962. In 1974, he published *The Production of Space*, which focused on the concept of space as a social product or construction that relies on values and the social production of meaning. He argued that politics and economics made—particularly

Top: Thomas More's, The Island of Utopia, 1516. Thomas More coined the term "Utopia" (from the Greek words *eu-topos* and *ou-topos*—meaning 'good place' and 'no place' respectively) to describe a fictional New World island community and its social and cultural customs. Written in Latin, the book was heavily influenced by Plato's classical model of the perfect republic and by the writer's work with Erasmus. The society was a perfect mechanism meant to cast doubt on the actual social, political and religious life of Europe and set a pattern and a style for the literary utopias that followed. The abolition of private property, the society's location in a distant, timeless land, the almost totalitarian obsession with order, control and uniformity—all these became defining features of Utopianism as the movement came to be defined

in the sixteenth and seventeenth centuries.

Opposite: Ettore Sottsass, The Planet as Festival: Study for a Large Dispenser of Waltzes, Tangos, Rock, and Cha-Cha, 1972–1973. Ettore Sottsass was a highly influential Austrian born architect and designer. In the early 1960s he became widely know as an industrial designer for Olivetti and was later associated with Italian radical architecture and the work of Superstudio and Archizoom. In 1972 he created The Planet as Festival, a series of drawings depicting a utopian, fantastical land free from the constraints of work. It remains one of the landmarks of visionary, unrealised architecture.

Following pages: Ambrogio Lorenzetti, *Allegory of Good Government: Effects of Good Government in the City*, 1338–1340. Among Ambrogio Lorenzetti's most significant

achievements is the fresco series that adorns the walls of the Palazzo Publico in Siena. It is considered to be the first panoramic city/countryscape of its kind since Antiquity.

urban—space more important than historical or personal time. A conclusion that was in direct conflict with Debord's theories. Lefebvre was interested in *détournement*, in which a built environment loses its original purpose and is re-appropriated for new uses. This was the case in les Halles, a central Paris market area that had been a haunt of the Situationists but which temporarily became a focus for celebration and leisure by Parisian youth after the 1968 student-led protests challenging the state's authority. However, Lefebvre also identified a wider society in which capitalism had appropriated space. The title of *The Production of Space* summarises a grand concept: that the social production of space is a top-down process, which imposes an environment on people, built by those in power, whether socialist or capitalist. "The state and each of its constituent institutions call for spaces—but spaces which they can then organise according to their specific requirements; so there is no sense in which space can be treated solely as an *a priori* condition of these institutions and the state which presides over them."[3]

For Lefebvre, there would be no 'church' without churches, for example. Within the framework of produced space, the city can be perceived as a method of controlling the population. In contrast, the social construction of space is a roots-up creation of the environment, in which the people themselves shape the space they live in. Another way of looking at this phenomena is in the form of planned cities and New Towns—implying that utopian ideals require produced space, where dystopias are constructed space. The reality, however, is not so clear-cut.

In 1967, another French thinker, Michel Foucault, wrote that utopias "are sites that have a general relation of direct or intended analogy with the real space of society... (they) preserve society itself in a perfected form". He went on to say that attempts to create utopias only extend the problems they seek to solve. Foucault also coined the term "heterotopia", to describe real places "which are something like counter-sites, a kind of effectively enacted utopia in which... all the other real sites that can be found within a culture are simultaneously represented, contested and inverted".[4] More explicit, taken from the term "heterogeneous", it entails space or places absent of a single ruling class or society, but what does this really mean? Like utopia, heterotopia is defined by society, but it is somewhere else, where social order is different to normal society. Places are juxtaposed in heterotopias (foreign languages are spoken in an immigrant community) and admission and exclusion policies are enforced. Foucault's own examples include Scandinavian saunas or Puritan colonies in America in the seventeenth century. Heterotopia also applies to modern urban places. Fast-developing cities in the Asian Pacific region follow a perceived model of the Western city, from the built environment of office towers and mass housing to the patterns of employment and amenities. It is as if they have recreated the Western model, re-imagined as a heterotopic structure.

TOWARDS GREEN AND PLEASANT URBAN UTOPIAS

What is the story of these attempts to build utopia? We have already seen how nineteenth century industrial cities exploded, with the working classes relegated to extreme conditions; ramshackle construction, bad sanitation and pollution from the very factories they served. Karl Marx' ideas about capital and class emerged from these very conditions, observed most dramatically in the urban proletariat of nineteenth century Cologne and London. But the first attempts to address industrial dystopia were actually late nineteenth century paternal industrialists rather than socialists, who built small integrated utopian towns for their workforces—the chocolate tycoon George Cadbury at Bourneville near Birmingham, England; the railway magnate George Pullman at Pullman near Chicago; and the head of the soap empire, WH Lever, at Port Sunlight, near Liverpool. These places gave workers decent housing, gardens, schools and shops, all situated within a picturesque environment. The English planner, Ebenezer Howard, reacted to the urban dystopia by extending this spirit of idealism to his regional plans for self-sufficient Garden Cities. Howard's utopian model fused the most positive elements of country and city living into one settlement, providing everything from social diversions, high wages, employment opportunity, natural beauty and low rent. The Garden City was a place in which the "town and country must by married, and out of this joyous union will spring a new hope, a new life, a new civilisation".[5] Letchworth's Garden City was the first such example. Completed in 1903, here was a place where land was communally owned, the sale of alcohol was banned, and (following the Cheap Cottages Exhibition in the town in 1907), houses were built in traditional cottage-style.

All these turn-of-the-century communities were characterised by buildings constructed on a human scale and styled to evoke an idealised near past. Nowadays, this quaint-looking idea of utopia is as strong as ever, but it is built for affluent conservatives who seek a tranquil refuge from the frenetic dystopian anarchy of the modern city proper. Two such picturesque utopias, each with built-in nostalgia, are Thames Town and the village of Poundbury—the latter, the brain-child of Prince Charles. Under construction since 1993, it is planned to house 5,000 people. Curiously, both are, in some sense, Dorset towns—Poundbury is located in the region while Thames Town's (the clone town situated near Shanghai,

Opposite top: Yona Friedman, *Spatial City*, 1958–1959. Friedman's *Spatial City* was a three-dimensional megastructure and one of the most significant applications of mobile architecture. Friedman's utopian city was user centred and meant to allow the inhabitants maximum freedom of movement. A quest away from the outdated, static realities of earlier modernist practice, it encapsulated Friedman's belief that architecture should refrain from imposing itself on the inhabitant, and called for a design that would allow for user participation.

Opposite bottom: Constant Nieuwenhuys, *Gezicht op New Babylonische sectoren*, 1971. Collection of the Gemeentemuseum, Den Haag, NL. In the 1950s Dutch artist Constant Nieuwenhuys started working on New Babylon, a visionary architectural plan for a future society. It was a situationist proposal

for the transformation of everyday life and the abolition of human labour through the full automation of production. Like Friedman's *Spatial City* it envisioned a nomadic city lacking an overall masterplan and being constantly recreated by its inhabitants.

Above: Superstudio, *12 Ideal Cities*, 1971. Superstudio was a radical architecture group founded in 1966 in Florence. With a strong situationist ethos and deeply affected by the events of May 1968, the group produced *12 Ideal Cities*, a series of brief metaphorical narratives and collages on the limits of utopia. Each city was meant to represent a coherent, totalising, 'flawless' and dystopian system, where individuals were completely deprived of any control over their own lives. As Superstudio's member, Piero Frassinelli, remarked: 'I sought to improve 12 models of cities, ridding them

of the incongruities, the mistakes, the perplexities that human weakness interposes.... I achieved city nightmares, perfect mechanisms, like the ones the Nazis designed to solve the Jewish 'problem'." Though often mistakenly understood as a last attempt to rescue the modernist monumental utopias, *12 Ideal Cities* was essentially a total re-examination and critique of the utopian project.

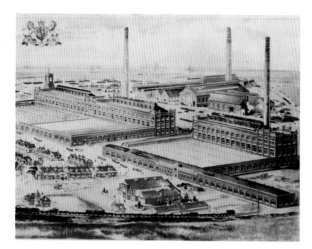

China, which emanates the style of English housing in its architecture) buildings have been appropriated from Dorset vernacular architecture. Few can afford to live in Poundbury or Thames Town, so if the common definition of utopia implies classlessness, these are definitely dystopias for many. Nevertheless, anyone can drive to these places. Indeed, despite Prince Charles' assertion that Poundbury's "entire masterplan was based upon placing the pedestrian, and not the car, at the centre of the design", its residents have a greater car use than adjacent Dorset settlements. Access to gated communities is, however, not so simple.

And the People, who hide themselves behind a Wall…

According to American Census Bureau's American Housing Survey of 2001, six per cent of those surveyed live in communities built behind walls and gates that control entry. That amounts to seven million households across the country, especially in the south and west of the country. When asked about the motivation behind sealing their community off from the rest of urban society, inhabitants cite security, privacy and sense of community as primary factors. The 'perfect' life of a gated estate resident was satirised in the 1998 film *The Truman Show*, filmed in the actual town of Seaside, Florida. *The Truman Show* focuses on the life of one Truman Banks, whose every move has been broadcast nationwide to thousands of viewers since the day of his birth. The fictional town of Seahaven is too perfect, its inhabitants too happy. Ultimately, it speaks of the control and restrictions set upon the inhabitants of environments over which they have little or no control. Seaside, the real settlement in Florida, is one of the many projects of New Urbanist town planning. Drawing on some of the principles put forward by Howard's Garden Cities, the members of the New Urbanist movement aim toward "the restoration of existing urban centres and towns within coherent metropolitan regions, the reconfiguration of sprawling suburbs into communities of real neighbourhood and diverse districts, the conservation of natural environments and the preservation of our built legacy".

In so doing, the New Urbanists conceived of the ideal domestic dwelling, the Traditional Neighbourhood Unit, in which the neighbourhood must have

> a centre and an edge. The optimal size of a neighbourhood [must be] a quarter mile from centre to edge. [It must have] a balanced mix of activities— dwelling, shopping, working, schooling, worshipping and recreation. The neighbourhood structures, building sites and traffic [will be organised] on a fine network of interconnecting streets. The neighbourhood [must give] priority to public space and to the appropriate location of public buildings.[6]

Even if these communities are utopias to their inhabitants, petty intolerances from neighbours objecting to, say, a party or a paint colour that doesn't conform to the plan, can sour their paradise. Research in Britain in 2002 found that crime levels were about the same in gated communities and ordinary suburbs. It is too early to tell if that will be the case with Holwood, a 2008 development that places terraced townhouses in crescents deep inside a private English forest (re-fulfilling the Regency architect John Nash's vision of urban terraces where everyone has a country view). Like those nostalgically-inspired towns, people in gated communities are often affluent conservatives, and they constitute a class separation on a far bigger scale than commonly seen in other urban environments.

Gated estates are also cropping up in poor countries. In the exploding megacities of the developed world, the middle classes feel under siege from poverty, disorder and often a breakdown of state agencies. One of the oldest is Alphaville, conceived in the 1970s and 23 kilometres from the centre of São Paulo. Here 30,000 people live in an environment peopled with nearly a thousand armed guards and, with a murder rate eight times that of New York, commuters use helicopters to literally skip over the ever-present dangers of crime.

The gated estate, like the ancient walled city, is defensible and sealed off from the threats and chaos outside, and the most extreme examples of defensibility make no illusions about their purpose. The biggest gated estate is the oil

Above: Anonymous, Port Sunlight, Works and Village, 1905. Unilever Historical Archives, Port Sunlight. Port Sunlight is a village in Merseyside, England. It was founded by William Hesketh Lever in 1888 to accommodate the employees of Lever Brothers' soap factory. Influenced by the Arts and Crafts Movement and by English writer, poet and socialist William Morris, it provided better housing conditions for the working class than typically available at the time.

Opposite: Seaside, Florida. Seaside, a masterplanned community in Florida, is often cited as the first truly New Urbanist town and was used as a model for the creation of other New Urbanist developments both in America and elsewhere. It has been both praised for its successful realisation of New Urbanist ideals.

Top: Frank Lloyd Wright's Broadacre City, 1934–1935. Broadacre City was a late creation by Lloyd Wright. He attempted to blur the distinction between the city and the countryside —Broadacre was a decentralised city with neither end nor beginning, stretching itself endlessly over the natural landscape. The Frank Lloyd Wright Foundation, Scottsdale, Arizona. © ARS, NY and DACS, London, 2008.

Bottom: An Industrial City: metallurgical factories, blast furnaces and public services, 1917, in Tony Garnier's, *Une Ville Industrielle, étude pour la construction des villes*, Lyons, 1919.

Opposite top: Le Corbusier's *La Ville Radieuse: The Contemporary City for Three Million Inhabitants*, 1933. Plan FLC 24909B © FLC/DACS, 2008 *La Ville Radieuse* was an unrealised

project indebted to the thought of nineteenth century French utopias such as Saint-Simon and Charles Fourier. It promised a future of clean air, giant residential units and green, landscaped spaces.

Opposite bottom: Le Corbusier, *Plan Obus*, project A, 1930. *Plan Obus* was an unrealised plan for the North African city of Algiers. © FLC/DACS, 2008.

town of Dhahran in Saudi Arabia, where 100,000 people are sealed off from the retrogressive religious country at large and the threat of terrorism it has engendered. Life is good for the many ex-patriate employees of the oil business and their families here—they live in comfort with servants and swimming pools. In Baghdad, the Green Zone is where the Iraqi government and coalition military and administrative personnel live and work. This sector, also known as 'The Bubble' or 'Emerald City', is defended by checkpoints, razor-wire, walls, earthworks, tanks and other armed military vehicles. Within its confines, the environment couldn't be more pleasant, trees bearing dates and other fruits dot tranquil, villa-lined streets.

THE EVOLUTION OF THE IDEAL SOCIAL ESTATE

The Communist Manifesto of 1848, was commissioned by the Communist League and written by Karl Marx and Friedrich Engels. The document proposed a course of action to facilitate removal of power and social order as implemented by the bourgeoisie, paving the way for a classless and stateless society. Marx and Engels go on to discuss the even distribution of people across the land, eliminating the difference between urban and rural. One of the great US architects of the twentieth century thought along similar lines. Frank Lloyd Wright proposed his Broadacre City in *The Disappearing City* of 1932. Wright envisioned a low-density built environment of 6.4 square kilometres where factory workers were allocated a farm plot of .4 hectares each, but used cars to drive to the factories that employed them. Just as the garden cities shaped English suburbia and other suburbs elsewhere, Broadacre City's principles can be seen in the suburban sprawl of American cities after the Second World War, albeit without the farms and the working classes.

New towns and public housing were seen as the 'New Jerusalem' after the Second World War, particularly in Europe, stemming from twentieth century socialist thinking typified by a drive to empower both worker and intellectual by providing equal opportunity of work, housing and cradle-to-grave welfare. One such example was a proposal made in 1907 by the radical French architect, Tony Garnier, whose suggestion for a holistic utopian city—*Ville Industrielle*—would see over 30,000 workers housed in a settlement with a built-in hygiene system facilitated by air and light. The workers in Garnier's proposal would have access to a city centre and transport links, but the settlement would do away with such institutions as the police force, the prison system and the church, deemed unnecessary given this new vision of the future city. There would be no private land ownership, and, in many ways, the zoning principles of the *Ville Industrielle* would anticipate the Athens Charter of some 30 years later. In the 1920s, the forces of modernism were proffering a new, utopian vision of living and the built environment, eager to sweep away past social hierarchies and classist structures. During this time the Swiss-born architect Le Corbusier produced utopian plans for entire cities. His 1922 Ville Contemporaine plan would have housed three million people in a 12-storey structure overlooking communal rectangles of greenery, all laid out on a grid around a nucleus of 60-storey office blocks. Le Corbusier's vision saw these blocks as office space or housing for the most wealthy, with a central transportation hub that would service all inhabitants by bus or train. Le Corbusier re-planned entire cities such as Algiers (in the guise of an extensive housing viaduct, parts of which were realised before the Algiers War in the 1950s and 60s). As one of the leading voices in CIAM, the *Congrès International d'Architecture Moderne*, a group of modernist architects formed in 1928, who believed that architecture must be functional to better serve humanity, rather than aesthetic to serve the demands of theory, he planned *La Ville Radieuse* where everything—including the roads—was raised on columns above the ground, and flats were stacked in long glass curtain-walled terraces. In a 1933 meeting, that took place on a boat sailing the Mediterranean, CIAM turned their attention to urban planning. The resulting Athens Charter spelt out a zoned built environment in which people lived in uncluttered rectilinear superblocks with flat roofs, separated by green space. The utopian vision of the Athens Charter was particularly influential on post-war public-sector architects, and the inner city social housing they designed quickly spread across Europe.

The result was the sink estates of the 1960s and 70s, such as Peckham in London, before its regeneration, Harlesden or Gospel Oak which replaced the Victorian slums but failed to replicate the close-knit community the original settlements encompassed. Their architecture was descended from Le Corbusier's, and revived the use of concrete in a Brutalist style. These estates would become the new dystopias, the dehumanising domains of disenfranchised, alienated youth and foster culture of crime.

The USSR should have provided a clean slate for the building of complete urban utopias, but the Soviets fared little better than their European or American counterparts. Constructivist avant-garde architects led the direction towards new, functionalist architecture based on scientific principles. In the 1920s they designed standardised communal living spaces, but when it came to planning a huge new steel town at Magnitogorsk, the Soviets chose a German architect, Ernst May. He had studied the English Garden Cities and had built functionalist housing developments in Frankfurt and was a member of CIAM. In 1928 he led a team of 14 to build 20 new towns in the USSR. At Magnitogorsk, however, he found that construction was already underway, and his plans were compromised. Stalin's Five Year Plans prioritised industry and great civil engineering projects over housing, resulting in vast 'identikit' estates of poor quality apartment blocks, with these also spreading into Central Europe's Warsaw Pact countries during the post-war period.

The visions for utopian state housing also spread to the East, with the most optimistic examples being devised and built in Singapore. From 1960, high-rise apartment blocks started to replace overcrowded slums, and were built—according to principles following those of CIAM architects—in holistically-planned estates with green spaces, local amenities and light industry. As of 2007, 84 per cent of Singaporeans lived in flats built by the Housing and Development Board (HBD), whose work now focuses on upgrading flats built before 1986, when spaces were smaller and the architecture plainer. Since 1964, home ownership of these state-built flats has been encouraged, which is a significant factor given the lack of

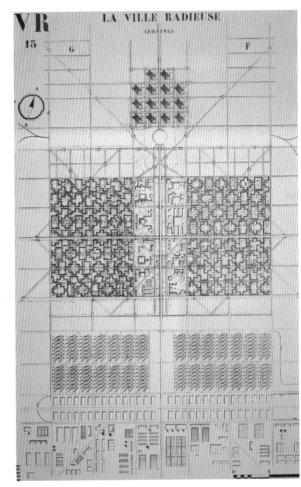

Top: One of the few modern utopias to be materialised, Habitat 67 is a housing complex and Brutalist architectural landmark on the Saint Lawrence River in Montreal, Quebec. It is composed of 354 prefabricated concrete modules and was designed by Moshe Safdie. Built as part of Expo 67, one of the world's largest universal exhibitions, it was meant to provide affordable, low rent housing and a strong sense of community through the creation of communal spaces, children's play areas and a series of interconnecting outdoor walkways or 'pedestrian streets'. By combining factory produced components with the vernacular structure of hillside villages, it embodied a humanistic alternative to the drab realities of earlier modernist housing.

Bottom: Digital view of Jumeirah island, an artificial island located off the Jumeirah coast of Dubai in the United Arab Emirates.

graffiti and vandalism in this spotless city state. Nowadays, the HBD increasingly function like a private developer, and their latest project, a string of 50-storey towers linked by skybridges, is being marketed with showflats and advertisements, just as luxury condominium developments are. In Singapore, the dystopic heritage of social housing has been gradually transformed into something closer to a utopian built environment.

INVESTING IN UTOPIAS FOR PROFIT

Today, it is the property developer who is leading the delivery of urban utopias. In the heart of rich cities across the world, finger-thin luxury residential skyscrapers reach up to break into already crowded skylines, with developers such as Beetham or Ballymore in Britain, or Donald Trump and Michael Shvo in America leading the pack. Entire downtown blocks are being redeveloped into upmarket residential complexes, evidenced by such new developments as the Candy Brothers' luxury housing projects at Knightsbridge, Fitzrovia and Chelsea in London. However substantial these undertakings appear, they are dwarfed by the plans of developers elsewhere in the world, particularly in Dubai. Emaar Properties are the developers of the world's tallest building, the Burj Dubai, and the 'Downtown Dubai' development that surrounds it. Their big rivals, Al Nakheel, site their prestige developments offshore, on manmade islands in a complex they have dubbed "The World", which comprises 300 residential islands configured into the shape of a world map. The three Palm developments, by contrast, are linked to Dubai's coast, and are palm-tree shaped land-masses surrounded by breakwater rings, and containing both residential and light industry areas. The Palm Jumeirah started construction in 2001 with the first residents moving in just five years later, with a monorail transit system running down the trunk of the palm currently under construction. The next development in the series will be Palm Jebel Ali, started in 2002, it is set to be twice the size of Palm Jumeriah, and a considerable degree denser than its predecessor, with a projected 1.7 million inhabitants by 2020. The final development, the Palm

Deira, may only house one million, but it boasts the largest area of the three Palm developments—an area five times that of Jebel Ali.

Developments such as these are projected utopias for the super-rich, but they conceal a mirror dystopia of the low-paid migrant workers that built and sustain them. Almost half a million foreigners work in construction in the United Arab Emirates (UAE), coming mainly from the Indian sub-continent. According to the 2006 Human Rights Watch report "Building Towers, Cheating Workers", their average monthly pay is US$175 a month—if they are paid at all. Indeed, withholding a month or two of pay is seen as a 'custom' by some construction companies, and since the workers arrive already indebted to unscrupulous recruitment agents, interest quickly accrues in what amounts to something like slave labour. Passports are confiscated and health and safety standards are low. In 2007, the UAE started to address some of the problems, for example by posting officials in Dubai's worker camps to address complaints, and by looking into the issue of minimum wages. However, as many more of these workers are on fixed-term contracts, their rights are limited. As in other places building rapidly, such as China, the almost exclusively male worker population live in poor-quality shared accommodation—often just temporary huts—with few or no amenities, and little recourse to employment or safety regulations.

From this survey, we may conclude that there is a certain truth in the words of the rationalist philosopher Karl Popper: "Those who promise us paradise on earth never produced anything but a hell." Certainly, utopia's socialist origins may have been lost in the emerging playgrounds of the rich, but the class divide utopia seeks to address are as wide as ever. The traditional concept of utopia might be a planned state of produced space, but its most common consequence—at least in the West—is the development of unplanned suburbia. Utopia proper may remain unrealised, but the heterotopias it produces are everywhere.

1. Bell, Julian, *Mirror on the World*, London: Thames and Hudson, 2007, pp. 146–147.

2. Ivain, Gilles, "Formulary for a New Urbanism", *Internationale Situationniste*, No. 1, October 1953.

3. Lefebvre, Henri, *The Production of Space*, Oxford: Blackwell Publishing, 1991.

4. Foucault, Michel, "des Espaces Autres" written in 1967 but published in 1984 in *Architecture-Mouvement-Continuité*.

5. Howard, Ebenezer, *Garden Cities of To-Morrow*, London, Faber and Faber, 1946.

6. New Urbanist Charter, 1993.

CUMBERNAULD

21 kilometres northeast of Glasgow on a windblown hilltop sits Cumbernauld, the New Town considered to be Britain's most concrete example of modernist architecture and town planning—in more ways than one. Tagged everything from "utopia" to "the Kabul of the north", "Stalinist" to "the most significant contribution to urban design in the western world", Cumbernauld has never been one for occupying the middle ground.[1]

There has been a settlement at Cumbernauld (Gaelic for "the meeting of the waters") since Roman times, but the present new town was constructed in the 1950s and 60s in response to overcrowding and bomb damage in Glasgow's dilapidated post-war city centre. Its population currently hovers around 52,000, making it the sixth largest urban conurbation in Scotland and the most populous town in North Lanarkshire.

Its history begins with paternalistic goodwill, but the road to hell, as the saying goes, is always paved with good intentions. The newly-elected Labour government had set up the New Towns Committee in 1945 with a view to solving the problems of urban congestion and squalid inner city housing conditions. As

part of the Scottish response to the problem, the Clyde Valley Regional Plan was put forward by Patrick Abercrombie and Robert Matthew in 1946, despite the opposition of the Glasgow municipal authorities. The Plan proposed rehousing up to a third of the population of Glasgow in newly-constructed satellite towns outside the city, preserving greenbelt land around the old city centre. Cumbernauld was designated a New Town in 1955 and construction began in 1957.

The planning and development of the town was handled by the non-political, government-funded Cumbernauld Development Corporation, which continued to manage its development until 1996. Under the supervision of Chief Architect and Planning Officer, Hugh Wilson, an expert and idealistic team of planners and architects sourced from all over the world began work designing what was to become one of the great modernist experiments of twentieth century Britain.

The New Towns project had its deepest roots in the Garden Cities movement of the early twentieth century, which advocated low-density development, traditional building styles and naturalistic landscaping as a

pathway to successful community-building in new housing projects. Cumbernauld's planners and architects, however, reacted against the suburban pattern set out in earlier English garden suburbs like Welwyn Garden City, instead taking very literally the First Report of the New Towns Committee's high-minded assertions that the building of the New Towns must be "experiments in building, as well as in living", and must "conduct an essay on civilisation".[2] Free from the financial constraints of more commercial developments, the project's architects and planners saw themselves as pioneers of a new set of social and architectural ideals. Cumbernauld was to be a town for the future that didn't only look different, but allowed people to live differently.

The town was designed centring around a single abstract-form, multi-purpose and multi-level 'megastructure' designed by architect Geoffrey Copcutt, which would house the town's municipal, commercial, leisure and business facilities as well as luxury penthouse apartments: the world's first multi-level covered shopping centre, catering to its 50,000 projected residents' every need. It included multi-functional entertainment spaces, which could be

CUMBERNAULD, DHAVARI AND THAMES TOWN

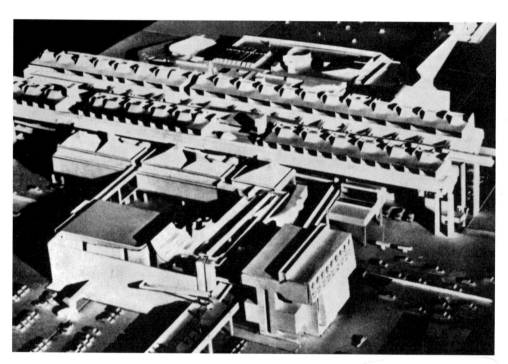

Model of
Cumbernauld city
centre, circa 1960s.

anticipated to reach 100 per cent). It was to be a haven for business and pleasure; minutes by walkway from open countryside and by expressway from the motorway network. Phase One of the project was completed in 1968.

Cumbernauld was a place to be bold; its public buildings were not wallflowers. In addition to Copcutt's megastructure, the town is also home to many notable modernist buildings by the now-defunct Scottish firm Gillespie, Kidd and Coia, most famous for St Peter's Seminary in Cardross. It should have been so successful; a modernist utopia built from the ground up in central Scotland. A roll-call of the awards and accolades the town has accumulated over the years, however, is an ambivalent affair to say the least. In 1967, Cumbernauld was awarded the RS Reynolds Award for Community Architecture by the American Institute of Architects. Cumbernauld was, the committee stated, "designed for the millennium—the dreams of the 1920s and 1930s... built on a hill near Glasgow".[3] Architects, planners and students came from all over the world to marvel at the bold new environment taking shape. Thousands of column inches were dedicated to its modernity and vision

redfined as the town's needs evolved. This structure was surrounded by high-density mixed high- and low-rise housing clusters, linked to the town centre by a system of raised pedestrian walkways and underpasses. The town's transport infrastructure was designed to segregate pedestrians and motor vehicles completely, with cars using high-speed expressways and enormous car parks; the aim being that a resident could walk from anywhere in Cumbernauld to the town centre buildings within 20 mintutes without ever crossing a road (though car ownership was in the world's architectural journals. Yet in 2001 and 2005, the town was awarded the distinctly less prestigious 'Plook on the Plinth' Carbuncle of the Year award for the Most Dismal Town in Scotland. Even more spectacularly, in December 2005, the entire town centre garnered a public nomination for demolition in the Channel 4 series *Demolition*, which ultimately voted it the worst building in Britain.

So what went wrong? The town centre megastructure itself has focused a lot of the debate surrounding Cumbernauld and its ultimate success or failure as a utopian project, and can serve to illustrate many of the town's failings in shorthand. Its all-encompassing concrete heft—in the abstract—is bold and imposing, clean and modern. In reality, subject to the harsh Scottish weather, it is damp, alienating and in need of constant maintenance. Its canopied walkways became wind tunnels, its retail units were never fully let and the well-heeled imagined occupants of the upper-level penthouse apartments never materialised. The confusing and frustrating system of raised walkways linking the residential areas to the town centre quickly became a magnet for vandalism and residents took to running

the gauntlet of high-speed expressways to reach what shops there were. Leisure activities were painfully limited, particularly for young people; one resident remembered that for most of the 1970s there was only one restaurant in the whole town, and no cinema. The multi-functional leisure spaces of the town centre stood empty, or were never built. The initial New Town ideal of "space, sunlight and privacy" too easily fostered isolation and, with a municipal lack of commitment to achieving Copcutt's original vision of a socially-sustaining infrastructure, the life had left the town centre before it had the chance to begin.

Funding problems have dogged the project, particularly in recent years, and the free spending of the initial phases of construction could not be repeated. The liberating potential for flexibilty Copcutt had written into his plan for the town centre buildings was never realised, and it became a costly, problematic monolith. Many phases of the Plan were never completed (the drawings for the next, never-realised phase of the town centre showed the ambition of Copcutt's social vision; it was to feature nurseries, a library, a social club, a hotel, a winter garden, and even small nooks for 'flea markets'); some were diluted

and modified beyond recognition; others were carved up and passed over to privately financed development companies. Natural decay continued unabated and a large section of the town centre fell into such disrepair that it had to be demolished.

Once Cumbernauld town centre had left the jurisdiction of the original architects, its original modernist utopian vision—requiring time and commitment—quickly gave way to the vagaries of market forces. Scheme followed scheme of retail quick-fixes, none of which succeeded in re-invigorating the town centre.

It would be unfair to suggest the fate of the megastructure mirrors that of the town as a whole. Cumbernauld's residential developments have been successful and still win awards, and housing areas like Seafar have the potential to become listed sites in the future. Socially and economically too, the statistics look good. Cumbernauld has an average gross household income above the national average, and below-average unemployment and child poverty rates. A number of international-scale businesses have bases just outside the town centre, and private investment is bringing new money to the area. A new phase in the regeneration of

Still from
Cumbernauld: Town for Tomorrow, 2003.
Video, animation,
sound, archive
material, variable
dimensions. Original
archive image courtesy
of North Lanarkshire
Archives. Created by
Gair Dunlop and Dan
Morton, this work is
an interactive vision of
the modernist utopia
and an exploration of
its architectural space.

CUMBERNAULD

the town centre—the £40 million Antonine Shopping Centre by Keppie Design for London and Regional Properties—was completed in 2007. Although all this private finance may seem at odds with the centralised utopian social vision of Cumbernauld, a key tenet of the New Towns movement was to create focal points for economic growth. A 2006 report by North Lanarkshire Council proposed a £6 million strategy for the redevelopment and regeneration of the town centre area (but this remains largely unrealised due to a lack, so far, of the necessary private finance). Although house prices in Cumbernauld remain below the national average, new housing developments—albeit largely exurban and low density—are being completed every year and are selling well.

People even seem to be slowly coming back round to Cumbernauld's aesthetic. In 2002, it was recognised by the International Council on Monuments and Sites (ICOMOS)—an advisory body to UNESCO, which recommends potential World Heritage Sites for preservation—as one of 18 sites in Britain to be considered for heritage site status. ICOMOS commented that: "Cumbernauld reflects the rewriting of the urban landscape that took place

in the last century. It is among the most important innovations."[4] It could be argued that Cumbernauld never really fell out of favour with those who appreciated it solely in terms of design; the objections came from those who had to live there. In 2007, however, a small breakthrough was made: the Royal Commission on the Ancient and Historical Monuments (RCAHM) of Scotland launched the 'Treasured Places' campaign. It asked the Scottish public to choose their favourite image from a selection of 100 Scottish landmarks. A drawing prepared by Michael Evans, circa 1963, of a small section of Geoffrey Copcutt's original design for the town centre came in tenth place.

This perhaps sums up the quandary of Cumbernauld; people can't quite find a place in their hearts for the reality of the Scottish 'Kabul' and its 'rabbit warren on stilts', but they are at least slowly beginning to recognise the value and even the beauty of the bold utopian ambition of its vision.

1. Reynolds, RS, Award of the American Institute of Architects committee, quoted in George Kerevan, "So how did we get from classical to carbuncle?", *The Scotsman*, 20 February 2005.
2. The New Towns Committee first report (1945), quoted in "Cumbernauld Town Centre", *From Here to Modernity* (Open University). See: http://www.open2.net/modernity/3_10.htm
3. Reynolds, RS, Award of the American Institute of Architects committee, quoted in Miles Glendinning and Diane Watters, "What's it Called? Cumbernauld!" *The Drouth Magazine*, Issue 10, Winter 2003.
4. A spokesman for ICOMOS quoted in Jim McBeth, "Cumbernauld: From Ugly Duckling to Swan", *The Scotsman*, 21 June 2002.

DHARAVI

Dharavi is a district of central Mumbai, India. Its boundaries are marked by two of the city's main commuter railway lines, the Western and Central Railways, and the expressway linking Mumbai with the city airport. It sits between the districts of Mahim and Sion, and is widely credited as one of Asia's most populous slums. Marked 'ZP' on the map for zopadpatti (slum), it is spread over an area of 175 hectares and has a population of more than one million people.

Mumbai is India's financial capital, home to both the Bombay Stock Exchange and the National Stock Exchange of India, together accounting for around 92 per cent of India's total share turnover. It is home to the Indian bases of many international financial and media corporations, India's Hindi film industry, and is the fashion, art and entertainment capital of the sub-continent. With the most millionaires of any city in India, it is the beating heart of the country's current economic boom and the cradle of a new and voracious commercial culture. With a total population of around 19 million in the wider urban agglomeration, half Mumbai's residents are estimated to live in the slum districts of the city.

Until the late nineteenth century, the Dharavi district was mangrove swamp inhabited by Koli fishermen. Later, the Kumbhars established a potters' colony and Tamils came from the south to set up leatherworking enterprises. In the twentieth century, thousands travelled from all over India to work in the textile industry. Despite its population of one million the area was an illegal settlement until 2004, and since its official recognition the authorities have yet to conduct an accurate headcount.

Dharavi's physical appearance could best be described as "informal". Its vernacular building style is opportunistic and improvised; its materials tarpaulin, tin, corrugated iron and concrete forming hutments and lean-tos. Having operated as a semi-legal community for so long there is no official streetplan and the district has organically grown outwards and even upwards to fill the available space. It has little transport infrastructure, and no formal sanitation arrangements. It has running water for an hour a day, and its electricity provision is largely makeshift.

There are a number of reasons for its existence and persistence as a slum district.

The official government census puts the number of new arrivals flooding into Mumbai (termed Mayanagri by many, Hindi for "the city of dreams") at 200 per day, and spiralling property prices preclude all but the wealthy making their homes in the more salubrious districts. A standard two bedroom flat in south Mumbai, overlooking Dharavi, can sell for £400,000. At the upper end of the scale, property prices exceed those of Manhattan. Decades of poor governance, a lack of strong policymaking concerning housing and welfare, and rapid and unequal economic development have all played their part in driving Dharavi's growth. And it is far from a static situation: the UN World Urbanisation Prospects Report predicts that Mumbai—now the world's fourth most populous city—will be second only to Tokyo with 22.6 million people by 2015.

It is a city of stark contrasts; whilst the millionaires live their luxury lifestyles, a 2006 report found that there is one functioning toilet per 1,440 people in Dharavi. The district inspires mixed reactions; to some, it is a diverse multi-cultural melting pot teeming with all human life; for others it is an insanitary eyesore which has already demonstrated its capacity

Top: Aerial view of
the slum housing in
Dharavi, Mumbai.

Bottom: The rubbish-
filled 'streets' between
lines of makeshift
housing, Dharavi slum,
Mumbai. Photographs
by Ayan Khasnabis.

to degenerate into criminality and violence. Its existence within the boundaries of the richest city in India makes manifest the contradictions in contemporary urban life in India; £4 million marble-clad penthouses overlooking streets of corrugated steel lean-tos, piles of rubbish and open drains. Dharavi could be seen as what journalist, Robert Neuwirth, has termed a "shadow city", the dark flipside to the glorious technicolour of Mumbai.

Dharavi and Mumbai's development is not, however, as inversely proportional as it might first appear. One might expect that, as Mumbai's rich get richer, its poor just get poorer, and yet, Dharavi is a space of contradictions in more ways than one; while not quite achieving the dizzying disposable incomes of some of the upmarket districts of the city, a new estimate has placed Dharavi's annual turnover at around £700 million. The district sustains a dynamic recycling industry in which thousands of tons of Mumbai's waste products—scrap plastic, metals, paper, cotton, soap and glass—are crushed, melted, reformed, repaired and repurposed in the workshops of Dharavi each year. This ultimate in self-sustaining industries is just one sector of the district's self-built

economy; Mumbai is a city that prides itself on its self-starting attitude and Dharavi is no different. From the traditional crafts of leatherworking and pottery to a thriving property rental and sales system, Dharavi has developed its own complex informal economy, a twilight zone of sub-legal enterprise and entrepreneurialism. Every square metre, as one journalist puts it, is an opportunity to start a business.

It may not have full sanitation, or a healthcare or educational infrastructure, or even room in most places for motor vehicles to pass along its streets, but this is not to say that the district is cut off from the trappings of a modern urban existence. Many of the one- and two-storey buildings crammed into its narrow streets function as bars, beauty parlours and even cyber cafes. A research study recently found that 85 per cent of residents own a television, 75 per cent a pressure cooker and a mixer, 56 per cent a gas stove, and 21 per cent a telephone; it was a local singer, Abhijit Sawant, who won the first Indian Idol contest.

It has been estimated that up to 70 per cent of Dharavi's buildings are now used for commercial purposes, like banks and

The heart of the Dhavari slum, where housing and the waste generated by its inhabitants collide. Image courtesy of Ayan Khasndbis.

restaurants. Many younger residents are studying business or computer science. Dharavi is far from a straightforward example of the slum stereotype, a backward and insular crime-ridden sinkhole whose residents have lost all hope; it is rather a dynamic entrepreneurial hub where making do has become an art form; a slum in its advanced creative stages.

The residents' tenure, however, is distinctly precarious and property 'rights' are largely unofficial. Many wrongly believe that they can lay claim to their housing and business plots under the provision of the Raj-era Vacant Land Tenancy Act, but this was repealed in 1974 and replaced in 1975 with an Act which gave the Maharashtra government the right to evict tenants without warning. Many of the dwellings in Dharavi have informally been passed through generations, becoming more permanent each time. Roots have taken hold in Dharavi, despite its privations, but the municipal rhetoric thus far has been of 'clearing'.

Dharavi's contradictions have inevitably split opinion on how to 'solve the problem' of the district; a problem that many residents don't want to see 'solved'. Still inextricably linked in the city's middle class, municipal and media's imagination with criminal activity, extreme poverty and violence—it was the scene of some of the worst outbreaks of the riots following the demolition of the Babri Masjid mosque in late 1992 to early 1993, and has suffered local 'mafia'-related activity in the past—the solution is often simplistically seen as razing the current settlement to the ground, and beginning again.

Dharavi's location makes the debate around its redevelopment more complicated. Traditionally slum areas are located on the outskirts of a city, in a liminal position where they can be ignored and don't cause much disruption to the day-to-day life of that city.

Dharavi's particular historical development, having been swallowed up gradually as Mumbai's borders crept ever outwards taking in more and more of the mangrove swamps surrounding it, means it now occupies prime land in the centre of the city. Its proximity to the new Bandra-Kurla business complex, representative of Mumbai's latest drive to become the Shanghai of the sub-continent, is symptomatic; Dharavi finds itself in the wrong place (or rather in the right place) at the right time. A 2003 report by consultants, Bombay First-McKinsey, laid out the 'Vision Mumbai' template for achieving the state government's ambition of transforming Mumbai into a 'world city' by 2013. Dharavi, as well as blighting the appearance of new developments like Bandra-Kurla, doesn't fit the profile of this ambition. Architects and planners speak of 'mainstreaming' the district, and the 'Vision Mumbai' report sets a target of reducing slum-dwelling in the city from 50 to 60 per cent to ten to 20 per cent, by providing new, affordable housing stock for lower-income residents (and of course, leaving the way clear for commercial redevelopment of former slum land).

The report's recommendations are currently being acted upon. A plan by America-trained urban designer and architect, Mukesh Mehta, has been accepted by the Maharashtra state government, and is to be implemented by the Slum Rehabilitation Authority (SRA).

The plan sees Dharavi split into zoned sectors—residential and commercial—to be completed by different developers selected by a state-run competition. It involves the construction of 30 million square feet of residential infrastructure to rehouse displaced current slum-dwellers in the residential sector, allocating 225 square feet of self-contained living space in relatively low-rise multi-storey dwellings free of charge to each family. The developers will absorb the cost of maintenance for these dwellings for a period of 15 years (a move prompted by the state of disrepair suffered by previous solutions offered by SRA, apartments in high-rises where lack of maintenance quickly transformed the buildings into alternative 'slums in the sky'). It also includes the development of 40 million square feet of residential and commercial space for open sale. The plan's housing provision, however, has been based on the official estimate extrapolated from the number of families included on the voters' list of 1995: 57,000. 13 years is a long time in demographics, particularly in 'informal' places like Dharavi; at best, this official figure is a gross underestimate. There are no plans to re-site the thousands of businesses currently successfully operating out of the slum, and the 225 square foot allocation applies regardless of how much floor space a family currently occupies. The redevelopment plans have been the source for much local controversy, with many residents questioning whether the plan's purported social objectives have been overshadowed by a clear opportunity for commercial profit which may see many residents homeless.

The plan does, however, include the implementation of amenities currently lacking in Dharavi: wider roads, reliable electricity and water supplies, schools, colleges, medical facilities, cultural centres, and legitimate commercial opportunities for further investment. It is easy to romanticise Dharavi's spirit of entrepreneurialism and make-do-and-mend approach, but its severe public health issues and the working conditions in its kaarkhanas, or sweatshops, coupled with its residents' lack of tenure, necessitates some form of redevelopment. Time alone will tell if what is currently underway will solve Dharavi's problems, or create a whole new set.

Top: The rooftops of Thames Town, with its red brick houses, Victorian-style cast iron lampposts, and local church.

Bottom: A street in Thames Town, modelled on the picturesque rural towns of Britain. Photographs by Huai-Chun Hsu.

THAMES TOWN

Thames Town is one of seven themed satellite towns nearing completion 32 kilometres outside Shanghai, China; built by the municipal government to deal with the city's swelling population. A key project in Shanghai's tenth Five Year Plan, Thames Town forms part of the Songjiang New City development which aims to re-house 500,000 people. This whole development is part of a mass urbanisation project being undertaken by the Chinese government; around 400 million people are expected to move into urban areas in the coming decade, which means China requires 3,000 new towns or cities by 2020. Built entirely from scratch, the £200 million Thames Town project—officially opened in October 2006—takes its aesthetic inspiration from five centuries of British architecture with just three years' construction time. The outcome is a perfect imitation of all that is picturesque and quaint in British culture, architecture and planning, Chinese-style.

Centred around a waterfront square, the mixed-use development consists of high-density low-rise housing for a projected population of 8,000 in the form of detached houses, townhouses and multi-storey

apartment buildings, and public and business amenities like a hospital, church, clinic, and supermarket. It will house universities relocated from around Shanghai, several high-tech plants and one of the world's largest shopping malls. A newly-opened rail link takes commuters into the centre of Shanghai within 20 minutes.

For a more distinctly British flavour, Thames Town also includes a pub, a fish and chip shop and a church modelled on one in Clifton, Bristol. A covered market echoes Covent Garden, and the sports facilities include several football pitches. In terms of its architectural style, eclectic is the word; mock-Tudor townhouses sit alongside Victorian-style warehouse developments and twentieth century low-rise apartment buildings, on cobbled streets around village greens.

The chief developer is Shanghai Songjiang New Town Developing and Construction Co. Ltd, with Shanghai Henghe Real Estate as developer and WS Atkins, a British firm, as supervising architects. Atkins won the international design competition in 2001 to build the British-themed town (the Songjiang New City project also includes towns with German, Dutch, Spanish, Italian, Canadian

and Swedish themes). The developers' reasons for theming the towns at Songjiang in this way—after some of the nineteenth century colonial quarters of Shanghai—are slightly opaque. Some journalists have speculated on Shanghai's desire to project a Westernised image to the world (on their terms, this time); others, that the town is a grotesque symptom of China's newly-capitalist excesses. The motivation is more likely to be the need for a unique selling point in the ferociously competitive and overheated Shanghai housing market. How many developers can offer the "unique flavour of the English way of life" with their three-bed detached luxury homes?[1]

Their desire for authentic detail certainly knows no bounds; Atkins conducted a thorough research study on the architecture of southern England prior to designing, and the developer insisted upon using imported materials for ultimate veracity. A 2002 press release from the developers assertively claimed: "Foreign visitors will not be able to tell where Europe ends and China begins."[2] British retail giants such as Tesco and Sainsbury have been approached to open stores in the town so as to make the British experience even more all-encompassing, and security guards for the development wear red greatcoats inspired the Queen's Household Cavalry.

Its perfection is, however, slightly too complete: there is a danger that Thames Town could become a British Disneyland of sorts, a pastiche which emulates its analogues a bit too precisely. British towns are the way they are because they have evolved over time ('organic growth' is a buzzword in the promotional material), but although they have recreated the multi-level roofline and variation in building styles of British towns, the Thames Town developers can't realistically replicate the effects and accretions of organic growth and ageing; a certain patination, the moss between the cobbles, is missing.

The developers' thirst for authenticity has resulted in some interesting copyright issues. The owner of a pub and neighbouring fish and chip shop in Lyme Regis was amazed to see an identical pair of buildings, with the same configuration and names in pictures of Songjiang in the British press. As the original buildings are centuries old and the owner did not have the deeds, no action could be taken.

Paul Rice, principal architect of the Atkins consultancy, said: "We are aware of the Disneyland implications. This could become a joke if built in the wrong way. But this is a working community. Compared with other Chinese towns, it will be a pleasant place to live."[3] It is true that Thames Town, on its own terms, is very different to the average Chinese overspill town. It is a low-rise development of 'moderate scale', as the developers put it, in contrast to the usual high-density high-rise concrete constructions. Out of character architecture is far from out of character for Shanghai; historically it has been home to any number of non-native architectures. In a strange sense, Thames Town is perfectly in keeping.

But although the ostensible aim of the New Songjiang City urbanisation project is to rehouse ordinary citizens, the high prices in Thames Town will ensure that it remains an exclusive development and is unlikely ever to house those whose needs the projects initially intended to address. With prices between £330,000 and £410,000 for a three bedroom villa—above average even at Shanghai prices—Thames Town remains beyond the reach of all but the very affluent.

Critics have attacked the model of instant development followed by projects like Thames Town as unsustainable. As Shanghai is often seen as a trendsetter for the rest of China, other cities may follow this model before its success has been proven. Shanghai's urban planners were not keen on the development from the outset, but it was a pet project of Huang Ju, Shanghai's former Communist Party Secretary, and it progressed unhindered despite opposition.

Where Thames Town might never become anything more than a themed residential enclave for the affluent, it appears to have found its niche: as a high-prestige television commercial location. Both Samsung and Volkswagen have shot advertisements there recently, no doubt playing on the connotations of 'authenticity' and 'culture' that the developers have worked so hard to incorporate.

1. See: http://www.thamestown.com/english/thamestown.htm
2. As cited in Beech, Hannah, "Ye Olde Shanghai", *TIME*, 7 February 2005.
3. Paul Rice cited in Watts, Jonathan, "Shanghai Surprise... a new town in ye olde English style", *The Guardian*, 2 June 2004.

Top left: Shopfronts in
Thames Town resemble
those that might be
found in Britain.

Bottom left: A red
public telephone
box on the streets of
Thames Town.

Right: Replica timber-
framed Medieval
housing in Thames
Town. Photographs
by Huai-Chun Hsu.

12 ULTIMATE CRITICAL STEPS TO SUDDEN URBAN SUCCESS

Shumon Basar

I'm fascinated by the phenomena of 'self-help' culture. Visit any contemporary bookshop, and you'll find a whole section devoted to titles such as *Brand New Me*, *Fat is a Feminist Issue* or *The Power of Now*. Television schedules are also crammed with programmes that are aimed at saving people from themselves and the barrage of ills that plague those living in late-capitalist, liberal democracies.[1] Self-help culture seeks to empower the individual subject by borrowing success formulae from others. There is nothing truly altruistic about this, though. Self-help is a billion dollar industry that creates consumers from weakened victims, and smiling, secular preachers who offer swift salvation. I've come to take the success of self-help as a telling symptom of developed civilisations that have attained a peculiar nirvana of liberal contentment. As Jean-Paul Sartre pointed out, the ultimate effect of true freedom is the tremendous alienation of realising you're an existentially free subject with no one or nothing to blame your misery on anymore. Shopping, as many have pointed out, has become one of the celebrated, contemporary panaceas for market-driven, liberal societies. Denuded of any vestige of religious guilt (in other words, that materialism is evil, greed is bad etc.), shopping is flaunted as both harmless distraction for the unsettled soul (where one more pair of shoes might make the magic number) and an economic bedrock for national and global markets to survive, and grow.

The logic of self-help seems to operate at a much larger scale too. Countries may look at one another (or, sometimes, precisely not look) to dig themselves out of social or economic quagmires. Cities have begun to do this too. New York has confirmed that it is set to install a version of London's Congestion Charge control mechanism to cut down its own choking traffic problems. But we always expect famous metropolises to learn from each other. It is an exclusive club of urban like-mindedness.

Rarely do Western cities look to developing, emerging or 'third-world' cities for self-help. Why would they? Progress, it is assumed, always migrates from the more developed to the less developed.

As we near the end of the first decade of the twenty-first century, resigned to the fact that humanity's future is in the future of the city, the fastest growing urbanities are less likely to be in Europe than in the Middle and Far East; and by growth, I don't necessarily mean population only. I mean percentage growth in office space, in residential blocks, in infrastructure, in airport runways, in towers and bays and the anxious flux of semi-indentured, migrant labour.

For the last 15 years, the former British desert colony of Dubai has been a site of unstoppable boom in tourism and business, fuelled by oil reserves that are now nearly dry and a global ambition bordering on hysterical hubris. The population has increased from 69,000 in 1969 to 1.5 million in 2007, which includes more than 200 nationalities living side by side. The city state clearly follows the dictum that nobody remembers who comes second. Dubai is home to the world's largest marina, the biggest motorway intersection and will soon house the world's biggest shopping centre. At this rate, it will soon break the record for the location with most world-breaking records.

Shiny, new, over-scaled, scaleless, pompous, obscene, tasteless, but very real, Dubai is Utopian without ever using the word. It is

visionary, but without the pesky obligation to be revolutionary. Sure, part of me that feels that the 'Dubai mission' should be denounced as a bling, bland and deeply superficial vision, one that equates size with sexiness, like those 1980s macho-mobiles seen in *Magnum PI* or *Miami Vice*. Perhaps we should chide Dubai for forgetting (or, worse still, ignoring) lessons Western Europe could provide about the way in which a city's history must be layered over time—vertically—as though history were geology. If Dubai wanted to genuinely prove its liberal lifestyle leanings, it would begin to set a course in the honourable tradition of the European Enlightenment: lots of museums, libraries and other symbols of democratic representation. But is that the ultimate idea of the city for the twenty-first century?

If you stand on the main boulevard/highway, Sheikh Zayed Road—perhaps the best barometer there is for measuring Dubai's transformation from desert to downtown—all you see is an endless line-up of multicoloured mirror glass skyscrapers: a city reflecting its own reflections, ad infinitum. Mirror glass is what architecture becomes when it wants to say something, but doesn't know what. Is there a more potent image of emptiness?

Yet there is a genuine attempt to construct the definition of a city-state in the twenty-first century which is fascinating to watch. Does Dubai simply press rewind? I don't think so. Unlike Berlin, which seems to long for a nineteenth century past it actually once had but probably will never be able to recuperate, Dubai isn't hankering for a past it once lost—mainly because it never really had one to lose. It is desperately, defiantly and daringly looking for a destiny that draws images of the past, present and future into one jaw-dropping (and, for some, deeply disturbing) synthesis. There is no lamentation. No remorse.

So, if, for a moment, we look at Dubai as seriously as it looks at itself, might we discover tactics and strategies that signal new paradigms for cities in the twenty-first century—for other 'cities from zero'. To put it another way: if Dubai were to write a best-selling, self-help book for other non-places desperate for a premium upgrade to the global stage, what might it suggest as the 'Ultimate Critical Steps to Sudden Urban Success'?

BE GEOGRAPHICALLY REMOTE
A location stuck between scorched desert on one side and sea on the other may not sound ideal as a site to build a city on. But Dubai turns apparent deficiencies into positive assets. Advantage one of a tabula rasa that was traipsed over by Bedouin tribes 100 years

ago is that there is no built history to contend with, no foundational forebears, no symbolic origins to tip-toe around. Advantage two is that there is nothing to limit growth. Like the fastest growing city sprawl in America—Las Vegas—Dubai has virginal space to expand into as and when it wants to. So far, it plans to do so in both directions, devouring desert and securing the sea.

ALREADY POSSESS SIGNIFICANT WEALTH
Dubai struck oil in the 1960s, but even then knew its supplies were relatively tiny next to those of neighbouring emirate Abu Dhabi. Dubai's gas and oil will last for 120 more years, but its oil is set to dry up by 2020. But who cares? By then it will have translated 50 years of oil-lubricated wealth into an ever-expanding portfolio of industries. According to the Director General of Economic Development in Dubai: "When compared to $6.2 billion in 2000 and $4.4 billion for the year 1996, 2005's GDP of $13.6 billion puts the accumulated annual growth of Dubai's economy in the last decade at among the highest rate of growth in the world."

THE FUTURE CITY SHOULD BE ENVISIONED FROM ABOVE
In the Nakheel Showroom, tucked away behind high security gates and set within flowing fountains and fauna, there is a meticulously Photoshopped aerial image of the Dubai that will take shape over the next 20 years. Sprouting off its coastline are three palm-shaped artificial islands, a crescent-shaped city for 750,000 people and an archipelago of islands known as The World. Inland, there is a 'city' planned in the shape of a falcon and another as a chessboard with 32 64-storey buildings for pieces. Everything is part of the big, planned picture. Sheikh Mohammed bin Rashid al-Maktoum, Dubai's Emir and visionary architect of change, is said to be a keen helicopter pilot. From his floating vantage point, the logic of Dubai's parts combines with a vision of the new city whole. This perspective—aloft, perpendicular to the quotidian ground—is an ancient, even celestial one for urban generation. Order once again comes from above.

YOUR NATURAL CLIMATE IS NO BARIIER TO THE ECOLOGIES YOU CAN
In December, Dubai can average 29°C. By summer, it gets as hot as 45°C. Its average annual rainfall is just 30 centimetres. But that is no reason not to have a rotating mountain that is snow-capped all year long or a waterworld with a 400 metre long galleon ship, or an artificially cultivated greenbelt strung around an artificially dug river. It is the logic of air conditioning and heating extended and amplified into a magic that can conjure up every ecology humans have ever coveted, and a few that have yet to be imagined.

Opposite left: A Dubai Properties model of the Business Bay development in Dubai, 2006.

Opposite right: Sheikh Zayed road, lined with tower blocks and skyscrapers.

Top left: An image of Sheikh Zayed bin Sultan Al Nahyan, the principal architect of the United Arab Emirates, as seen from Sheikh Zayed Road. He was president of the United Arab Emirates from 1971 until his death in 2004.

Top right: View of The World, 2006, an artificial archipelago of 300 islands off the coast of Dubai.

PEOPLE LOVE HISTORY

There are three tenses in Dubai: new-new, new-old and old-new. When Bastikiya—an 'old' neighbourhood from the early 1900s with single-storey houses and courtyards—was being destroyed in the mid-1990s, someone evidently made the shrewd observation that: "Tourists like old stuff, so we need to keep some history. Let's rebuild Bastikiya!" And so they did. It may feel like it has just been removed from its shrinkwrap, but its narrow streets nevertheless invoke a more innocent time, countering the strident skyscraperlust that pervades everywhere else. Next to the Burj Dubai, the slick 800 metre tower that is already the world's tallest building even during construction, is another development by the same company, Emaar Developments. 'Old Town' will be Medieval and castellated in its looks and boast bubbling fountains and underground parking for every resident. In other parts of Dubai, English suburbia, American ranch-life and Arabian summer palaces will all exist and provide copy and paste memories; and 'The Lost City' (for fans of Indiana Jones) will not be miraculously found but built from scratch.

A CITY SHOULD CONSIST OF MANY CITIES, VILLAGES AND WORLDS

Everything—from the smallest scrap of site to the largest planned development is given an ennobling name that evokes a village, a city, a land or a world: Knowledge Village, Dubailand, Gidtland, Eastland, Humanitarian City, Maritime City, Textile City, Media City, internet City, Healthcare City, Industrial City, The Lost City, City of Gold, Waterworld, World Gold Council, The World. Such appellations transcend locality and nationality. Each 'land' or 'world' is now the summation of the idea by which it is prefixed, part of a new and absolute index of place-identities. From here, pedestrians and motorists traversing Dubai become everyday travellers charting a strange, scaleless geography.

INVITE THE SUPER-RICH TO VISIT AND MOVE-IN FIRST

A room at the Burj Arab hotel costs $5,000 per night. Its 'seven star' status is just clever PR hyperbole that was coined to convey its dedication to elite, luxury lifestyle. Each suite comes with its own butler, gold and chrome fittings are standard; Michael Jackson drops in but doesn't stay over. David Beckham and his English football teammates were said to be some of the first celebrities to buy in Dubai. Since then, Donald Trump, Versace and Giorgio Armani have decided to invest with their own branded hotels. Tax exemptions, perfect weather, golf courses, a doting and endless service class and a ruling class that exemplifies ostentatious wealth make Dubai the new gated attraction for the world's most visibly affluent. There is nothing filthy about being rich here. Monaco should be very scared.

Above: View of the China court in Ibn Battutta Mall. Split into six different sections, Ibn Batutta Mall is themed around the travels of a fourteenth century Arabian explorer. Image courtesy of Nakheel Dubai.

Opposite: A labour camp building in Dubai, living accommodation for some of the city's many migrant workers.

ARCHITECTURE MUST BE SKIN DEEP (AND THAT'S NOT SUPERFICIAL THINKING)

At Dubai Marinas, 200 towers have been built. Each one was cast in concrete. The collective effect during construction (especially at night) was of a coven of dark figures conspiring to attack. But their dull, atonal physiques were soon transformed. In Dubai, architectural individuality comes in cladding options. Applied like make-up for buildings, cladding comes flatpacked and is stuck on to the concrete. Bronzed steel, aqua blue glazing or pink granite finish? Instant differentiation! What is better still is that when the building is sold to a new owner, the cladding can be peeled off and replaced with a newer pattern. The modernist rubric claimed the outside should be a function of the inside; Dubai, however, declares that the two have nothing in common, that they can live parallel lives.

INSTALL AN ALTERNATIVE TO PARTICIPATORY DEMOCRACY

Is it coincidence that the world's fastest-growing economies— China and Dubai—both eschew participatory democracies and espouse a hybrid form of state-controlled free-market capitalism? Both the Chinese Communist government and the United Arab Emirates' ruling tribal family believe the minds of the select few should map national visions for the many. Once decided upon, plans for the future are mobilised almost instantly into direct action. Any resistance to the vision goes unheard and is therefore useless. While cities like London and Rome are often held hostage by their history and those who insist on preserving it, Dubai encounters no such resistance to its grandiloquent strokes. Accountability comes only in the form of guaranteeing a lifestyle good enough for everyone to sacrifice their electoral representation.

DESIGNATE CONTROLLED ZONES OF EXCEPTIONAL LIBERALISM

At its heart, Dubai is an autocratic Islamic state that closely monitors its media and its citizens. If this were its primary public face, it would hardly make for the best place in which to bask on the beach in a bikini or to run Reuters' Middle East operations. One of the first signs of legislative fine tuning came when Dubai allowed non-nationals temporary citizenship in order to buy certain new properties. From then, more 'Freezones' were set up as legal lacunae excepted from the Emirate's primary social, economic and media orders. In Media City, now home to BBC, Al Jazeera and CNN, there is no interference from the Dubai authorities in any of the transmissions. At internet City, you can surf through any areas of the web you wish, a privilege not granted to the rest of Dubai's residents. The hotels that line the coast merrily serve alcohol to the skimpily dressed designer-clad crowd, where the chances of encountering an Eastern European prostitute are considerably higher than anywhere else. For those that take their freedom for granted, Dubai ensures that freedom is easily available.

IMPORT AN ENDLESS SUPPLY OF LABOURERS AND SERVICE CLASS FROM ABROAD

Some 400,000 labourers are building Dubai every day of every year. Most originate from Pakistan, India or Bangladesh, though now, the source countries are diversifying to avoid the build-up of an ethnic majority where there are only really minorities. In addition to the construction workers, recognisable by their blue jumpsuits, hundreds of thousands of other immigrants will and do form the service foundation for the expanding hospitality and finance industries. Labourers live in the forlornly named 'Labour Camps' of Al Quoz and Sunapur, gated ghettoes unmarked on any of the grand plans of Dubai. Non-unionised, bereft of any representational recourse to workers' rights, and housed in

questionable living conditions, the throng that is building Dubai is in a semi-voluntary state of economic-human subjugation. Already the subject of scores of newspaper articles over the world, the plight of the migrant worker has begun to win a number of small, critical victories. Bad PR is like the plague for Dubai. In fact, 'Labour City' is already planned, proving that nothing in Dubai is unthinkable as thematisation or spectacle. Call it all an abject system of modern slavery, and those who work within it will tell you that here, at least, they earn money that would be unthinkable in their homelands. Such relativism is also the ultimate argument put by those shepherding this globally mobile workforce.

REBUILD THE WORLD—ONLY BETTER THAN IT EVER WAS

"Our World is not a political world", explains one of the representatives from Nakheel, the company responsible for laying out 300 manmade islands in the shape of the world map. Countries and states are on sale, at prices ranging from $6 millon to $40 million, for which you get a lump of sand and permission to start your own micro-nation. Elsewhere in Dubai, plans are afoot for a 1:1 scale Eiffel Tower, the Pyramids of Giza, and a perennially wintry snowdome. It is going to be the world's 'best of', a Greatest Hits of cherished geographies and icons. By rebuilding the world, Dubai hopes to sieve away the danger, the dirt and the dross. It wants to start over again. It is like Pimp My World. To repeat: there is no lamentation, no remorse. Maybe that's the troubling thing for many academics and critics from Western Europe.[2] Dubai's guiltless and shameless thrust forward is not weighed down by an adherence to anyone's past. Where we in the West see huge postmodern quotation marks around everything that happens there, Dubai sees none. It sees the authentic production of the 'new', only bigger, and better, than anywhere else. Perhaps the doom-mongers are wrong, and Dubai isn't a freakish one-off, but the very first of very many twenty-first century cities from zero. And my guess is that the self-help guide is going to be a veritable blockbuster.

1. An indicative and impossible paradoxical example of this societal anxiety is the spectre of body-image crisis. On the one hand, magazines tell us that morbid obesity is on the rise, therefore we should eat less. At the same time, the media bellows about the pernicious dangers of 'size zero' aspiration that the fashion world 'forces' upon young girls—so beware of not eating enough. The 'too fat/too thin' crisis also exists for cities: codified in the diagnoses of 'super-cities' that are 'obese' with too many people and too few resources; and 'shrinking cities', that have atrophied under post-industrial failure or post-socialist disarray.
2. See my essay, "The Story of the Story", *Bidoun*, Issue 11, summer 2007, where I explore the idea that the West's denunciation of places like Dubai and China must be seen in light of the West's waning economic dominance in the century that is now unfolding.

FANTASY

| REALITY

Artists have long since drawn inspiration from the city. Representations in fiction and the visual arts may be a reflection—or a reaction to—actual cities, but often they are entirely new environments, or projections of the future city. These fantasies are, in some sense, instant cities, and they can often shape the character of real cities, through their influence on architects and designers. Artistic intervention has continually made its mark on the city throughout all of recorded history, whether it be through bizarre building forms, exquisite murals or startling graffiti.

URBAN CANVASES

In the twentieth century, Western painters continued a tradition of illuminating aspects of urban life, but they had new energies, politics and moods to explore in the modern metropolis. For example, George Grosz painted a version of Berlin after the First World War that satirised its decadence, hustle and bustle and social conflict, exposing the perversions of rich men and the deflation of soldiers returned from war. His *Metropolis*, 1917, is a cityscape that is giddy and ominous in mood, reflecting a city awash with festivity, as the scene is set for the slide to Nazism. By contrast, the paintings of Edward Hopper are apolitical, offering a voyeuristic view of America from the 1920s to 50s that depicts an isolated, melancholy and meditative culture. In *Nighthawks*, 1942, a diner is still serving as the city sleeps, while in *Office in a Small City*, 1952, an office worker stares motionless at a roofscape that could conjure up any number of small cities in America in the 1950s. Hopper offers a realist depiction of urban life, but reflects the paradox of alienation in cities that were more populous and diversion-rich than ever before.

The Surrealists were famous for positing an alternative reality that flew in the face of everything from politics to the laws of physics, and the city often featured in their representations. Max Ernst's *The Whole City*, 1935, depicts an archeological ruin forming a wide ziggurat-like stone structure, suggesting eternal qualities

Above: Archigram, *Instant City Airships*, 1968. Designed by Peter Cook in 1968, *Instant City* was a temporary megastructure consisting of modular, mobile parts drifting into the air. Through the use of installations, audiovisual devices and other latest technological developments transported by colossal airships, the 'sleeping' provincial town below was meant to be transformed into an active metropolitan

city, offering the inhabitants the cultural delights of urban life. © Peter Cook, Archigram. Image Courtesy of Archigram Archives.

Opposite: Pieter Bruegal, *Tower of Babel*, 1563. Brughel's oil painting was meant to demonstrate the dangers of pride and depicts a 'city' that is simultaneously being built as it is destroyed. Kunsthistorisches Museum Vienna.

that transcend human lifespans. Rene Magritte uses urban backdrops that are
reassuringly ordinary and, as such, deepens the contrast with his strange visions,
such as bowler-hatted men falling like rain in *Golconda*, 1953. Abstract painters
may have been inspired by the city, but (of course) abstracted it to a distorting
degree—for example, Pieter Mondrian's *Broadway Boogie-Woogie*, 1943, evokes
the glitz and jazz of Manhattan with a grid on which blocks of colour play. The
Futurists, the Italian movement pre-occupied with emerging machinery and
the speed of modern experience, offered a technology-focused urban vision, re-
imagining existing cities far into the future. The Futurists lead the way for the
science fiction view of the city, which has hitherto been engaged in a long dialogue
with the constraints of reality.

FUTURE CITY FANTASIES

The Tower of Babel, painted in 1563 by the Flemish artist Pieter Bruegal,
represents a mythical attempt to build the first skyscraper, before, as Genesis
accounts, God intervenes by making the languages of its builders mutually
unintelligible. Bruegal's tower has similarities to Rome's Colosseum. Both
structures can be seen to be related to a science fiction view of the city in that
they exaggerate the scale and form of existing architecture to a degree never
before seen.

The science fiction city, by no coincidence, proliferated in the 1920s, when the real
cities of New York and Chicago were building skyscrapers of ever dizzying height,
and the radio, the telephone and the movies were redefining culture. In 1926
the artist, Montague Black, was commissioned by London Transport, the newly-
constituted public transport authority, to imagine the city in a century's time. His
painting, *London 2026 AD*, shows office towers reaching into the sky, interspersed
with hundreds of airborne vehicles. Look carefully, though, and these towers are
neo classical; disguised with historic decorative elements, just like the actual early
twentieth century American skyscrapers.

Above: Archizoom, *Utopia della qualità*, 1972. Archizoom's work was an ironic take on both consumer society and architectural modernism. Image courtesy of Centro Studi e Archivio della Comunicazione, Università di Parma.

Opposite top: Archigram, *Plug-In City*, 1964. Image courtesy of Archigram Archives.

Opposite bottom: Superstudio, *12 Ideal Cities, Città 2000*, 1971. Illustration representing the 'first' ideal city.

OFFICES

INFORMATION SILOS

A2

RAILSTOPS

PLAZA

EXHIBITIONS

THEATRE

CAR SILO

CAR SILO

MUSIC THEATRE

B1

ROUTE 'B'

'PLUG-IN CITY'
MAX PRESSURE AREA
© 1964 PETER COOK

X76 | X77 | X78 | X79 | X80 | X81 | X82 | X83 | X84 | X85 | X86 | X87 | X88 | X89 | X90 | X91 | X92 | X93 | X94

K J H G F E D C B A

In 1914, the Italian Futurist, Antonio Sant' Elia, drew a new city of soaring blocks, crossed with great traffic arteries, in which the human scale was overwhelmed by the massive requirements of industry, offices and transport. In 1919, the Bauhaus Proclamation marked the start of a German academy led by Walter Gropius who wanted to dispense with sentiment in architecture and eliminate the distinction between form and function. Elsewhere, Russian Constructivists (whose priorities were a commitment to complete abstraction, both in art and architecture) were developing a 'scientific' architecture that combined advanced engineering and technology with Communist principles. At the same time le Corbusier was about to start planning the utopian metropolis in the guise of such projects as *Une Ville Contemporaine*. These amounted to a great shift in architectural vision, driven by technology as much as by the politics of empowering the working class. The themes taken up in this real-life architecture are spectacularly mirrored in the dark vision of Fritz Lang's 1927 film *Metropolis*. Here, the future city is dominated by buildings of immense mass, below which highways snake above and across each other in a bewildering complex of movement, industry and human suffering. The city is vertically layered, with the elite located at its rarified upper levels and the great mass of workers toiling (literally) beneath them. Society here is a dystopian inversion of modernist architectural visions, with the pervasive view of technology positioning humans as subservient to machines. The scale of Lang's city and the threat of technology set the template for the cinematic future city.

Lang's city was not just a dark cautionary tale. It also, in some sense, reflected the reality of the city. In America, this reality is best represented by Art Deco, a movement in architecture and design that dispensed with the European embellishments of neo classical design, but retained something of the romantic and decorative, as expressed through the excitement of the Jazz Age. This transition is neatly encapsulated in the examples of Raymond Hood-designed New York skyscrapers—his American Radiator building, 1924, is neo Gothic, but the McGraw-Hill Building, 1931 and Rockerfeller Center designs, 1933, are Art Deco. Manhattan skyscrapers soared to command views over the booming metropolis, occupied by those who commanded the burgeoning economy that underpinned it. This was literally 'high society', with everything from glamorous penthouse apartments to sky-high ballrooms, such as New York's Starlight Room at the Waldorf-Astoria. As for the streets, the *Unter-* and *Übermenschen* of *Metropolis* shared the same sidewalks in the reality of Manhattan.

The classic science fiction city has an ambiguous relationship with both reality and the socially inspired visions of avant-garde architects. Most science fiction city visions that followed were, in one way or another, variations of *Metropolis*. The Flash Gordon cartoons, started in 1934, contained cities of towers that looked rather like laboratory apparatus, based on cylinders and cones adorned with antennae. This budget version of the future city would find countless variations in space comics and B-movies. Meanwhile, Batman's home town, Gotham City, originally portrayed in a 1941 comic, is an exaggerated, gothic version of New York—its creator Dennis O'Neil citing Manhattan's 14th street on a winter night as his inspiration for this particular visionary city.

DESIGN FEEDBACK LOOPS

So, did the classic science fiction fantasy city feed back into architecture? Technology continued to inspire radical architects to generate brilliantly bizarre urban visions, however less concerned with political class ideals they appeared to be. As early as 1927, Buckminster Fuller, the American engineer and scientist, applied engineering principles from bridge-building and aircraft design to produce an efficient structure he called the Dymaxion House. He went on to conceive the geodesic dome and in 1962, he envisioned covering Midtown Manhattan, protecting it from the growing problems of pollution. The Metabolists, formed in 1959 in Japan, conceived modules that could be added to constantly growing megastructures to alleviate the national problem of overcrowding, and later, compact modular pods to be stacked as living units (concepts that were put into practice in such projects as Unabara, a floating city in the sea, and Kiyonari Kikutake's Marine City and Kisho Kurokawa's 'Helix City' and Nakagin Capsule Tower).

Opposite top: Buckminster Fuller, *Geodesic Dome Over Manhattan*, 1962. Fuller envisioned his Dome as a solution to the problem of energy waste. It was meant to consist of a hemisphere two miles in diameter and one mile high at its centre. Better energy conservation, more stable atmospheric conditions, cleaner water and brighter daylight would have been some of its advantages. Image courtesy of the Buckminster Fuller Estate.

Opposite bottom: Erich Kettelhut, *Metropolis*, set design, 1925.

Following pages: Ludwig Hilberseimer, *Berlin Development Project: Friedrichstadt District*, 1928. Hilberseimer's planning for Friedrichstadt, Berlin was a rational, modernist proposal, though partly indebted to Ebenezer Howard's Garden Cities.

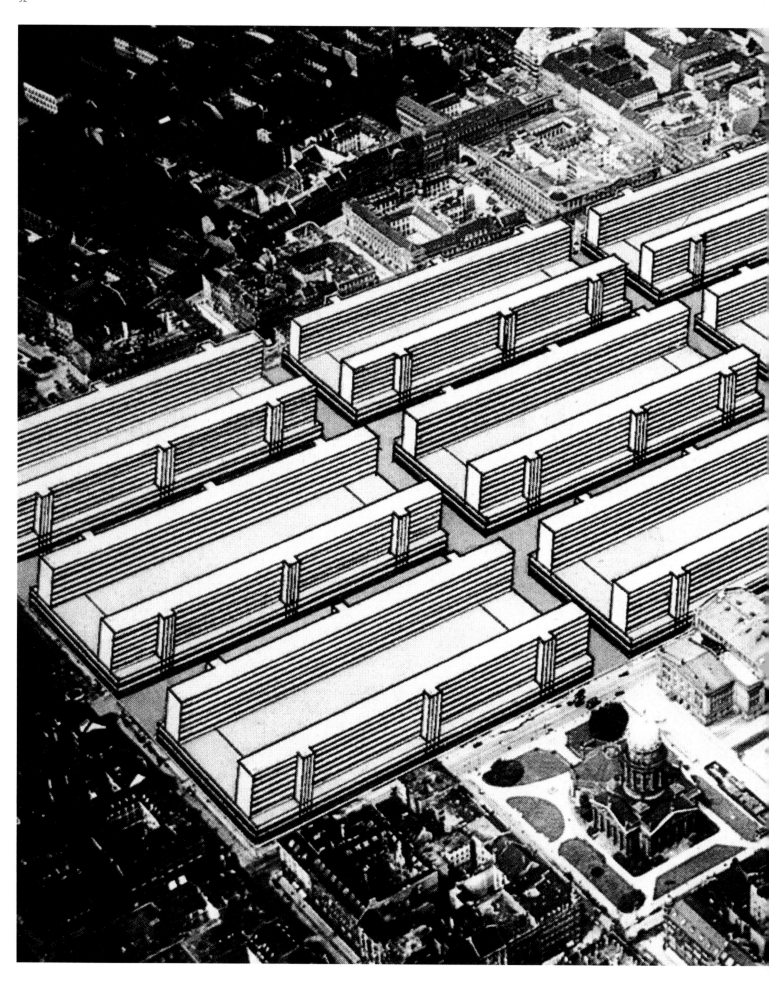

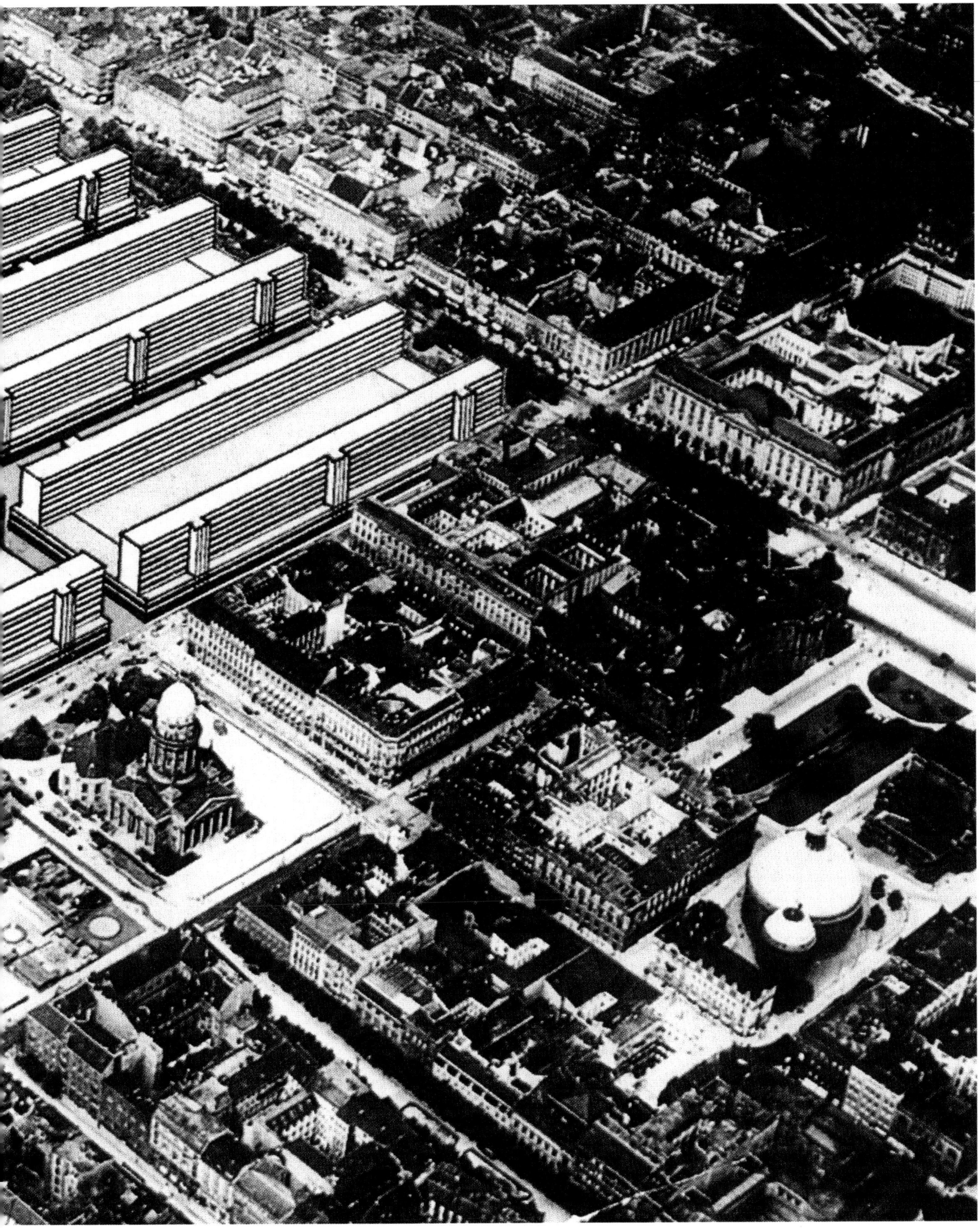

In the 1960s, Archigram, the avant-garde group of British architects, promoted concepts like *Walking City*, 1964, a massive mobile community on telescopic legs, *Plug-in City*, 1964, in which modules were hung in huge frames. The ongoing *Instant City*, which 'floated' from location to location, like a travelling urban fair, leaving new infrastructure behind when it moved on is another enduring Archigram vision of the city. Indeed, *Instant City* is echoed in the twenty-first century airbourne installations of Tomas Saraceno, in which people live in fluid configurations of balloons, as floating nomads, and it was eventually Archigram's designs that would most typically reflect the constant state of flux characterised by the urban experience, and pose the most sustained challenge to the architectural orthodoxy of the day.

Following them, two Florence-based groups produced more conceptual challenges, which together they exhibited as *Superarchitettura*. ArchiZOOM's No-Stop City, 1968, imagined a space in which people freely generate their own organic dwellings within a rectilinear, air conditioned, artificially-lit endless continuum. Superstudio produced *Il Monumento Continuo*, 1971, which comments on the blandness of modernism by visualising a huge anodyne structure that pierces and constricts Lower Manhattan, threatening to extend its reach across the planet. Their montages which anticipated environmental concern, such as *12 Ideal Cities*, 1972, depicted semi-spherical artefacts floating above a huge field full of sheep, the centre of which is occupied by a gigantic mirror.

BEYOND MODERNISM

These fantasies were created to challenge the reality of post-war architecture, as expressed by Brutalism in Europe, and the march of the ubiquitous plain glass boxes that threatened to engulf the downtowns of many American cities. These modern cityscapes looked very different to the almost baroque fantasy cities of science fiction or visionary architects. But what would actually follow modernism?

In Europe, the radical architecture of the 1960s inspired the high-tech of Richard Rogers, whose great cultural centre designed with Renzo Piano, the Centre Pompidou in Paris, opened in 1977. In structure and function, it draws upon Cedric Price's unbuilt Fun Palace project, a bid to provide the public with a steel structure in which spaces were ever changeable and in which people could participate in or view a variety of cultural activities. The Fun Palace had an Archigram look-and-feel, resulting from service structure like lifts, escalators and pipework being placed on the outside of the building, rather than the inside. Rogers' Lloyds Building in London, 1986, and Foster+Partners' Hongkong and Shanghai Bank Building in Hong Kong, 1985, firmly rooted this new high-tech trend in architecture.

Meanwhile, in 1984, American architect, Philip Johnson, a key player in the rise of modernism, is quoted as saying that by the late 1970s, "we were getting bored with boxes". He made this comment as his AT&T Building was completed in Manhattan. At almost 200 metres high it looked, to some, like a marble-clad Chippendale cabinet. This was a stylistic fantasy made reality, and was one of the key buildings that heralded the arrival of postmodernism in America, in which decorative elements were re-instated in the form of pitched and sculpted roofs, voids, ledges, loggia, ground-level arcades and the cladding of exteriors with marble and stone. Postmodernism did not restrict itself to historical elements. Johnson went on to pioneer a retro-futurist look in Manhattan's Lipstick Building, in which pink oval sections telescope upwards with all the easy plasticity of a Flash Gordon structure. The distinctive retro-styled glass spires of Helmut Jahn, such as Philadelphia's One Liberty Place, 1987, seem to be inspired by *Metropolis* imagery while the Taiwan-based CY Lee's eclectic local skyscrapers such as the Tumtex Tower, 1997, and Taipei 101, 2004, are spectacular testaments to the latent reality of urban fantasy. In the heterotopic cityscapes of China, the retro-futurist look has almost become a vernacular, from KY Cheung's Shun Hing Square in Shenzhen, completed in 1996, to the recurring flying-saucer-like structures that top Shanghai skyscrapers.

Richard Rogers and Partners, a nighttime view of Lloyds in London. Image courtesy of Richard Stirk Harbour and Partners. Photograph by Richard Bryant. © Richard Bryant/arcaid.

UPDATING THE FUTURE

Just as reality in architecture had caught up with the classical science fiction city, the paradigm was updated in Ridley Scott's film *Blade Runner*, 1982, based on a novel by Philip K Dick. It offered a future image of Los Angeles, complete with amplified realities of the contemporary city, such as its social mix and the rise of advertising images in public space. As in *Metropolis*, technology unleashed dangerous androids in Dick's vision, called "replicants". Power and money still occupy the heights—the sanctum of the sinister Tyrell Corporation's head is at the peak of a pyramid-like building on an immense scale. Street level, however, exaggerates the demi-monde of the new reality of the American inner city, a multi-ethnic space babbling with different tongues in bustling, garishly illuminated markets. Away from the crowds, the dispossessed and the strange occupy dirty, decaying and dangerous neighbourhoods.

Blade Runner is the postmodernist idea of the science fiction city. In parallel, William Gibson's *Necromancer* novel, 1984, gave rise to cyberpunk fiction, in which characters of ambiguous morality battle dark forces in a world dominated or subverted by data and surveillance. The genre synthesised the romance of classic hard-boiled detective heroes such as Raymond Chandler's Philip Marlowe with a decidedly pessimistic view of the future city. These were visually represented in comics from *2000AD*, which anticipated dystopian city life in Mega City One (the fictional city-state from the comic *Judge Dredd*) as early as 1977, to *Transmetropolitan*, 1997–2002. The Japanese vision of future cities relates strongly to *Blade Runner's* Los Angeles because Tokyo, with its blur of dense urban fabric, commercial images and technology, was already similar to the fictional vision Dick had posited. Manga series like Katsuhiro Otomo's *Akira*, 1982–1995, set in a Tokyo Bay city in 2030, and Masamume Shirow's *Ghost in the Shell*, 1989, are further examples of the emerging cyberpunk genre. Modern science fiction is not wholly comprised of dysopian visions and cautionary tales, Matt Groening's cheerful television cartoon *Futurama*, has the backdrop of a city evoking the retro-

futurism of *Flash Gordon*, and in the credits, an airborne vehicle crashes into a mid-level advertising hoarding borrowed from *Blade Runner*.

The science fiction city, the ideas of radical architecture, and the reality of the built environment, then, are like a triangle in which any corner has lines or bridges to the others, connecting fantasy and reality. But in the postmodern world, a new agent has arisen which changes everything on all three planes. Cyberspace became an ingredient in science fiction from the 1980s. Virtual reality was also on the rise in architecture and as a play zone for society at large as video games leapt from flat plane play modules to three-dimensional simulated space. As architect Rem Koolhaas noted: "Cyberspace will provide not only a one-way path into screenland but special effects at your table. The future is here, it just hasn't been evenly distributed (yet)."[1] Koolhaas' 1978 conceptual project for New York, *The City of the Captive Globe*, exactly predicts the look of a city that anyone can now fashion using the 1993 computer game, SimCity 2000.

Digital intervention is not just the stuff of fantasy in the postmodern world, indeed, today, the real built environment is in some sense computer-generated. In the 1970s, CAD programmes offered designers the ability to make two-dimensional drawings using computers as a drawing tool. Three-dimensional line or wire frame drawings followed and, by the 1980s, solid modelling was in place. This development led to digital prototyping which, in industrial product design, allowed practitioners to test their designs in virtual reality without having to build physical prototypes. In architecture, the equivalent developments allowed architects to simulate structural engineering parameters, as well as view, in detail, every angle of a building's proposition. By the mid-1990s, multi-megapixel images with a full palette of colours allowed three-dimensional virtual walkthroughs of architectural designs that conveyed a sense of movement through an ultra-clean version of reality. Oddly enough, walking through big postmodern developments today can feel strangely similar to moving through the virtual reality of a computer model.

This confusion of reality with simulation is an example of the sequence of steps that society has taken away from reality, as described by the French philosopher Jean Baudrillard. He argued that reality has been replaced by a hyper-reality, "the product of an irradiating synthesis of combinatory models in a hyperspace without atmosphere".[2] Essentially, he considered a story by the Argentine writer Juan Luis Borges in which an emperor commissions a 1:1 scale map of his domain, which, of course, covers all of it. From this he developed the idea of how images have passed through the stages of empirically reflecting a basic reality, then selectively representing reality, then masking it, and finally replacing it. When what we see reaches this final stage, it is a simulacrum. After the experience of walk-through renderings, there is something Baudrillardian about how an actual building or complex can feel too similar to its rendering. The building, it may be argued, has become a simulacrum, indeed, Baudrillard posited Disneyland and most of Los Angeles as just that, a replacement of reality. The 1999 film, *The Matrix*, in which reality is disguised by an all-encompassing simulated experience, is said to be based on Baudrillard's theoretical framework.

In this century, parametric modelling has enabled the detailed design of buildings on greater scales than ever before. After 9/11, New Yorkers entered into a variety of alternative realities, rendered in three dimensions, representing competing schemes for Ground Zero. An aspect of parametric modelling is that the shapes of buildings are becoming increasingly bizarre, and the fantasy of an artistic vision is now easier to translate into the design of a structure.

Cities have always been mapped, but now the map can be images from above that anyone can view on Google Earth. There are three-dimensional virtual models of cities that architects work on to plan big projects so that they can see, for example, sight lines that protect historic views. In some cities such as London, physical models open to the public show future building projects spread across entire stretches of the metropolis. Cartography itself has become three-dimensional, for example the mapping of underground structures like utility lines or metro lines, or multi-level circulation schemes. Except to specialists, this sort of representation of reality might become overloaded with such information uncomfortably traversing our psychological boundaries of fantasy and reality.

The urban landscape
in Fritz Lang's
Metropolis, 1927.
Image courtesy of
Ronald Grant Archive.

1. Koolhaas, Rem, and Bruce Mau, *S, M, L XL*, New York: Monacelli Press, 1995.
2. Baudrillard, Jean, *Simulacra and Simulations*, Michigan: University of Michigan Press, 1994.

THE METABOLISTS

At the 1960 World Design Conference held in Tokyo, a group of young architects, designers and critics launched their manifesto to the design world: *Metabolism 1960—a Proposal for a new Urbanism*. The series of papers contained in this self-published pamphlet outlined an approach to the future of the urban environment that was both an architectural theory and a critical social theory from a spatial perspective; a manifesto which aimed to change the way that people inhabited, thought about and built in urban space. Metabolism, as the movement was termed by critic, Noboru Kawazoe, was to have a relatively brief flowering—officially between the 1960 conference and the 1970 Osaka Expo—but some of the ideas it put forward about space, technology and society have gone on, often unacknowledged, to influence twenty-first century design practice. Most of what the group designed was never realised, or was not even 'realisable', although a few seminal examples of the Metabolist architecture were built in the 1970s.

The movement's main exponents were a multi-disciplinary group: architects Kiyonori Kikutake, Noriaki 'Kisho' Kurokawa, Masato Otaka, Fumihiko Maki, critic Noboru Kawazoe, industrial designer Kenji Ekuan, and graphic designer Awazu Kiyoshi, but it was the architectural theory and practice of the group that attracted most attention. It was contemporaneous with—and aesthetically and ideologically connected to—other radical architectural movements of the 1960s, particularly the work of the Archigram group in Britain, France's Paul Memon, Yona Friedman's *Spatial City* and the work of the Superstudio and Archizoom practices in Italy. These groups all reacted to the changed spatial and social conditions of 1960s urban space. In Japan's case, it was an economic boom, overcrowding and poorly thought-out post-war reconstruction that shaped the Metabolists' vision.

Kawazoe's term for the Metabolist movement came out of their vision of the future city as conceived like the human body, composed of cellular elements that each individually develop, mutate, decay and regenerate in a 'metabolic' cycle. The metropolis was, in their eyes, in a constant state of flux and self-renewal, and their aim was to create a dynamic built environment that could be flexible enough to accommodate

THE METABOLISTS AND SECOND LIFE

Arata Isozaki,
Re-Ruined Hiroshima,
photomontage from
Electric Labyrinth,
1968. Isozaki's
rendering of Hiroshima
in ruins was a
metaphor for the
endless collapse
and regeneration
of future cities. Image
courtesy of Arata
Isozaki Associates.

its constantly changing state. The cities and buildings they designed—and, more rarely, built—were engineered to go beyond traditional fixed forms and functions, and instead were composed of mobile and flexible elements—capsules—that could be moved, detached, replaced and repurposed according to need. Their urban spaces would behave organically and responsively, rather than remaining static 'containers' of human life. This transformation of space would in turn bring about a social transformation, with a new focus on individuality in society. As Kurokawa put it:

> Future society should be constituted of mutually independent individual spaces, determined by the free will of the individuals.... Each space should be a highly independent shelter where the inhabitant can fully develop his individuality. Such space is a capsule.... The capsule aims at diversified society.[1]

Beyond this commitment to dynamic, individualised and impermanent architecture, Metabolism was far from a monolithic architectural school. Rather, it was an amalgamation of the urban projections of a group of like-minded people who explored complementary (and sometimes contradictory) ideas about space and society. The founding vision of Metabolism—that the city was a living space and, in the future, technology, architecture and urban design could facilitate rather than stifle its life—opened many different doors for its exponents. Some members of the group, like Kiyonori Kikutake, envisioned the sea and the sky as future human habitats, or looked at the creation of entirely artificial environments; others became more interested in the juxtaposition of urban elements and the natural world; others looked more closely at the interaction of humans and technology in urban spaces. Fumihiko Maki became interested in the different ways that buildings can be grouped, and the intermediary new urban spaces created between 'group forms'. Kisho Kurokawa designed cities based on DNA-like organic formations. What remained constant throughout all these differing experiments and visions, however, was the concept of modular building—individual capsules surrounding a core—and this form's intrinsic and liberating potential for flexibility and mobility.

The metabolic cycles of these architects' vision of the city found a corollary in contemporary assembly-line industrial production. One of the only built examples of the Metabolist vision is Kisho Kurokawa's Nagakin Capsule Tower, 1972, located in the upmarket Ginza district of Tokyo. Individual capsule units (140 2.3 x 3.8 x 2.1 metres each), made from modified shipping containers, were stacked at angles around two central reinforced concrete cores of 11 and 13 storeys. The one-man capsules—each with one circular window and a built-in bed and bathroom unit, and complete with built-in television, alarm clock, radio and telephone, even a built-in calculator—were pre-assembled in a factory off-site and then hoisted by crane and attached to the core shaft. Each unit was attached using only four high-tension bolts, a system designed by Kurokawa, making them easily detachable and replaceable. The tower's service infrastructure is exposed on the outside of the building for ease of replacement and repair. The Sony Tower in Osaka, 1976, also by Kurokawa, uses a similar construction method, but its capsules were made of stainless steel.

These rare built examples have not, unfortunately, fared well. The Sony Tower was demolished in 2006 and is to be replaced with a plate glass office building, and it seems as though the Nagakin Tower's

fate is similarly sealed: on 15 April 2007, the building's management company approved a new 14-storey building to replace it, though a demolition date is yet to be scheduled. Before his death in October 2007 Kisho Kurokawa fought tirelessly to save his creation from demolition, even standing for the post of Mayor of Tokyo in an unsuccessful last-ditch attempt to rescue it. The building's capsules have latterly been rented out as micro-offices for around 70,000 yen (about £350) a month—in a city where space is money it was far less efficient in terms of yield than an equivalent modern office building on the same footprint. Current tenants expressed concern at its state of disrepair, the asbestos used in its construction and its safety in earthquake conditions.

Kurokawa told *Building Design* that he would have liked to see the building maintained to his original modular theory, unplugging each capsule and replacing it with an updated unit leaving the base towers untouched as was always intended. "Every year I have proposed maintenance", he said. "In 33 years they didn't do this." Japan's four major architectural organisations, including the Japan Institute of Architects, supported this

scheme, and the building has been on the Docomomo recommendation list for UNESCO protection since 1996. The building is a major Tokyo tourist attraction and, in 2005, a World Architecture News poll showed 95 per cent of architects from around the world believed the tower should be saved. Where the Japanese government are particularly active in ensuring the conservation of the country's Edo-era architectural treasures, their beneficence doesn't extend to the gems of the twentieth century; it has declined to offer protection.

The Metabolists' vision, in contrast, lives on—recently the British government has argued that a modified version of their modular housing concepts could be utilised to meet targets for the building of new affordable homes.

1. Kurokawa, K, "Capsule declaration", in Kurokawa, K, *Metabolism in Architecture*, London: Studio Vista, 1977, pp. 75–86.

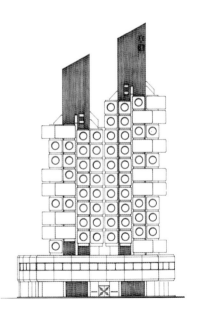

Left: Drawing of the *Nagakin Capsule Tower* as designed by Kisho Kurokawa of the Metabolists. Built in 1972, the tower was conceived to house individual living capsules that could be prefabricated, 'fitted' to the building, and were eventually interchangeable.

Right: Exterior view of the *Nagakin Capsule Tower* living units. Photographs by Tomio Ohashi.

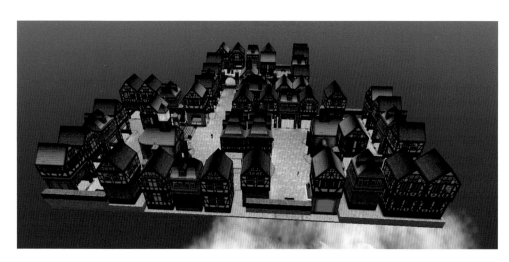

Aerial view of Arcadia,
a floating Tudor village
in Second Life.

SECOND LIFE

Second Life (commonly abbreviated as SL) is an internet-based virtual world developed by Linden Research, Inc and launched in 2003.[1] The creation of Philip Rosedale—who was first inspired to create a virtual universe by Neal Stephenson's 1992 science fiction novel *Snow Crash*—Second Life is one of a new breed of "metaverses", to use Stephenson's terminology, fully immersive and interactive virtual three-dimensionally rendered spaces which take massive multi-player online role-playing games (MMORPGs) to a whole new level. The recent increases in bandwidth and graphic capabilities in home computing have enabled the development of metaverses with an ever more convincing aesthetic and far greater capacity for millions of simultaneous logins all over the real world. Linden Labs themselves describe Second Life as "a three-dimensional virtual world entirely built and owned by its residents", a "vast digital continent, teeming with people, entertainment, experiences and opportunity".[2]

Second Life is unique in that it is entirely open-source, and absolutely all content— houses, clothing, cars, flowers, everything— is user-generated (Linden provide some three-dimensional modelling tools for creating objects, and users retain intellectual property rights on what they create). Second Life is different to other MMORPGs that have been popular in the past, like World of Warcraft, as it has no embedded narrative, goals or objectives; the objective for users is purely and simply to live an alternative online virtual life, however they choose to do so. Beginning as essentially empty webspace, users themselves populate, build and manipulate the online environment. Users or 'Residents' (Residents—argues Linden Labs' Robin Harper—"seems most descriptive of people who have a stake in the world and how it grows") are represented in-world by their avatars, humanoid simulations that can be named, given individual physical characteristics and manoeuvred as Residents see fit.[3] Residents can walk around, explore and socialise, create and trade items, property, land and services, even attend classes and conferences, fly and teleport.

What began as an online space for niche communities looking for like-minded individuals and an escape from everyday life—the elf community, for example, was one of the first that emerged, closely followed by the Furries, people who like to take on the identity of a small rodent in-world—has quickly become a full-blown ubiquitous media phenomenon. In Spring 2006, when media attention was first piqued by Second Life, it encompassed almost 165,000 Residents. By September that year, there were 780,000 virtual inhabitants. At Linden's last count in February 2008, there were 12.7 million Residents—approximately the same population as Mali or Senegal. This is not a particularly accurate figure as it includes all Second Life profiles that have ever been registered, but even the number of individual logins in the first two months of 2008—1.35 million—is still impressive. An important aspect of Second Life is its conventional spatial organisation; despite its digital, virtual nature, maps are available of its population distribution and building density. Its spaces are simulations of real-world physicality; its users build and dwell as they would normally. Second Life is organised into the 'mainland'—where land rights are administered by Linden—and private estates, regions and islands administered by private companies and, to all extents and purposes, outside the

jurisdiction of Linden Labs. Residents can, subject to a monthly fee, purchase 'land' and build on it what they wish; individual plots can be added endlessly to the matrix, as the virtual environment expands ever outwards. (No figures are currently available for Second Life's equivalent real world total dimensions, but each plot is meticulously allocated in square metres.)

Just as in the real world, this organisation has spawned its own industry relating to the built environment—virtual architects and builders—in the form of development companies like InWorld Momentum and Clicks and Links and, because of Second Life's open source nature, enterprising individuals become in-world 'Artist Builders' or 'Land Terraformers', property developers and land brokers. Many Residents can turn a tidy profit from such enterprises: Second Life has its own microcurrency, the Linden Dollar (L$), which can be exchanged with American dollars or euros at the in-world LindeX exchange, or via third party sites. Its exchange rate remains relatively stable at around L$266 to US$1, and there are rumoured to be several Second Life property millionaires; Anshe Chung, for example, allegedly made her

real life fortune through her Dream Worlds virtual land brokering business.

Second Life offers an interesting case study in this sense. Many see it as offering Residents the chance to inhabit a utopian space completely free of real world constraints, to enact a fantasy life and reinvent their identity. The only limitation here is the user's imagination, and the speed of their broadband connection. And yet, apparently relieved of these constraints, people demonstrate a touching attachment to the real world environment and its economics, and to the urban environment in particular: Second Life Residents live in houses, they work as property consultants and construct digital paeans to real world cities.

Linden Labs provide three-dimensional modelling tools to create any object in-world and, with some skill, Residents can sculpt and script the 'physical' virtual environment around them. Primitive objects, or 'prims', can be cloaked in 'sculpted textures' to create realistic objects. Second Life also includes a scripting language called LSL, which can be used to add autonomous behaviour to the objects created, such as making doors open when approached. (Why

doors should be necessary at all in a virtual world is seemingly never questioned. In the same way, Residents design and build cars for transport, when they could equally 'fly' or teleport to their desired destination.) LSL has been used to create advance autonomous fantasy systems, like the artificial life experiment on the island of Svarga where a whole ecological system (weather systems, plant and animal life) runs autonomously. But largely, sculpties (or sculpted prims), LSL-scripted movements, and the appearance and functionality of the built environment are based on real world realities.

So despite this apparent freedom, life in Second Life can seem surprisingly quotidian—mundane even—for a virtual 'dream' world, where utopia might be achievable. Second Life Residents still tend to adhere to, or recreate, recognisable strategies for physical organisation and societal structures, norms and values. Neighbourly disputes over personal space crop up with just the same regularity as in the real world. (According to *Los Angeles Times*, one Resident joined Second Life to escape the pressures of everyday life—building a home with good sea views—only for her virtual idyll to be ruined when

someone moved in next door and built a giant refrigerator that blocked her light.)

So where does this leave cities and the specifically urban environment in Second Life? There has been a trend of developers trying to recreate exact replicas of contemporary cityscapes. You can now visit a virtual Munich, a Manchester, several Venices and Parises, a version of Beijing, of London, and so on. These simulations vary in quality: bloggers and metaverse commentators don't hold back in complaining when absolute veracity is not achieved, or when buildings are left as simulated skins with no functioning interior space. There are a number of reasons why a real life city might develop a presence in Second Life: some of these sims are constructed in a fit of zeitgeisty enthusiasm by a country's tourist board in order to encourage real world tourism; others, like 'Paris 1900' or the simulated pre-Hurricane Katrina New Orleans, offer a glimpse of a past that can no longer be obtained in the real world. Some city authorities, like Copenhagen, have used the potential of Second Life in a more integrated sense, to project and promote development initiatives still ongoing in the real world.

Real world corporations were quick to seize upon Second Life's popularity and its Residents' spending power, buying up retail and advertising space. Among the companies to develop presences and even mirror businesses in-world are Reebok, Toyota, Adidas, IBM, Philips, Coca Cola and American Apparel, while Vodafone have developed an in-world SMS service. This, relatively new, commercialism emerging in the Second Life experience has angered and frustrated many early adopters, creating an all-too-real, unwanted interface with the real world. At the height of the media's interest in Second Life news agency, Reuters, stationed a full-time journalist in-world, and bands like U2 and Duran Duran have staged in-world concerts.

This interaction between the real world and in-world was seen as the future for Second Life; the development of an 'interreality', the physical and the virtual converging until you could take a virtual item off a shelf in an in-world supermarket, and it would be delivered to your real-world door. But the cynical focus on the commercial aspects of this proposition, rather than the social and cultural possibilities it opens up, has resulted in a backlash. Big businesses like

Above: View of one of the many pedestrian streets in Arcadia, Second Life.

Opposite: An urban cityscape-environment in Second Life.

Dell have abandoned their islands, shutting up virtual shop; others became insolvent. Bemused avatars wait in queues for in-world ATMs that can no longer dispense money. It has been argued that Second Life has been suffering the same fate as comparable real-world urban environments; over-commercialisation, over-development, social tensions, abandonment, and a pernicious property speculation industry. The spatial organisation implemented by Linden Labs at the outset has come to mirror suburban sprawl, with vast areas now lying abandoned or given over to what are diplomatically termed 'mature' virtual pursuits. The old guard have even set up their own body for political resistance: the Second Life Liberation Army. In 2007, they staged numerous protests culminating in planting bombs outside Reebok and American Apparel (in-world, of course).

And yet the possibilities that Second Life offers—as an incubator for innovation, an experimental virtual lab for rapid prototyping and a space for creative collaboration—have not been completely abandoned. Some initiatives have even taken the current sorry state of Second Life's 'physical' environment as their starting

point. At the 2007–2008 Shrinking Cities—Nine Urban Ideas exhibition at the Deutsches Architektur Museum (DAM) in Frankfurt, one strand of the display exhibited the outcome of a 2007 competition that re-imagined the possibilities of urban space in Second Life in the future. Entries ranged from a proposal to reorganise the space of Second Life along thematic rather than traditional spatial means, using keywords to organise content into categorised areas, to looking at further mirroring real world urban development by building upwards (but generating the shape and height of the resulting towers democratically by locating the most popular, more frequently visited content higher up in the construction). An organisation called Studio Wikitecture are currently utilising the Second Life platform for applying the open-source paradigm to architecture and urban planning, in much the same way that the online user-generated Wikipedia enables a self-organising network of contributors to collaborate on content creation, and more sophisticated AutoCAD import tools are being developed all the time to bring real-world architectural design in-world.

Despite Second Life's conspicuous and rapid boom and bust, some still see virtual worlds

and 'interreality' as the way forward. The Thai government, for example, have recently underwritten the $250 million development of a so-called Cyber City in Chiang Mai to be, among other things, a home for the new CGI department of Creative Kingdom, Inc. (CKI, the real world themed architectural designers responsible for the Palm and World Islands developments in Dubai, UAE). The maiden project for this new media hub will be the creation of a virtual planet within the Entropia Universe MMORPG, with CKI hoping to "bring the specificity and rigour of its architectural practice to a purely fantastic destination".[4]

1. www.secondlife.com

2. http://secondlife.com/whatis/

3. Harper, Robin (aka Robin Linden), "Origin of the term 'Resident'", 23 February 2007. See: http://wiki.secondlife.com/wiki/Origin_of_the_ term_%27Resident%27

4. Reuters, "Creative Kingdom, Thai Government Collaborate on Landmark Cyber City Development in Chiang Mai; CKI to Craft Planet", 19 February 2008. See: http://www.reuters.com/article/pressRelease/ idUS197137+19-Feb-2008+MW20080219

THE EXPLOSION OF SPACE: ARCHITECTURE AND THE FILMIC IMAGINARY

Anthony Vidler

> I am kino-eye. I am a builder. I have placed you, whom I've
> created today, in an extraordinary room which did not exist
> until just now when I also created it. In this room there are
> 12 walls shot by me in various parts of the world. In bringing
> together, shots of walls and details, I've managed to arrange
> them in an order that is pleasing and to construct with
> intervals, correctly, a film-phrase which is the room.[1]
>
> —Dziga Vertov, 1923

In this essay, I want to examine that aspect of film which has
acted, from the beginning of this century, as a sort of laboratory
for the exploration of the built world; of, that is, architecture and
the city. The examples of such experimentation are well known
and include the entire roster of filmic genres: science fiction,
adventure, film noir, action films, documentaries. Film, indeed,
has even been seen to anticipate the built forms of architecture
and the city: we have only to think of the commonplace icons of
Expressionist utopias to find examples, from *Das Cabinet des
Dr Caligari* to *Metropolis*, that apparently succeeded, where
architecture failed, in building the future in the present. The
installation of a recent exhibition in Los Angeles by the Viennese
architectural firm Coop Himmelblau even suggested a moment
of contemporary closure when, at last, architecture might have
been seen to have caught up with the imaginary space of film. In
recent years, other designers, searching for ways to represent
movement and temporal succession in architecture, have
similarly turned to the images forged by the Constructivist and
Expressionist avant-gardes, images themselves deeply marked
by the impact of the new filmic techniques. From the literal
evocations of Bernard Tschumi in his Manhattan Transcripts, 1980,
and projects for the urban Parc de la Villette in Paris to more
theoretical and critical work on the relations of space to visual
representation in the projects of Elizabeth Diller and Ricardo
Scofidio, the complex question of film's architectural role is again
on the agenda. In their new incarnation, such neo Constructivist,
Dadaist, and Expressionist images seem to reframe many earlier
questions about the proper place for images of space and time in
architecture, questions that resonate for the contemporary critique
of the 'image' and the 'spectacle' in architecture and society.

And yet the simple alignment of architecture and film, as the
following discussion will confirm, has always posed difficulties,
both theoretically and in practice. On the one hand, it is obvious
that film—the modernist medium *par excellence*—has been the site
of envy and even of imitation for those more static arts concerned
to produce effects or techniques of movement and space-time

interpenetration. Painting, from Duchamp's *Nude Descending the
Staircase*; literature, from Virginia Woolf's *Mrs Dalloway*, poetry,
from Marinetti's *paroles en liberté*; architecture, from Sant' Elia
to Le Corbusier—all have sought to reproduce movement and the
collapse of time in space, and montage, or its equivalent, has been
a preoccupation in all the arts since its appearance, in primitive
form, with rapid-sequence photography. On the other hand, it
is equally true that modernism's roots in the Enlightenment
insured that film, as well as all the other arts, were bound, in the
manner of Gotthold Ephraim Lessing, to draw precise theoretical
boundaries around the centres of their conceptually different
practices—practices understood as distinct precisely because
of their distinct media, each one, like Lessing's own poetry and
painting, more or less appropriate to the representation of time
or space. Thus, despite the aspirations of avant-garde groups—
from Dada to Esprit Nouveau—to syncretism and synaesthesia,
the relations of the arts still could not be conceived without
their particular essences being defined. As if the arts were so
many nations, romantically rooted in soil and race, each with
characteristics of its own to be asserted before any treaties might
be negotiated. Of all the arts, however, it is architecture that has
had the most privileged and difficult relationship with film. An
obvious rote model for spatial experimentation, film has also been
criticised for its deleterious effects on the architectural image.

When, in 1933, Le Corbusier called for film aesthetics that
embodied the "spirit of truth", he was only asserting what many
architects in the 1920s and, more recently, in the 1980s saw
to be the mutually informative, but properly separate realms

of architecture and film. While admitting that "everything is Architecture" in its architectonic dimensions of proportion and order, Le Corbusier nevertheless insisted on the specificity of film, which "from now on is positioning itself on its own terrain… becoming a form of art in and of itself, a kind of genre, just as painting, sculpture, literature, music, and theatre are genres".[2] In the present context, debates as to the nature of 'architecture in film', 'filmic architecture', or filmic theory in architectural theory are interesting less as a guide to the writing of some new *Laocoön* that would rigidly redraw the boundaries of the technological arts than they are to the establishment of possibilities of interpretation for projects that increasingly seem caught in the hallucinatory realm of a filmic or screened imaginary—somewhere, that is, in the problematic realm of hyperspace.

CINEPLASTICS

The obvious role of architecture in the construction of sets (and the eager participation of architects themselves in this enterprise), and the equally obvious ability of film to 'construct' its own architecture in light and shade, scale and movement, allowed from the outset for a mutual intersection of these two 'spatial arts'. Certainly, many modernist filmmakers had little doubt regarding the cinema's architectonic properties. From George Méliès' careful description of the proper spatial organisation of a studio in 1907 to Eric Rohmer's re-assertion of film as "the spatial art" some 40 years later, the architectural metaphor—if not its material reality—was deemed essential to the filmic imagination.[3] Equally, architects such as Hans Poelzig (who together with his wife, the sculptor Marlene Poelzig, sketched and modelled the sets for Paul Wegener's *Der Golem wie er in die Welt kam* and Andrei Andreiev (who designed the sets for Robert Wiene's *Raskolnikoff*, 1923) had no hesitation in collaborating with filmmakers in the same way as they had previously served theatre producers.[4]

As the architect Robert Mallet-Stevens observed in 1925:
It is undeniable that the cinema has a marked influence on modern architecture; in turn, modern architecture brings its artistic side to the cinema. Modern architecture does not only serve the cinematographic set (decor), but imprints its stamp on the staging (*mise-en-scène*), it breaks out of its frame; architecture plays.[5]

Of course, for filmmakers (like Sergei Eisenstein) originally trained as architects, the filmic art offered the potential to develop a new architecture of time and space unfettered by the material constraints of gravity and daily life.

Out of this intersection of the two arts a theoretical apparatus was developed that at once saw architecture as the fundamental site of film practice, the indispensable real and ideal matrix of the filmic imaginary and, at the same time, posited film as the modernist art of space *par excellence*—a vision of the fusion of space and time. The potential of film to explore this new realm, seen as the basis of modernist architectural aesthetics by Siegfried Giedion, was recognised early on. Abel Gance, writing in 1912, was already hoping for a new "sixth art" that would provide "that admirable synthesis of the movement of space and time".[6] But it was the art historian, Elie Faure, influenced by Fernand Léger, who first coined a term for the cinematic aesthetic that brought together the two dimensions: "cineplastics". "The cinema", he wrote in 1922, "is first of all plastic. It represents, in some way, an architecture in movement which should be in constant accord, in dynamically pursued equilibrium, with the setting and the landscapes within

Opposite: Diller Scofidio + Renfro's Blur Building at Expo O2 in Yverdon.

Left: Antonio Sant' Elia, The New City, 1914.

which it rises and falls."[7] In Faure's terms, "plastic" art was that which "expresse[d] form at rest and in movement", a mode common to the arts of sculpture, bas-relief, drawing, painting, fresco, and especially dance, but that perhaps achieved its highest expression in the cinema.[8] For, as Faure put it, "the cinema incorporates time with space. Even better, time, in this way, really becomes a dimension of space."[9] By means of the cinema, Faure claimed, time became a veritable instrument of space, "unrolling under our eyes its successive volumes ceaselessly returned to us in dimensions that allow us to grasp their extent in surface and depth".[10] The "hitherto unknown plastic pleasures" thereby discovered would, finally, have the effect of creating a new kind of architectural space, akin to that imaginary space "within the walls of the brain":

The notion of duration entering as a constitutive element into the notion of space, we will easily imagine an art of cineplastics blossoming which would be no more than an ideal architecture where the 'cine-mimic' will... disappear, because only a great artist could build edifices that constitute themselves, collapse, and reconstitute themselves again ceaselessly by imperceptible passages of tones and modelling which will themselves be architecture at every instant, without our being able to grasp the thousandth part of a second in which the transition takes place.[11]

Such an art would, Faure predicted, propel the world into a new stage of civilisation, one in which architecture would be the principle form of expression based on the appearance of mobile industrial constructions, ships, trains, cars, and airplanes together with their stable ports and harbours. Cinema would then operate, he concluded, as a kind of privileged "spiritual ornament" to this machine civilisation, as "the most useful social play for the development of confidence, harmony, and cohesion in the masses".[12]

SPACES OF HORROR
Critics of the first generation of German Expressionist films had already experienced such a "cineplastic" revolution in practice. The spate of immediate post-war productions in 1919 and 1920, including Wegener's *Golem*, Karl-Heinz Martin's on *Morgens bis Mitternachts* and, of course, Robert Wiene's *Caligari*, demonstrated that, in the words of the German art critic and *The New York Times* correspondent, Hermann G Scheffauer, a new "stereoscopic universe" was in the making. In a brilliant analysis published at the end of 1920, Scheffauer hailed the end of the "crude phantasmagoria" of earlier films and the birth of a new space:

Space—hitherto considered and treated as something dead and static, a mere inert screen or frame, often of no more significance than the painted balustrade-background at the village photographer's—has been smitten into life, into movement and conscious expression. A fourth dimension has begun to evolve out of this photographic cosmos.[13]

Thus, film began to extend what Scheffauer called "the sixth sense of man, his feeling for space or room—his *Raumgefühl*", in such a way as to transform reality itself. No longer an inert background, architecture now participated in the very emotions of film. The surroundings no longer surrounded, but entered the experience as presence: "The frown of a tower, the scowl of a sinister alley, the pride and serenity of a white peak, the hypnotic draught of a straight road vanishing to point—these exert their influences and express their natures; their essences flow over the scene and blend with the action."[14] The "scenic architect" of films such as *Caligari* had the ability to dominate "furniture, room, house, street, city, landscape, universe". The "fourth dimension" of time extended space into depth,

the plastic [was] amalgamated with the painted, bulk and form with the simulacra of bulk and form, false perspective and violent foreshadowing were introduced, real light and shadow combat[ted] or reinforce[d] painted shadow and light. Einstein's invasion of the law of gravity [was] made visible in the treatment of walls and supports.[15]

Scheffauer provided a veritable phenomenology of the spaces of *Caligari*, all constructed out of walls that were at once solid and transparent, fissured and veiled, camouflaged and endlessly disappearing, and all presented in a forced and distorted perspective that pressed space both backwards and forwards, finally overwhelming the spectator's own space, incorporating it into the vortex of the whole movie. In his description of the film's environments, Scheffauer anticipated all the later commonplaces of expressionist criticism from Siegfried Kracauer to Rudolf Kurtz:

A corridor in an office building: wall veering outward from the floor, traversed by sharply defined parallel strips, emphasising the perspective and broken violently by pyramidal openings, streaming with light, marking the doors; the shadows between them vibrating as dark cones of contrast, the further end of the murky corridor, giving vast distance. In the foreground a section of wall violently tilted over the heads of the audience, as it were. The floor cryptically painted with errant tines of direction, the floor in front of the doors shows cross lines, indicating a going to and fro, in and out. The impression is one of formal coldness, of bureaucratic regularity, of semi-public traffic.

A street at night: yawning blackness in the background— empty, starless, abstract space, against it a square, lopsided lantern hung between lurching walls. Doors and windows constructed or painted in wrenched perspective. Dark segments on the pavement accentuate diminishing effect. The slinking of a brutal figure pressed against the walls and evil spots and shadings on the pavement give a sinister expression to the street. Adroit diagonals lead and rivet the eye.

An attic: it speaks of sordidness, want and crime. The whole composition a vivid intersection of cones of light and dark, of roof lines, shafts of light and slanting walls. A projection of white and black patterns on the floor, the whole geometrically felt, cubistically conceived. This attic is out of time, but in space. The roof chimneys of another world arise and scowl through the splintered windowpane.

A room; or rather a room that has precipitated itself in cavern-like lines, in inverted hollows of frozen waves. Here space becomes cloistral and encompasses the human—a man reads at a desk. A triangular window glares and permits the living day a voice in this composition.

A prison cell: a criminal, ironed to a huge chain attached to an immense trapezoidal 'ball'. The posture of the prisoner sitting on his folded legs is almost Buddha-like. Here space

Exterior shot of Diller Scofidio + Renfro's recently designed ICA building in Boston. Photograph by Christopher Peterson.

turns upon itself, encloses and focuses a human destiny. A small window high up and crazily barred, is like an eye. The walls, sloping like a tent's to an invisible point, are blazoned with black and white wedge-shaped rays. These blend when they reach the floor and unite in a kind of huge cross, in the centre of which the prisoner sits, scowling, unshaven. The tragedy of the repression of the human in space—in trinity of space, fate and man.

A white and spectral bridge yawning and rushing out of the foreground; it is an erratic, irregular causeway, such as blond ghouls might have built. It climbs and struggles upward almost out of the picture. In the middle distance it rises into a hump and reveals arches staggering over nothingness. The perspective pierces into vacuity. This bridge is the scene of a wild pursuit.

Several aspects of the market place of a small town... the town cries out its will through its mouth, this market place.[16]

Caligari, then, produced an entirely new space, one that was both all-embracing and all-absorbing in depth and movement.[17] But the filmic medium allowed the exploration of other kinds of space than the totalising plasticity modelled by Walter Röhrig, Walter Reimann, and Hermann Warm for Wiene's film. Scheffauer identified the "flat space" of Martin's *Van Morgens bis Mittermachts*, designed by Robert Neppach, which—rather than being artificially constructed in the round like *Caligari*—was suggested in black, white, and gray as "a background, vague, inchoate, nebulous".[18] Above and around this inactive space that made the universe into a flat plane, there was only "primeval darkness"; all perspective was rendered in contrasts of white planes against blackness. There was also the "geometrical space" found in Reimann's film fantasy *Algol*; here, "the forms are broken up expressionistically, but space acts and speaks geometrically, in great vistas, in grandiose architectural culminations. Space or room is divided into formal diapers, patterns, squares, spots, and circles, of cube imposed upon cube, of apartment opening into apartment."[19] Finally, there was what Scheffauer termed "sculptural" or "solid" space, such as that modelled by the Poelzigs for Wegener's *Golem*:

Professor Poelzig conceives of space in plastic terms, in solid concretions congealing under the artist's hand to expressive and organic forms. He works, therefore, in the solid masses of the sculptor and not with the planes of the painter. Under his caressing hands a weird but spontaneous internal architecture, shell-like, cavernous, somber, has been evolved in simple, flowing lines, instinct with the bizarre spirit of the tale.... The gray soul of Medieval Prague has been molded into these eccentric and errant crypts.... Poelzig seeks to give an eerie and grotesque suggestiveness to the flights of houses and streets that are to furnish the external setting of this film-play. The will of this master architect animating facades into faces, insists that these houses are to speak in jargon—and gesticulate![20]

PAN-GEOMETRIES

In assimilating filmic space with the theoretical types of *Raum* adumbrated in German philosophy and psychology since Theodor Vischer, and in proposing the relativity of spatial forms in the face of continuous optical movement in a way that reminds us of

the historical relativity of optical forms demonstrated by Alois Riegl, Scheffauer seems also to have been anticipating the more scholarly account of perspectival history developed between 1923 and 1925 by Erwin Panofsky. Panofsky's essay "Perspective as Symbolic Form" set out to show that the various perspective systems developed from Roman times to the present were not simply "incorrect" instances of representing reality, but were instead endowed with distinct symbolic meanings of their own, as powerful and as open to reading as iconographical types and genres. Panofsky even took note of the modernist will to break with the conventions of perspective, seeing it as yet another stage of perspective vision. He cited the Expressionist resistance to perspective as the last remnant of the will to capture "real, three-dimensional space", as well as El Lissitzky's desire to overcome the bounds of finite space:

Older perspective is supposed to have 'limited space, made it finite, closed it off', conceived of space 'according to Euclidian geometry as rigid three-dimensionality', and it is these very bonds which the most recent art has attempted to break. Either it has in a sense exploded the entire space by 'dispersing the centre of vision' ('Futurism'), or it has sought no longer to represent depth intervals 'extensively' by means of foreshortenings, but rather, in accord with the most modern insights of psychology, only to create an illusion 'intensively' by playing colour surfaces off against each other, each differently placed, differently shaded and, only in this way, furnished with different spatial values (Mondrian and in particular Malevich's 'Suprematism'). The author believes he can suggest a third solution: the conquest of 'imaginary space' by means of mechanically motivated bodies, which by this very movement, by their rotation or oscillation, produce precise figures (for example, a rotating stick produces an apparent circle, or in another position, an apparent cylinder, and so forth). In this way, in the opinion of El Lissitzky, art is elevated to the stand point of a non-Euclidian pan-geometry (whereas in fact the space of those 'imaginary' rotating bodies is no less 'Euclidian' than any other empirical space).[21]

Despite Panofsky's skepticism, it was, of course, just such a "pan-geometric" space that architecture hoped to construct through abstraction and technologically induced movement. Architects from Lissitzky to Bruno Taut were to experiment with this new "pan-geometry", as if—in Ernst Bloch's words—it would enable them finally "to depict empirically an imaginary space".[22] For Bloch, the underlying Euclidian nature of all space offered the potential for architecture to approach "pan-geometry" in reality; basing his argument on Panofsky's essay, he commended the Expressionists for having generated rotating and turning bodies that produced "stereometric figures... which at least have nothing in common with the perspective visual space (Sehraum)". Out of this procedure emerged "an architecture of the abstract, which wants to be *quasi-meta-cubic*".[23] For Bloch, this potential allowed modern architecture to achieve its own "symbolic allusions", even if these were founded on the "so-called Euclidian pan-geometry" criticised by Panofsky.[24] In this illusion, the architects were encouraged by cinematographers, who, at least in the 1920s, and led by Fritz Lang and FW Murnau, accepted the practical rulings of the Universum Film AG, or Ufa, whose proscription against exterior filming supported the extraordinary experimentation in set design of the Weimar period.

PSYCHO-SPACES

But the attempt to construct these imaginary new worlds was, as Panofsky noted, not simply formalistic and decorative; its premise was from the outset psychological, based on what Rudolf Kurtz defined as the "simple law of psychological aesthetics that when we feel our way into certain forms exact psychic correspondences are set up".[25] Hugo Münsterberg, in his 1916 work *Film: A Psychological Study*, had already set out the terms of the equation film = psychological form.[26] For Münsterberg, film differed from drama by its appeal to the "inner movements of the mind":

To be sure, the events in the photo-play happen in the real space with its depth. But the spectator feels that they are not presented in the three dimensions of the outer world, that they are flat pictures which only the mind molds into plastic things. Again the

events are seen in continuous movement; and yet the pictures break up the movement into a rapid succession of instantaneous impressions... the photoplay tells us the human study by overcoming the forms of the outer world, namely space, time, and causality, and by adjusting the events to the forms of the inner world, namely, attention, memory, imagination, and emotion.[27]

Only two years later, in one of his first critical essays, Louis Aragon was to note this property of film to focus attention and reformulate the real into the imaginary, the ability to fuse the physical and the mental, later to become a Surrealist obsession. Seemingly anticipating the mental states of André Breton's *Nadja* or of his own *Paysan de Paris*, but revealed in film, Aragon meditated on "the door of a bar that swings and on the window the capital letters of unreadable and marvellous words, or the

vertiginous, thousand-eye facade of the 30-storey house".[28] The possibility of disclosing the inner "menacing or enigmatic meanings" of everyday objects by simple close-up techniques and camera angles, light, shade, and space established, for Aragon, the poetic potential of the art: "To endow with a poetic value that which does not possess it, to willfully restrict the field of vision so as to intensify expression: these are two properties that help make cinematic decor the adequate setting of modern beauty."[29] To accomplish this, however, film had no need of an artificially constructed 'decor' that simulated the foreshortening of perspective or the phobic characteristics of space; the framings and movements of the camera itself would serve to construct reality far more freely. In his 1934 essay "Style and Medium in the Motion Pictures", Panofsky himself argued against any attempt to subject the world to "aesthetic prestylisation, as in the expressionist settings of *The Cabinet of Dr Caligari*", an exercise he characterised as "no more than an exciting experiment". "To prestylise reality prior to tackling it amounts to dodging the problem", he concluded. "The problem is to manipulate and shoot unstylised reality in such a way that the result has style."[30]

THE LURE OF THE STREET

In such terms as these, from the mid-1920s on, critics increasingly denounced what they saw as the purely decorative and staged characteristics of Expressionist film in favour of a more direct confrontation with the 'real'. If, as Panofsky asserted, "the unique and specific possibilities of film" could be "defined as dynamisation of space and, accordingly, spatialisation of time", then it was the lens of the camera, and not any distorted set, that inculcated a sense of motion in the static spectator and thence a mobilisation of space itself: "Not only do bodies move in space, but space itself does, approaching, receding, turning, dissolving and recrystallising as it appears through the controlled locomotion and focusing of the camera and through the cutting and editing of the various shots."[31] And this led to the inevitable conclusion that the proper medium of the movies was not the idealisation of reality, as in the other arts, but "physical reality as such".[32] Marcel Carné's frustrated question "When Will the Cinema Go Down into the Street", calling for an end to artifice and the studio set and a confrontation of the 'real' as opposed to the 'constructed' Paris, was only one of a number of increasingly critical attacks on the architectural set in the early 1930s.[33]

Among the most rigorous of the new realists, Siegfried Kracauer, himself a former architect, was consistent in his arguments against the 'decorative' and artificial and in favour of the critical vision of the real which film allowed. From his first experience of film as a pre-First World War child to his last theoretical work on the medium, published in 1960, Kracauer found the street to be both site and vehicle for his social criticism. Recalling the first film he had seen as a boy, entitled, significantly enough, *Film as the Discoverer of the Marvels of Everyday Life*, Kracauer remembered being thrilled by the sight of

... an ordinary suburban street, filled with lights and shadows which transfigured it. Several trees stood about, and there was in the foreground a puddle reflecting invisible house facades and a piece of sky. Then a breeze moved the shadows, and the facades with the sky below began to waver. The trembling upper world in the dirty puddle—this image has never left me.[34]

Film stills from Robert Wiene's 1920 silent film *The Cabinet of Dr Caligari*. Images courtesy of BFI Stills.

For Kracauer, film was first and foremost a material—not purely formal—aesthetics that was essentially suited to the recording of the fleeting, the temporally transient, the momentary—that is, the modern—and that possessed a quality that made 'the street' in all its manifestations an especially favoured subject. If the snapshot stressed the random and the fortuitous, then its natural development in the motion picture camera was "partial to the least permanent components of our environment", rendering "the street in the broadest sense of the word" the place for chance encounters and social observation.[35] But for this to work as a truly critical method of observation and recording, the street would first have to be offered up as an "unstaged reality"; what Kracauer considered film's "declared preference for nature in the raw" was easily defeated by artificiality and "staginess", whether the staged "drawing brought to life" (*Caligari*) or the more filmic staging of montage, panning, and camera movement. Lang's *Metropolis* was an instance in which "a film of unsurpassable staginess" was partially redeemed by the way in which crowds were treated "and rendered through a combination of long shots and close shots which provide exactly the kind of random impressions we would receive were we to witness this spectacle in reality".[36] Yet for Kracauer, the impact of the crowd images was obviated by the architectural settings, which remained entirely stylised and imaginary. A similar case was represented by Walter Ruttmann's *Berlin, die Sinfonie der Großstadt* (Berlin, Symphony of a Great City), 1927, in which—in a Vertov-like manipulation of shot and montage—the director tried to capture

> simultaneous phenomena which, owing to certain analogies and contrasts between them, form comprehensible patterns... he cuts from human legs walking in the street to the legs of a cow and juxtaposes the luscious dishes in a deluxe restaurant with the appalling food of the very poor.[37]

Such formalism, however, tended to concentrate attention not on things themselves and their meaning, but on their formal characteristics. As Kracauer noted with respect to the capturing of the city's movement in rhythmic shots, "tempo is also a formal conception if it is not defined with reference to the qualities of the objects through which it materialises."[38]

For Kracauer, the street; properly recorded, offered a virtually inexhaustible subject for the comprehension of modernity; its special characteristics fostered not only the chance and the random, but, more importantly, the necessary distance, if not alienation, of the observer for whom the camera eye was a precise surrogate. If in the photographs of contemporaries of Eugène Atget one might detect a certain melancholy, this was because the photographic medium, intersecting with the street as subject, fostered a kind of self-estrangement allowing for a closer identification with the objects being observed:

> "The dejected individual is likely to lose himself in the incidental configurations of his environment, absorbing them with a disinterested intensity no longer determined by his previous preferences. His is a kind of receptivity which resembles that of Proust's photographer cast in the role of a stranger."[39]

Hence, for Kracauer and his friend Walter Benjamin, the close identification of the photographer with the *flâneur*, and the potential of *flânerie* and its techniques to furnish models for the modernist filmmaker:

Image still from *Der Golem*, a 1920 silent horror film by Paul Wegener.

> "The melancholy character is seen strolling about aimlessly: as he proceeds, his changing surroundings take shape in the form of numerous juxtaposed shots of house facades, neon lights, stray passers-by, and the like. It is inevitable that the audience should trace their seemingly unmotivated emergence to his dejection and the alienation in its wake."[40]

In this respect, what Kracauer saw as Eisenstein's "identification of life with the street" took on new meaning as the *flâneur*-photographer moved to capture the flow of fleeting impressions, what Kracauer's teacher, Georg Simmel, had characterised as "snapshots of reality". "When history is made in the streets, the streets tend to move onto the screen", Kracauer himself concluded.

FILMING THE CITY

Other critics were more optimistic about the potential of filmic techniques to render a version of reality that might otherwise go unrecorded, or better, to reconstrue reality in such a way that it might be critically apprehended. Thus, Benjamin's celebrated eulogy of the film as liberation of perception in "The Work of Art in the Age of Mechanical Reproduction" was a first step in the constitution of the filmic as the modern critical aesthetic:

> By close-ups of the things around us, by focusing on hidden details of familiar objects, by exploring commonplace milieus under the ingenious guidance of the camera, the film, on the one hand, extends our comprehension of the necessities which rule our lives; on the other hand, it manages to assure us of an immense and unexpected field of action. Our taverns and our metropolitan streets, our offices and furnished rooms, our railroad stations and our factories appeared to have us locked up hopelessly. Then came the film and burst this prison world asunder by the dynamite of the tenth of a second, so that now, in the midst of its far flung ruins and debris, we calmly and adventurously go travelling. With the close-up, space expands; with slow motion, movement is extended... an unconsciously penetrated space is substituted for a space consciously explored by man.... The camera introduces us to unconscious optics as does psychoanalysis to unconscious impulses.[41]

Unconscious optics, the filmic unconscious, was, for Benjamin, itself a kind of analysis, the closest aesthetic equivalent to Freud's *Psychopathology of Everyday Life*, 1901, in its ability to focus and deepen perception. In this characteristic, film obviously outdistanced architecture. Benjamin's remark that "architecture has always represented the prototype of a work of art the reception of which is consummated by the collectivity in a state of distraction" was made in this very context: the assertion of the 'shock effect' of the film as that which allows the public, no longer distracted, to be once more put in the position of the critic. Thus, the only way to render architecture critical again was to wrest it out of its uncritically observed context, its distracted state, and offer it to a now attentive public—that is, to make a film of the building or of the city. In an evocative remark inserted apparently at random among the unwieldy collection of citations and aphorisms that make up the unfinished *Passagen-Werk*, Benjamin opened the possibility of yet another way of reading his unfinished work:

> Could one not shoot a passionate film of the city plan of Paris? Of the development of its different forms [Gestalten]

in temporal succession? Of the condensation of a century-long movement of streets, boulevards, passages, squares, in the space of half an hour? And what else does the *flâneur* do?[42]

In this context, might not the endless quotations and aphoristic observations of the *Passagen-Werk*, carefully written out on hundreds of index cards, each one letter-, number-, and colour-coded to cross-reference it to all the rest, be construed as so many camera shots ready to be montaged into the epic film *Paris, Capital of the Nineteenth Century*, a prehistory of modernity, finally realised by modernity's own special form of mechanical reproduction?

While obviously no 'film' of this kind was ever made, an attempt to answer the hypothetical question: "What would Benjamin's film of Paris have looked like?" would clarify what we might call Benjamin's 'filmic imaginary'. Such an imaginary, overt in the *Passagen-Werk* and his contemporary essay "The Work of Art in the Age of Mechanical Re-production" and covert in many earlier writings from those on German Baroque allegory to those on historical form might, in turn, reveal important aspects of the theoretical problems inherent in the filmic representation of the metropolis. For in the light of Benjamin's theories of the political and social powers of mechanical reproduction as outlined in his "Conversations with Berthold Brecht", it is clear from the outset that any project for a film of Paris would in no way have resembled other urban films of the inter-war period, whether idealist, Expressionist, or Realist. Rather, it would have involved Benjamin in an act of theoretical elaboration which, based on previous film theory and criticism, would have constructed new kinds of optical relations between the camera and the city, film and architecture. These would no doubt have been based on the complex notion of "the optical unconscious", an intercalation of Freud and Riegl, which appears in Benjamin's writings on photography and film from the late 1920s and early 30s.

On one level, Benjamin's fragmentary remark is easily decipherable. What he had in mind was evidently an image of the combined results of the *flâneur's* peripatetic vision montaged onto the history of the nineteenth century and put in motion by the movie camera. No longer would the implied movement of Bergsonian mental processes or the turns of allegorical text have to make do as pale imitations of metropolitan movement; now the real movement of the film would, finally, merge technique and content as a proof, so to speak, of the manifest destiny of modernity. In this sense, Benjamin's metaphor of a Parisian film remains just that: a figure of modernist technique as the fullest expression of modernist thought, as well as the explanation of its origins.

It is certainly not too difficult to imagine the figure of Benjamin's *flâneur*, Vertov-like, carrying his camera as a third eye, framing and shooting the rapidly moving pictures of modern life. The etchings of Jacques Callot, the thumbnail sketches of Saint-Aubin, the 'tableaux' of Sebastien Mercier, the rapid renderings of Constantin Guys, the prose poems of Baudelaire, the snapshots of Atget, are all readily transposed into the vocabulary of film, which then literally mimics the fleeting impressions of everyday life in the metropolis in its very techniques of representation. Indeed, almost every characteristic Benjamin associated with the *flâneur* might be associated with the film director with little or no distortion. An eye for detail, for the neglected and the chance; a penchant for joining reality and reverie; a distanced vision, set apart from that distracted and unselfconscious existence of the crowd; a fondness for the marginal and the forgotten: these are traits of *flâneur* and filmmaker alike. Both share affinities with the detective and the peddler, the rag-picker and the vagabond; both aesthetise the roles and materials with which they work. Equally, the typical habitats of the *flâneur* lend themselves to filmic representation; the *banlieu*, the margins, the zones and outskirts of the city; deserted streets and squares at night; crowded boulevards, phantasmagoric passages, arcades, and department stores—the spatial apparatus, that is, of the consumer metropolis.

On another level, however, if we take Benjamin's image literally rather than metaphorically, a number of puzzling questions emerge. A film of Paris is certainly conceivable, but what would a film of "the plan of Paris" look like? And if one were to succeed in filming this plan, how then might it depict the development of the city's 'forms'—its boulevards, streets, squares, and passages—at the same time 'condensing' a century of their history into half an hour? How might such a film, if realised, be 'passionate'? If, as Benjamin intimated, the model of the film director was to be found in the figure of the *flâneur*, how might this figure translate his essentially nineteenth century habits of walking and seeing into cinematographic terms? It seems that, step by step, within the very movement of Benjamin's own metaphor, the ostensible unity of his image is systematically undermined, as if the result of making a film of the plan of Paris were to replicate the very fragmentation of modernity the metropolis posed, the *flâneur* saw, and the film had concretised. Benjamin's image thus emerges as a complex rebus of method and form. Its very self-enclosed elegance, beginning with the film and ending with the *flâneur* as director (a perfect example of a romantic fragment turning in on itself according to the rules of the German philosopher Schelling), seems consciously structured to provoke its own unravelling. It is as if Benjamin inserted his cinematographic conundrum into the formless accumulation of the *Passagen-Werk's* citations and aphorisms to provoke, in its deciphering, a self-conscious ambiguity about the implied structure of his text and, at the same time, a speculation on the theory of film which he never wrote.

It was not simply that the *flâneur* and the filmmaker shared spaces and gazes; for Benjamin, these characteristics were transferred, as in analysis, to the spaces themselves, which became, so to speak, vagabonds in their own right. He spoke of the phenomenon of the "colportage or peddling of space" as the fundamental experience of the *flâneur*, in which a kind of Bergsonian process allowed "the simultaneous perception of everything that potentially is happening in this single space. The space directs winks at the flaneur."[43] Thus, the *flâneur* as rag picker and peddlar participates in his surroundings, even as they cooperate with him in his unofficial archaeology of spatial settings. And, to paraphrase Benjamin, "what else does the filmmaker do" for a viewer now opened up "in his susceptibility to the transient real life phenomena that crowd the screen?"[44]

ARCHITECTURAL MONTAGE

Here, we are returned to Eisenstein's "street", reminded, in Benjamin's desire to have shot a "passionate" film, of Eisenstein's own long analyses of the notion or filmic "ecstasy", the simultaneous cause and effect of movement in the movie. The "ecstatic" for Eisenstein was, in fact, the fundamental shared characteristic of architecture and film. Even as architectural styles had, one by one, "exploded" into each other by a kind of inevitable historical process, so the filmmaker might force the shot to decompose and recompose in successive explosions. Thus, the

... principles of the Gothic... seem to explode the balance of the Romanesque style. And, within the Gothic itself, we could trace the stirring picture of movement of its lancet world from the first almost indistinct steps toward the ardent model of the mature and post mature, 'flamboyant' late Gothic. We could, like [the art historian Heinrich] Wölfflin, contrast the Renaissance and Baroque and interpret the excited spirit of the second, winding like a spiral, as an ecstatically bursting temperament of a new epoch, exploding preceding forms of art in the enthusiasms for a new quality, responding to a new phase of a single historical process.[45]

But Eisenstein went further. In an essay on two Piranesi engravings for the early and late states of the Carceri series, he compared architectural composition itself to cinematic montage, an implicit "flux of form" which holds within itself the potential to explode into successive states.[46] Building on his experience as architect and set designer, Eisenstein developed a comprehensive theory of what he called "space constructions" that found new meaning in the romantic formulation of architecture as "frozen music":

At the basis of the composition of its ensemble, at the basis of the harmony of its conglomerating masses, in the establishment of the melody of the future overflow of its forms, and in the execution of its rhythmic parts, giving harmony to the relief of its ensemble, lies that same 'dance' that is also at the basis of the creation of music, painting, and cinematic montage.[47]

For Eisenstein, a kind of relentless vertigo was set up by the play of architectural forms in space, a vertigo that is easily assimilable to Thomas De Quincey's celebrated account of Coleridge's reaction to Piranesi's Carceri or, better, to Gogol's reading of the Gothic as a style of endless movement and internal explosions.[48]

And if Eisenstein was able to "force"—to use Manfredo Tafuri's term—these representations of architectural space to 'explode' into the successive stages of their 'montage' decomposition and re-composition, as if they were so many 'shots', then it was because, for Eisenstein, architecture itself embodied the principles of montage; indeed, its special characteristics of a spatial art experienced in time render it the predecessor of film in more than simple analogy.

In his article "Montage and Architecture", written in the late 1930s as part of his uncompleted work on montage, Eisenstein set out this position, contrasting two 'paths' of the spatial eye: the cinematic, in which a spectator follows an imaginary line among a series of objects, through sight as well as in the mind—"diverse positions passing in front of an immobile spectator"—and the architectural, in which "the spectator move[s] through a series of carefully disposed phenomena which he observe[s] in order with his visual sense".[49] In this transition from real to imaginary movement, architecture is film's predecessor. Where painting "remained incapable of fixing the total representation of an object in its full multi-dimensionality", and "only the film camera had solved the problem of doing this on a flat surface", "its undoubted ancestor in this capability [was]... architecture".[50]

Here, Eisenstein, former architect and an admitted "great adherent of the architectural aesthetics of Le Corbusier", turned to an

example of the architectural 'path' which precisely parallels that studied by Le Corbusier himself in Vers une architecture, 1923, to exemplify the promenade architecturale: the successive perspective views of the movement of an imaginary spectator on the Acropolis constructed by Auguste Choisy to demonstrate the 'successive tableaux' and 'picturesque' composition of the site.[51] Eisenstein cited Choisy's analysis at length with little commentary, asking his reader simply "to look at it with the eye of a filmmaker": "[I]t is hard to imagine a montage sequence for an architectural ensemble more subtly composed, shot by shot, than the one which our legs create by walking among the buildings of the Acropolis."[52] For Eisenstein, the Acropolis was the answer to Victor Hugo's assertion of the cathedral as a book in stone: "The perfect example of one of the most ancient films."[53] Eisenstein found in the carefully sequenced perspectives presented by Choisy the combination of a "film shot effect", producing an obvious new impression from each new, emerging shot, and a "montage effect", in which the effect was gained from the sequential juxtaposition of shots. The Russian filmmaker speculated on the desirable temporal duration of each picture, discovering the possibility that there was a distinct relationship between the pace of the spectator's movement and the rhythm of the buildings themselves, a temporal solemnity being provoked by the distance between buildings.

Le Corbusier, who was apparently less faithful in his reproduction of Choisy's sequence, concentrated on the second perspective, shown together with the plan of the visual axis of entry from the Propylea to the former statue of Athena.[54] For the architect, this demonstrated the flexibility of Greek 'axial' planning as opposed to the rigidity of the academic Beaux Arts: "[F]alse right angles have furnished rich views and a subtle effect; the asymmetrical masses of the buildings create an intense rhythm. The spectacle is massive, elastic, nervous, overwhelming in its sharpness, dominating."[55] The plan of the mobile and changing ground levels of the Acropolis was only apparently "disordered". There was an inner equilibrium when the entire site was viewed from afar. In this common reliance on Choisy, we might be tempted to see the final conjunction of architectural and filmic modernism; the rhythmic dance of Le Corbusier's spectator (modelled no doubt on the movements of Jacques Dalcroze) anticipating the movement of Eisenstein's shots and montages. For both analysts, the apparently inert site and its strangely placed buildings were almost literally exploded into life, at once physical and mental. For both, the rereading of a canonical monument provided the key to a 'true' and natural modernist aesthetic.

Giovanni Battista Piranesi, *Carceri d'Invenzione*, plate seven, etching, 1780.

And yet, as both writers ceaselessly reiterated, such correspondences were, when taken too literally, false to the internal laws of the two media, architecture and film. If Le Corbusier agreed that "everything is Architecture", he also called for film to concentrate on its own laws; Eisenstein, similarly, abandoned a career as an architect and stage designer precisely because the film offered a new and different stage of representational technique for modernity. For Le Corbusier, architecture was a setting for the athletic and physical life of the new man, its objects and setting the activators of mental and spiritual activity through vision; for Eisenstein, architecture remained only a potential film, a necessary stage in aesthetic evolution, but already surpassed.

Both would have agreed with Robert Mallet-Stevens, who was troubled by the invasion of the decorative into filmic architecture, by the potential to create 'imaginary' forms that illustrated rather than provided settings for human emotions. Mallet-Stevens warned against the tendency to view architecture as a photogenic aid to film, thereby creating a 'foreseen' dynamic that in real space would be provided by the human figure: "[T]he ornament, the arabesque, is the mobile personage who creates them."[56] Rather than expressionist buildings imitating their cinematic counterparts, he called for a radical simplification of architecture which would, in this way, offer itself up naturally to filmic action, always preserving the distance between the real and the imaginary: "Real life is entirely different, the house is made to live, it should first respond to our needs."[57] Properly handled, however, architecture and film might be entirely complementary. Mallet-Stevens cited a screenplay by Ricciotto Canudo that would perhaps realise this ideal:

> It concerned the representation of a solitary woman, frighteningly alone in life, surrounded by the void, and nothingness. The decor: composed of inarticulate lines, immovable, repeated, without ornament; no window, no door, no furniture in the 'field' and at the centre of these rigid parallels a woman who advanced slowly. Subtitles become useless, architecture situates the person and defines her better than any text.[58]

In this vision of a cinematic architecture that would through its own laws of perspective return to the essential characteristics of building, Mallet-Stevens echoed Le Corbusier and anticipated Eisenstein. He also, in his depiction of a decor framed as the very image of isolation, agoraphobic or claustrophobic, answered those in Germany who were attempting to 'express' in spatial distortion what a simple manipulation of the camera in space might accomplish.

Such arguments between two possibilities of filmic architecture have hardly ceased with the gradual demise of cinema and the rise of its own 'natural' successors, video and, more recently, digital hyperspatial imaging. That their influence on architecture might be as disturbing as those observed by Le Corbusier and Mallet-Stevens is at least possible to hazard, as buildings and their spatial sequences are designed more as illustrations of implied movement or, worse, as literal fabrications of the computer's eye view. It is certainly possible to develop an all-too-easy critique of contemporary attempts to construct 'virtual reality' as simply replicating the perspectival forms of previous 'reality representations'. But there is one consideration that makes the contemporary question entirely different from that of the 1920s or the 1940s, or even from that of Lessing's 1750s: the fact that the technologies and means of representation have changed once again, this time bringing architecture and film closer than ever before. Where in the 1920s and after, film and architecture were, in a fundamental sense; entirely different media utilising their respective technologies, the one to simulate space, the other to build it, now, by contrast, the increasing digitalisation of our world has rendered them if not the same, at least coterminous.

And in this condition, we are no longer, or not for long, talking about 'virtual reality', but rather about 'virtual space'—in the sense of William Gibson's *Virtual Light*, 1993. Virtual space (and not hyperspace, or cyberspace, those confections of the 1970s and 80s) would be that space that is neither flat nor deep; neither surveyed nor unsurveyed; neither changing nor unchanging. It would be, and perhaps be for the first time, a space that was entirely indifferent to any differences among bodies, things, and positions. Constituted of endless strings, represented on apparently flat screens, it would exist without us and would not expect us to exist. Here, the dynamic interplay of subject and object, object and space, assayed by modernism would give way to an endless *mise-en-abyme*, where not even the myth of interactivity could dispel the unease of a wall that looked back—but not at you. Jeremy Bentham would not be at home in this space, nor would Mike Davis, who relies on Bentham's model of surveillance, nor even would Gibson himself, to whom we must attribute its first imagining. Rather, no one is or could be at home here, where the old fashioned cowboy hacker, the mutant, the cyborg, and the postmodernist, post-humanist subject are simply revealed as themselves mutations of the old, well-worn subject of Cartesian origin. If for Georg Lukács, the post-technological world of modernism was one of transcendental homelessness, then the world of digital encoding does not even afford this vagabond-like identity, where, for example, the space of the everyday and the space of DNA are merged and morphed with diabolical effect. Physico-spatial metaphors like nets and highways fail in the face of such totalising absorption, leaving us with only a screen imaginary, or perhaps a screen nostalgia, that we may believe for an instant positions us in front of it, subjects in front of a screen, and not, as is more probably the case, it in front of us.[59]

1. Vertov, Dziga, *Kino-Eye: The Writings of Dziga Vertov*, Annette Michelson ed., Kevin O'Brien trans., Berkely and Los Angeles: University of California Press, 1984, p. 17.

2. Le Corbusier, "Esprit de vérité", *French Film Theory and Criticism: A History/Anthology*, Richard Abel trans., Princeton: Princeton University Press, 1988, Vol. 2, pp. 111–113.

3. Méliès, George, "Les Vues cinématographiques", *L'intelligence du cinématographe*, Paris: Editions Corea, 1946, pp. 178–187; Rohmer, Eric "Cinema, The Art of Space", *The Taste for Beauty*, Cambridge University Press, 1989, pp. 19–29.

4. For the best discussion of the architectural contribution to set design in the context of the Expressionist 1920s, see Eisner, Lotte H, *L'écran démoniaque*, Paris: Eric Losfeld, 1965.

5. Mallet-Stevens, Robert, "Le Cinema et les arts: L' Architecture", *L'Herbier*, p. 288.

6. Gance, Abel, "Qu'est-ce que le cinématographe? Un Sixième Art", *L'Herbier*, p. 92.

7. Faure, Elie, "De la cinéplastique", *L'Herbier*, p. 268. The English translations in this paragraph are my own.

8. Faure, "De la cinéplastique", p. 268.

9. Faure, "De la cinéplastique", p. 275.

10. Faure, "De la cinéplastique".

11. Faure, "De la cinéplastique", p. 276.

12. Faure, "De la cinéplastique", p. 278.

13. Scheffauer, Herman G, "The Vivifying of Space", *Introduction to the Art of the Movies*, Lewis Jacobs ed., New York: Noonday Press, 1960, pp. 76–85. The essay appeared in Scheffauer's collection of essays, *The New Vision in the German Arts*, New York: BW Huebsch, 1924. As Dietrich Neumann has noted, Scheffauer was considerably indebted to Heinrich de Fries, who published an article entitled "Raumgestaltung im Film" in *Wasmuths Monatshefte für Baukunst*, Nos. 1–2, 1920–1921, pp. 63–75, even to the extent of repeating de Fries' mistakes as well as paraphrasing entire passages (see pp. 133–134).

14. Scheffauer, "The Vivifying of Space", p. 78.

15. Scheffauer, "The Vivifying of Space", p. 79.

16. Scheffauer, "The Vivifying of Space", pp.79–81.

17. Scheffauer's analysis was echoed by the art critic Rudolf Kurtz:

Perpendicular tines tense towards the diagonal, houses exhibit crooked, angular outlines, planes shift in rhomboidal fashion, expressed in perpendiculars and horizontals, are transmogrified into a chaos of broken forms.... A movement begins, leaves its natural course, is intercepted by another, led on, distorted again, and broken. All this is steeped in a magic play of light, unchaining brightness and blackness, building up, dividing, emphasising, destroying....

(Kurtz, Rudolf *Expressionismus und Film*, as cited in Prawer, Siegbert Solomon, *Caligari's Children: The Film as Tale of Terror*, New York: Da Capo Press: 1988, p. 189.)

18. Prawer, *Caligari's Children: The Film as Tale of Terror*, p. 82.

19. Prawer, *Caligari's Children: The Film as Tale of Terror*, p. 83.

20. Prawer, *Caligari's Children: The Film as Tale of Terror*, p. 84.

21. Panofsky, Erwin, *Perspective as Symbolic Form*, Christopher S Wood trans., New York: Zone Books, 1991, p. 70. Panofsky's essay "Die Perspektive als symbolische Form" was first published in *Vorträge der Bibliothek Warburg 1924–1925*, Leipzig and Berlin: BG Teubner, 1927, pp. 258–330.

22. Bloch, Ernst, "Die Bebauung des Hohlraums", *The Utopian Function of Art and Literature: Selected Essays*, Jack Zipes and Frank Mecklenbur trans., Cambridge, MA.: MIT Press, 1988, p. 196.

23. Bloch, "Die Bebauung des Hohlraums".

24. Bloch referred directly to Panofsky's essay (Bloch, "Die Bebauung des Hohlraums", p. 96).

25. Kurtz, cited in Prawer, *Caligari's Children: The Film as Tale of Terror*, p. 189.

26. Münsterberg, Hugo, *Film: A Psychological Study*, New York: Dover Publications, 1969. For a general study of his theory, see Fredericksen, Donald L, *The Aesthetic of Isolation in Film Theory: Hugo Münsterberg*, New York: Arno Press, 1977.

27. Münsterberg, cited in *Film Theory and Criticism: Introductory Readings*, Gerald Mast and Marshall Cohen eds., New York: Oxford University Press, 1985, p. 332.

28. Aragon, Louis, "Du décor", *French Film Theory and Criticism: A History/Anthology*, Vol. 1, p. 165.

29. Aragon, "Du décor", p. 166

30. Panofsky, Erwin, "Style and Medium in the Motion Pictures", *Film Theory and Criticism: Introductory Readings*, Gerald Mast and Marshall Cohen eds., p. 232.

31. Panofsky, "Style and Medium in the Motion Pictures", p. 218.

32. Panofsky, "Style and Medium in the Motion Pictures", p. 232.

33. Carné, Marcel, "Quand le cinéma descendrat-il dans la rue?", *French Film Theory and Criticism: A History/Anthology*, Vol. 2, pp. 127–129. Carné himself, however, continued to rely on sets built in the studio, meticulously imitating the real streets of Paris.

34. Kracauer, Siegfried, *Theory of Film: The Redemption of Physical Reality*, London: Oxford University Press, 1960, p. xi.

35. Kracauer, *Theory of Film: The Redemption of Physical Reality*, p. 52. Kracauer elaborated:

The affinity of film for haphazard contingencies is most strikingly demonstrated by its unwavering susceptibility to the 'street'—a term designed to cover not only the street, particularly the city street, in the literal sense, but also its various extensions, such as railway stations, dance and assembly halls, bars, hotel lobbies, airports, etc..... Within the present context the street, which has already been characterised as a centre of fleeting impressions, is of interest as a region where the accidental prevails over the providential, and happenings in the nature of unexpected incidents are all but the rule.... There have been only a few cinematic films that would not include glimpses of a street, not to mention the many films in which some street figures among the protagonists [p. 62].

36. Kracauer, *Theory of Film: The Redemption of Physical Reality*, p. 62.

37. Kracauer, *Theory of Film: The Redemption of Physical Reality*, p. 65.

38. Kracauer, *Theory of Film: The Redemption of Physical Reality*, p. 207.

39. Kracauer, *Theory of Film: The Redemption of Physical Reality*, p. 17.

40. Kracauer, *Theory of Film: The Redemption of Physical Reality*, p. 17.

41. Benjamin, Walter, "The Work of Art in the Age of Mechanical Reproduction", *Film Theory and Criticism: Introductory Readings*, pp. 689–690.

42. Benjamin, Walter, "Das Passagen-Werk", *Gesammelte Schriften*, Frankfurt am Main: Suhrkamp, 1982, p. 135.

43. Benjamin, "Das Passagen-Werk", p. 527.

44. Kracauer, Siegfried, *Theory of Film: The Redemption of Physical Reality*, London: Oxford University Press, 1960, p. 170.

45. Eisenstein, Sergei, *Nonindifferent Nature*, Herbert Marshall trans., Cambridge: Cambridge University Press, 1987, p. 122.

46. Eisenstein, *Nonindifferent Nature*, pp. 123–154. For a discussion Eisenstein's filmic interpretations of Piranesi in the context of the European avant-garde, see Tafuri, Manfredo, *The Sphere and the Labyrinth*, Cambridge, MA: MIT Press, 1990, pp. 55–64.

47. Eisenstein, *Nonindifferent Nature*, p. 140.

48. See Eisenstein, *Nonindifferent Nature*, pp. 159–165, for an analysis of Gogol's "On the Architecture of Our Time", 1831, along the same lines as his discussion of Piranesi.

49. Eisenstein, Sergei, "Montage and Architecture", *Towards a Theory of Montage*, Michael Glenny and Richard Taylor eds., London: BFI Publishing, 1991, p. 59.

50. Eisenstein, "Montage and Architecture", p. 60.

51. Choisy, Auguste, *Histoire de l'architecture*, Paris: E Rouveyre, 1899, Vol. 1, p. 413.

52. Eisenstein, "Montage and Architecture", p. 60.

53. Eisenstein, "Montage and Architecture".

54. Le Corbusier, *Vers une architecture*, Paris: G Cres, 1923, p. 31.

55. Le Corbusier, *Vers une architecture*.

56. Mallet-Stevens, "Le Cinema et les arts: L'Architecture", p. 289.

57. Mallet-Stevens, "Le Cinema et les arts: L'Architecture", p. 290.

58. Mallet-Stevens, "Le Cinema et les arts: L'Architecture", p. 288.

59. This essay is based on an article published under the same title in *Assemblage*, No. 21, 1993, pp. 45–59.

NUCLEAR

| DISTRIBUTED

Above: Rendering of the Arcosanti project situated in the high desert of Arizona, conceived in the 1970s by architect Paolo Soleri. Designed to provide for 5,000 people, the project seeks to demonstrate sustainable town planning principles, while improving quality of life for its potential inhabitants.

Opposite: Plan of La Défense, located just outside of Paris, this CBD was created to service the French capital's commercial sector, and is currently the largest purpose-built business district in Europe. The area has recently revealed plans to build several sustainable, development style skyscrapers, furthering the project's aims to increased energy efficiency.

Urban Morphology can be broadly explained as an attempt to describe the physical configuration of a city; not only in terms of the interaction between its built environment and its citizens, but also in the interaction and relationship between its own constituent parts. The history of the modern metropolis can be seen as a conflict between the centre and the suburbs for population, resources and vitality. There are three great twentieth century geographical models to describe the zoning that results from the study of urban morphology and they serve as maps across which this conflict has been played out. So far, these models have essentially been two-dimensional, However, the twenty-first century may provide a new aspect to them.

The Concentric Model was developed in 1925 by the sociologist Ernest W Burgess to explain land values in Chicago. The Central Business District, or CBD, is surrounded by an industrial ring, which in turn, is surrounded by a residential ring housing industrial workers and beyond that, an outer residential ring from which the middle classes commute into the CBD. Population density is low at the centre, highest near it and falls as it spreads into the suburbs. Traditionally, the main driver of industrial and suburban spread in America had been railways and trams, however by the time the economist Homer Hoyt published his model for the city in 1939, rail had been overtaken by motorised vehicles. Different forms of transport have different practical applications and Hoyt, who studied 142 American cities to create his model, suggested zoning following radial transport routes emerging from the Central Business District. Put simply, where Burgess' model was based on distance from the city centre, Hoyt's was based on transit time to the centre. This was a step forward, however both models had a basic similarity in that they both describe a nuclear city.

The satellite business district is an increasingly widespread phenomenon, and is part of the third classical morphology model, which describes a distributed model of the city. In 1945, Chicago geographers Chauncey Harris and Edward Ullman

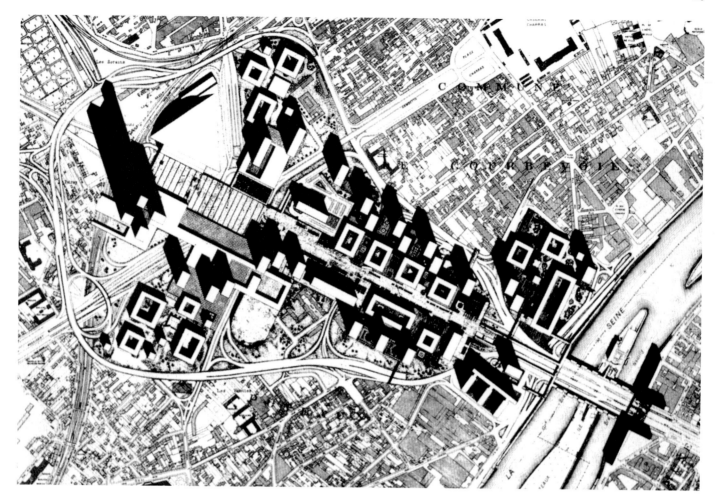

published *The Nature of Cities*, which posited the 'Multiple Nucleus' or 'Poly-Nuclear' model. In the Poly-Nuclear city, different activities congregate around nodes spread across the conurbation so that, for example, an industrial district may be embedded in the suburbs, while business may have a sub-centre in the inner city. This model neatly accommodates what Los Angeles-based urban geographer Edward Soja termed the "Exopolis"; outer urban concentrations that function like mini CBDs and arise when intense commercial processes are focused beyond the traditional centre. It even describes separate cities that have grown into each other, such as Minneapolis and St Paul in America. The reality of cities, especially large ones, is that all three classic sector models are in play and city nuclei and outlying areas compete as locations for a wide range of revenue-generating functions—corporate business, shopping, entertainment, culture and affluent (and less affluent) residents. It is urban density that is the dynamic centre's key defence against suburbia.

BATTLE OF THE BUSINESS DISTRICTS

Croydon in the distant southern suburbs of London became a business district in the 1960s as the government encouraged industry to relocate out of the city centre. This is an early example of a major satellite business district, which emerged as a competitor to the CBD for office location. In the 1980s, as the world recovered from a recession and financial trading went electronic, demanding vast trading floors, CBDs across the West revived, driving inner city redevelopment. However, old city centres are generally packed with historic buildings, accompanying heritage issues and local regulations to protect them. Cities began to plan bigger and brighter satellite business districts. In the 1990s, Paris's La Défense and London's Canary Wharf were powerful enough to attract corporate headquarters rather than the sub-offices handling business support functions such as IT or customer service, that had previously been devolved to satellite locations.

Globally, new CBDs challenge the old order as global business locations and have taller and bulkier skyscraper clusters. The most ambitious example of this is in Shanghai. The traditional centre of business is the colonial riverside stretch of The Bund and when the city awoke from its Maoist slumber in the 1980s, the CBD naturally expanded around it. In 1992, however, Deng Xiaoping stood across the river from the Bund in the undeveloped farmlands of Pudong and declared that there, China's new financial sector would rise. Business in Pudong's gleaming towers is now the driving force behind Shanghai's meteoric rise but, despite this, China's leading business metropolis is still Hong Kong and the district called "Central" is its CBD. However across Victoria Harbour, in Kowloon, the International Commerce Centre with the city's tallest skyscraper, has begun to challenge its more venerable neighbour, such is the competition between these fast-growing cities.

Further examples of spectacular new CBDs can be found all over the globe. One of the fastest-growing is "Dubai Downtown" or "Business Bay" which currently houses the start of what is projected to be the world's tallest building, the Burj Dubai. Construction began in 1994 and is expected to finish in 2009. Designed by Skidmore, Owings and Merrill, (who also worked on the Sears Tower in Chicago and the Freedom Tower in New York), its height on completion has yet to be revealed. It proposes to house over 30,000 residents, nine hotels and parkland. The rapid development of this building and the other structures in Dubai Downtown, ensures that it is currently one of the fastest growing cities in the world.

In a similar position is the Moscow International Business Centre (the former Moscow City), situated in the Presnensky district of the city just four kilometres from the Kremlin. The Russian government is currently spending over US$12 billion on transforming this city so that it might rival other such CBDs worldwide. Conceived in 1992, this CBD is expected to be a 'city within a city' encompassing work, living and leisure facilities. It will comprise Tower 200, Tower Imperia, Naberezhnaya Tower and a Russia Tower, among others, as well as a 'central core', which connects a number of different structures throughout the centre and contains its own transport terminal.

These satellite CBDs are unconstrained by the small physical area of individual leases in the traditional city centre. This results in a convergence, a massing of the older parts of the city and satellite CBDs and an erosion of the intimate scale of the traditional city centre. This is seen in its most extreme in Chinese cities, where scores of traditional buildings are being bulldozed to be replaced by new ones.

DOWNTOWN AMERICA

The city nucleus is more than business, of course. But where exactly is 'downtown'? In Manhattan, Downtown is the most southern part of the island, where the old city of New Amsterdam was established by the Dutch in 1624. North of Houston Street, cross streets ascend in number as you go Uptown. There is a general correlation between the age of a neighbourhood and how uptown or downtown it is. The vocabulary was already understood before New York's subways were built at the start of the twentieth century; to go to the centre of any large American city would be to go downtown. Yet New York's entertainment centre (as well as its burgeoning corporations) had been moving uptown along Broadway since the nineteenth century. 42nd Street had become New York's new theatre district by the 1920s and the point where Broadway cut across it at Times Square, became known as "The Crossroads of the World".

Heading downtown in the 1960s was likely to offer a very different experience to such 24-hour glitz. At night, the furthest part of downtown Manhattan, around the Battery, was a dead zone of dark office blocks, empty streets and closed businesses. In the great traditional manufacturing cities, Downtown started to shut down more profoundly after the war. In Detroit, car manufacturers were relocating and downtown department stores were closing their doors as business went to suburban shopping malls, serviced by

Top: Shanghai taken by Olivo Barbieri. Barbieri is an Italian photographer of urban environments, known for creating minature still photography from actual landscapes. He creates the illusion of shallow depth through the pioneering use of shift-lens photography.

Bottom: The skyline of Canary Wharf. This urban regeneration programme saw what was once the West India docks transformed into a Central Business District (CBD) in less than 20. Today, Canary Wharf boasts a pleasant working environment complete with parks, squares, promenades and a full range of services.

Opposite: The traffic circulation and skyscrapers of a possible New York, as depicted in *l'illustrazione italiana*, 31 August 1913. This illustration playfully presents a solution to the overcrowding of New York, resulting in a distinctly 'nuclear' hub of architecture and activity.

Following pages: Photograph of the Walt Disney Concert Hall. Located in downtown Los Angeles, the Frank Gehry designed building was completed in 2003 and stands as one of the four halls in the Los Angeles Music Center.

the rapidly expanding freeway system. Similar processes were working across America and not just in the northeastern industrial cities. As properties were abandoned, they fell into disrepair, affecting adjacent property values and fuelling a process that would condemn entire streets and subsequently, entire neighbourhoods. Low property prices, coupled with low employment levels meant crime in the inner city rocketed, further driving out the middle classes.

The reversal of inner city decline involves understanding the causes of the factors driving it, such as crime. In New York in the 1990s, Mayor Rudolf Giuliani introduced his 'Zero Tolerance' policing policies and its success would later lead to architectural design solutions to crime prevention. These are design strategies that helped inner cities revive in the 1990s such as a return to traditional street-fronted housing rather than high-rise blocks. An example is the southwestern quarter of Yonkers, bordering the New York city borough of the Bronx, a part of town that was characterised by similar population densities, tower block public housing and levels of poverty, crime and gang activity to its contiguous neighbour. Here, against vested political interests and a suspicious and vocal local community, 'row housing' was built in the 1990s for residents previously in high-rises. When the houses were finally occupied, it was found that street crime virtually evaporated.[1]

Downtown Detroit also resisted the suburbs; in the guise of the John Portman-designed Renaissance Center, a glass skyscraper hotel and office complex opened in 1977. Downtown Los Angeles, whose lack of vitality was summed up by urban writer, Robert Fulton, stating that "since its peak in the 1920s, downtown has eroded in most Angelenos' mental maps from the centre of civic life to little more than a footnote", found revival after the construction of the Pei-Cobb designed American Bank Tower.[2]

Gentrification of previously run-down inner city housing took place in many American cities, but it was only in 1999 that legislation was passed in Los Angeles to encourage the conversion of old commercial buildings to residential; exploiting the boom in loft dwellings that had been revitalising the American downtown elsewhere for 20 years.

CULTURE MAGNETS

If 'downtown' once represented the central quarter of culture, it now faces stiff competition across the distributed city, from purpose-built complexes in non-central locations. At the end of 2007, the O2 Arena, originally designed by Richard Rogers as the ill-fated Millennium Dome, was poised to become the world's busiest live music venue. According to *Forbes Magazine*, the third most visited museum in California is the Paul Getty Museum, opened in 1997 and situated over 20 kilometres west of Downtown Los Angeles off the San Diego Freeway.

These are by no means the norm, however, and there will always be the traditional draw of downtown. The Frank Gehry-designed Walt Disney Concert Hall, completed in 2003, is bringing classical culture to downtown Los Angeles. Its expressive, fluid design of massive melting blocks and curves, is at the forefront of modern, inner city regeneration. Gehry has been credited with kickstarting this movement with the spectacularly successful design for the Guggenheim Museum in Bilbao, opened in 1997. The museum single-handedly turned around a moribund industrial city into an international tourist destination and has become an iconic part of the city's identity. The downtown waterside location, the regenerative effect upon the city and even the look of the Bilbao Guggenheim are not unlike what Sydney had achieved with its Jörn Utzon-designed Opera House 25 years before. Nevertheless, it is 'The Bilbao Effect' (that is, the subsequent regeneration of an entire area of a city as promoted by an iconic building such as the Guggenheim), that drive architectural commissions today, as evidenced in the work Santiago Calatrava, Renzo Piano, Foster+Partners, Daniel Libeskind, Zaha Hadid, or other contemporary 'superstar' architects who know how to fashion abstract shapes into reality.

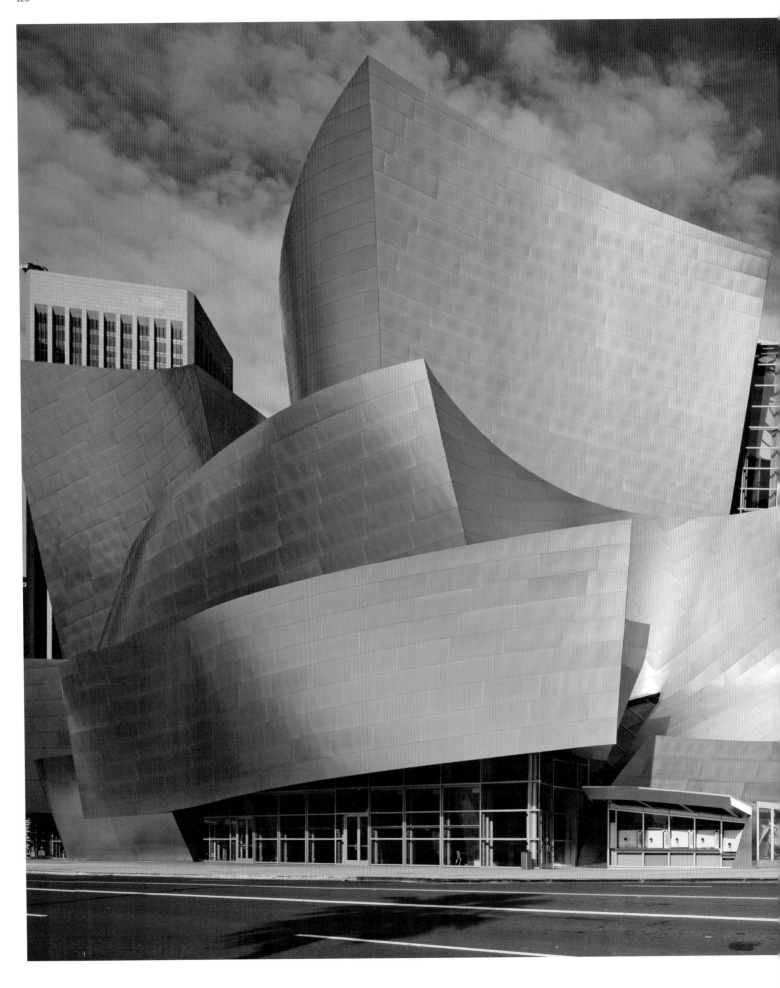

Top: Photograph of the Centre Georges Pompidou in Paris, France. Constructed in 1977, the Pompidou houses a large public library, the Musee National d'Art Modern and a centre for music and acoustic research. © Katsuhisa Kida.

Bottom: West Edmonton Mall, Canada. "The largest shopping mall in the world", West Edmonton is almost an all-encompassing city in itself. Facilities include 800 stores

and services as well as over 100 restaurants. Those who wish to stay overnight can chose from one of two options; the local camping grounds or the Fantasy Land Hotel. Also housed in the Mall is a mini golf course, ice skating rink and waterpark as well as a European style boulevard and its own 'Chinatown'.

Opposite: Celebration Town, Florida, designed by Robert Stern. Conceived by Walt Disney as

part of his EPCOT (Experimental Prototype Community of Tomorrow) project, Celebration was made realisable through Stern's town planning, which was strongly anti-modernist in design. Not dissimilar to the underlying concept of the New Towns of Ebenezer Howard, it nostalgically nods at the typical American old town and all that it encompasses.

SHOPPING TRANSFERS

Commerce and culture have often been called the new religion and as cathedrals marked what we would now call downtown in pre-industrial Europe, commercial skyscrapers or cultural trophy buildings do the same in the nuclear city. The activity that draws people in and is more popular than culture or religion, is shopping. If 'downtown' is where the shops are, the chances are that there are bigger shops in weather-proof malls in the suburbs.

In twenty-first century Europe, the market shadow of huge shopping malls and their disastrous transfer of business from local shops and town centres has increasingly been recognised. A greenbelt shopping mall may be a more powerful magnet than the city itself. Bluewater, which opened in 1999 almost 30 kilometres from London's centre, describes itself as "Europe's largest retail and leisure destination" with 330 stores. Bluewater attracts 27 million visitors a year, beating Oxford Street with its 22 million or so shoppers and Camden Town's market, which attracts 300,000 every weekend. The Netherlands was the first country to stop construction of new shopping malls and attitudes to them are changing across Europe, but their spread is booming in places like China.

Victor Gruen, the Austrian-born socialist—with an immense dislike of suburban sprawl—proposed shopping malls that were meant to be perfect downtowns where not just retail congregated, but schools, parks and apartments as well. Strangely, Gruen's ideals have parallels to the mall's nemesis, the 'New Urbanists'.

TAKING THE BATTLE TO THE SUBURBS

New Urbanism is a movement that started in the 1980s, rejecting the bland, suburban sprawl of the 'boomburgs' in favour of more compact, pedestrian-friendly and diversified development. As the New Urbanist architects at their 1996 Congress declared:

Communities should be designed for the pedestrian and transit as well as the car; cities and towns should be shaped by physically defined and universally accessible public spaces and community institutions; urban places should be framed by architecture and landscape design that celebrate local history, climate, ecology, and building practice.[3]

In the case of the suburbs, this implies bringing together elements that make traditional downtowns lively, people-friendly places—a return to the ideal of US small-towns in this century, governments and citizens have accepted that there is a looming global environmental crisis and the big environmental gains made by car-free urban activity has made New Urbanists major promoters of another sort of distributed nucleus—the Transit Orientated Development (TOD) or Transit Village. Here, suburban developments are deliberately clustered around public transport nodes, especially metro or tram stops.

EDGE CITIES AND LINEAR CITIES
The "Edge City" itself is a concept that was defined in 1991 by journalist Joel Garreau to describe suburban retail and office complexes above a certain size that have arisen adjacent to the highways via which all goods and people reach them. His criteria dictate that there must be almost half a million square metres of office and the same again of retail and that the complex must be less than 30 years old. The archetypal example of the Edge City is Century City, developed since the 1960s, 15 kilometres west of downtown Los Angeles off the Santa Monica Boulevard. Here, entertainment giants congregate in skyscrapers just as financial sector giants congregate in London's Canary Wharf, the difference being that Century City is still reliant on the freeway to connect it.

Places such as Century City, however, are nuclei within the conurbation, whilst the term "edge city" suggests a location on the fringes. Major airports may not

meet Garreau's office space or age threshold, but with their vast staffing levels, retail spaces, hotel and conference facilities and car parks, they are urban nuclei that exist at or beyond the city's edge and they can annex suburbs to make them part of their own zones, analogous to inner city worker dormitory rings or warehousing sectors. They can be a distance from the metropolis as a whole and are better described as Exurbs—Stansted is 48 kilometres from London and Narita 60 kilometres from Tokyo, for example. Such airports parallel a process that happened to old port towns when they became satellite terminals for certain cities in the heyday of the passenger liners. Southampton is an example situated 120 kilometres from London, or Yokohama, which was 30 kilometres from Tokyo, but now has become part of a single continuous conurbation. Tianjin prospered as the port for Beijing 115 kilometres away and despite the world's largest airport terminal, designed by Foster+Partners and opening in 2008 at the existing Beijing Airport, a second has been approved that is likely to be at a distance of about 60 kilometres.

Special zoning by state or national governments can create more mixed exurbs or satellite cities on the edge of conurbations. Examples include Noida, whose name is the acronym of "New Okhla Industrial Development Authority"; a city of over half a million inhabitants, south of Delhi, which was created at the behest of Sanjay Gandhi in 1976 to encourage new industry but now consists mainly of call centres. Even the megacity of Shenzhen could until recently be considered a cross-border satellite city of Hong Kong. It was the direct result of Deng Xiaoping's Special Economic Zone, initiated to kickstart China's economy.

Hoyt did not envisage downtown as one of his 'Linear Sectors', but that is what is happening in fast-growing linear cities. Las Vegas is probably the best known example. Although Downtown Las Vegas refers to a few blocks around Freemont Street and Casino Center Boulevard, hotels and casinos stretch along The Strip, making downtown effectively seven kilometres long but rarely more than a few blocks wide. More recently, however, tourism has driven linear growth most explosively along coastlines—examples include Australia's Gold Coast, which had no airport until 1981 but where hotels now service a continuous 40 kilometres of surfing beach. Not that such urban transformations are new—the British holiday-maker caused Brighton and Blackpool to develop this way in the nineteenth century, and exported the phenomenon to resorts like Benidorm in Spain during the 1970s.

HYPER-DENSITY

Cities are essentially flat structures and the greatest conurbations are merely blots on the Earth's surface as seen from space. Even the tallest skyscrapers melt into the horizon in the wider urban vista. When New York's 541 metre high Freedom Tower is completed in Manhattan, it will be just a fortieth of the length of Manhattan island, while the world's tallest skyscraper at over 800 metres, the Burj Dubai, will be just a fiftieth of the length of Dubai's urban spread between its coastal extremities at Al Heera and the Palm Jebel Ali project. But what if downtown and uptown actually had a vertical meaning?

Nuclear cities have an ultimate form to challenge horizontally-distributed cities—the mono-block vertical city. Like the first geographical flat models of Burgess and Hoyt, the vertical city vision starts in Chicago, where Frank Lloyd Wright conceived the original idea in 1956. His Mile-High City (1,609 metres), also known as The Illinois, was designed to accommodate 100,000 people and provide space for living, work and recreation in 528 storeys. Wright had imagined an orderly car-driven suburban spread in his decentralised Broadacre City, 1932, and Mile High City was his reaction to the increasing horror of unchecked suburban sprawl. The economic concerns aside, there were two questions hanging over his plan's feasibility. Firstly, no one had built a mixed-use skyscraper before, in fact, it wasn't until 1969 that Chicago's 344 metre high John Hancock Building offered vertically zoned offices and apartments. This multi-use construction has many advantages, not least from a developers point of view, where bringing in different markets to find anchor tenants, spreads the development risk. Even taller buildings such as the Jin Mao in

Above: The John Hancock Building. Situated in Chicago, Illinois, the John Hancock building was the tallest structure outside of New York City when it was completed in 1969. It currently ranks as the third tallest skyscraper in Chicago, and the fifth tallest in America.

Opposite top: View of the John Hancock Building.

Opposite bottom: X-SEED 4000, designed by the Taisei Corporation. The X-SEED 4000 is the tallest building that has ever been envisioned. If realised it would reach 4,000 metres in height and could house up to one million inhabitants.

Shanghai, which combines hotels and offices, and The Shard in London, both over 300 metres in height, will contain apartments with gardens. The second question is that of technical feasibility, even with this having been mitigated recently with resistance to wind-shear or having enough floorspace for lifts gradually being overthrown by technological advances in material science, structural engineering and design software. The 154-storey mixed-use Burj Dubai, designed by Chicago-based Adrian Smith and due for completion in 2009, will be over 800 metres tall and have evacuation procedures for 35,000 people.

From the late 1980s, several plans for a self-contained skyscraper city were commissioned by Japanese corporations, so as to address the issues of overcrowding familiar to Tokyo, many of these were located in Tokyo Bay—just as the Metabolist megastructures, such as Kiyonori Kikutake's Marine City, were imagined in 1958. Foster+Partners' 170-storey Millennium Tower project, 1989, is the most thought through of these later schemes, and even anticipated issues like carbon footprinting with his tower generating its own energy. Other Tokyo plans, more visionary than practical designs, include Sky City 1000 (one kilometre high and housing 35,000 residents and 100,000 workers), Aeropolis 2001 (a two kilometre high tower for 300,000 residents), the Shimizu Mega City Pyramid (a two kilometre high pyramid complex for 750,000), and the most ambitious, X-Seed 4000, a four kilometre high structure in the shape of Mount Fuji that could accommodate as many as one million people.

Today architects are still designing for the vertical city. Spanish architects, Cervera and Pioz, have designed what they call "bionic architecture" which, like 'biomimetic' architecture, seeks to apply biological lessons to buildings. Their 1,220 metre high Bionic Tower, designed for 100,000 inhabitants, is highly sustainable and has attracted interest from planners in Hong Kong and Shanghai and as the reality of a vertical city draws nearer, questions about its cultural and sociological impact arise.

For instance, what implications would there be regarding social structure, corporate and individual identity, quality of life and so on? Frank Lloyd Wright said about The Illinois, "no-one can afford to build it now, but in the future, no-one can afford not to build it". When this century's equivalent to The Illinois is built, downtown and uptown will at last take on their literal meaning.

CIVIL SOCIETY IN THE CITY

The downtown regeneration of cities has coincided with a population revival. Urban density is recognised as the key to the modern city's success, although the highest densities are in the developing countries and are sometimes analogous to the slums of the West's Industrial era. In America, "Smart Growth" is a general term to counter-act suburban sprawl, whether directing development downtown or increasing densities at suburban Transit Orientates Developments and employing New Urbanist principles to create pedestrian-friendly, diverse communities.

The British architect, Richard Rogers, has a similar vision with the 'Compact City', which relies not only on density and development as the key to future cities, but on a civil society that is founded on urban life in the city's built common spaces, the public realm. Rogers evangelises about the pedestrianisation of the city. His inspiration is taken from the vibrant street life of contemporary Florence and it's function as a meeting place for the exchange of ideas during the Renaissance. When he and Renzo Piano designed perhaps Europe's most successful cultural trophy building, the high-tech Centre Pompidou, which opened in 1977, half of the site was given over to a new plaza. It is now one of the most vibrant spaces in Paris.

The vertical city offers many solutions in an overpopulated world, but ultimately the future may lie in the construction of a more socially interactive space, a distributed city with strong nuclei with the needs and lifestyle of their inhabitants at the forefront. As Rogers told the Megacities Foundation in his lecture in The Hague in 2001: "A well-designed sustainable city will attract people back into its centre. I believe city living lies at the heart of our society, for cities are conceived as meeting places for people—friends or strangers."

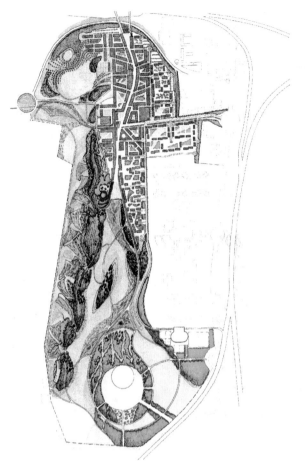

1. Fulton, William, "The Taking of Parcel K", *The Reluctant Metropolis: The Politics of Urban Growth in Los Angeles*, Baltimore: The Johns Hopkins University Press, 2001.

2. Jencks, Charles, *The Iconic Building*, London: Frances Lincoln Ltd, 2005.

3. *Charter of the New Urbanism*, © 1997–2007 Congress for the New Urbanism.

Opposite: Photograph of Jin Mao Tower, China, by Guillaume Gilbert. Designed by Chicago-based architects Skidmore, Owings & Merrill, the Tower occupies an area of 24,000 square metres and is situated near the station of Lujiazui. It houses a number of restaurants, a Jazz club, fitness centre and swimming pool as well as many offices and hotels.

Above: Rogers concept of the 'Compact City' is clearly apparent in this plan of the Piana di Castello. All facilities and housing are conglomerated closely together, assuming only a quarter of the entire area delegated for planning (the rest being comprised largely by green spaces and parks). © Rogers Stirk Harbour and Partners.

ATLANTA: SPRAWL CITY

The city of Atlanta is the capital of and the most populous city in the southeastern American state of Georgia. From the mid-1990s it was widely touted by the media as the new 'poster child' for the phenomenon of urban sprawl, with its frequent smog alerts, among the longest and most congested commutes in America and its seemingly unchecked suburban expansion across open country at a rate of more than two square kilometres a week. On the various 'sprawl indexes' issued by study groups and universities across America Atlanta is consistently one of the worst offenders, coming fourth in one recent study.

For the past 20 years, Atlanta has been a boomtown in terms of economic growth, population increase and rapid development. Since 1980 the population of the metro area has increased by 70 per cent and, in the 1990s, was the most rapidly populating city in America. One million new jobs have been created in the metro area since 1980, and 1.3 million more are predicted by 2025. In 2006, the population of the metro area was over five million. As this population has increased and become more affluent so the demand for suburban housing has increased. House

buyers want large individual properties on large plots on safe, quiet streets, and the developers have been only to happy to oblige. To cater to these new sub-urbanites, Atlantan developers built countless big box malls, strip malls, suburban office parks, enormous sub-divisions (housing estates) and the city built the roads to people's doors. Absorbing all or part of 13 counties of north central Georgia, the metro Atlanta region has expanded physically at a rate which far outstrips its population growth, leading to a very low density spread; as a comparison, the Atlanta region has approximately 700 people per square kilometre, where the Los Angeles metro area has around 2,400 (a hyper-dense urban area like Hong Kong has around 29,400 people per square kilometre).

The growth experienced by the city's suburban areas has not been mirrored by Atlanta's inner city districts. In 2006, the city of Atlanta had a population of 490,000 against a metro area population of 5.1 million. The environmental and human consequences of this continuous growth are now catching up with the city, and forcing its residents and the city authorities to make some tough choices. Reaction to the city's corrective policies has been symptomatic of

a longstanding friction between American citizens' desire for suburban comforts and a free housing market, and the dire need for well-managed development.

Atlanta's land use patterns throughout this period of expansion have cultivated a very particular type of development which has, in turn, fostered a very specific lifestyle. "Sprawl" is a term often used, but rarely broken down. It is characterised by very low-density development, which is 'leapfrogged' across open undeveloped land and joined to other suburbs by fast, arterial roads. Developments are zoned for single use (that is, housing, retail and office developments are rigidly separated) and zoning regulations require a set distance between them to be observed. This distance isn't walkable, and so walking or even cycling are not viable options; most of Atlanta's suburbs don't have pavements. All of these factors combine to create a dependence on the automobile for all journeys (even just for buying a newspaper or going for coffee); driving becomes a necessity and not an option. As everyone tends to have a car because of this, there is no demand for a public transport system, so only a token skeleton service is provided and the freeways are expanded

ATLANTA, MOSCOW CITY AND STAPLETON

to cope with the increased traffic volume. This is the cycle of sprawling development, which has been repeated again and again as the metro Atlanta area has swallowed up more and more land each year. Developers misleadingly call their new sub-divisions 'towns' and 'villages', but don't provide the infrastructure—shops, schools, parks—that such names imply.

As the metro area expands outwards the city's downtown remains the prime employment site, and so people drive further and further distances to work. According to a 2000 daytime population estimate by the Census Bureau, over 250,000 people commuted into Atlanta on any given workday, boosting the city's estimated daytime population to 676,431. This is an increase of 62.4 per cent over Atlanta's resident population, making it the largest gain in daytime population in the country among cities with fewer than 500,000 residents. Even those workers who don't commute into the city tend to work relatively far from home elsewhere in the metro area; more than half the area's workers live in one county and work in another. Despite this huge number of journeys, estimates put the proportion made by public transport at a mere two to three per cent.

The Sprawl Index, 2002, and its accompanying report, Measuring Sprawl and its Impact, produced by researchers at Cornell and Rutgers universities on behalf of Smart Growth America, rates cities' sprawl according to a sophisticated scale which takes many factors into account: residential density, mix of homes, jobs and services, strength of town centres/downtowns, and accessibility of the street network. Metro Atlanta was rated fourth most sprawling of the 83 metro areas measured, below average in each of the key measures for its lack of compact, convenient housing, for its segregation of homes from offices and shops, its weak activity centres like town centres and downtown, and for its street network marked by large blocks and poor accessibility. The report's list of 'affected outcomes' in the city shows the real effects of sprawl on day-to-day life, with each and every resident of Atlanta driving on average 56 kilometres a day (50 per cent further than residents of Los Angeles, for example). Implicitly, sprawl development also has a negative impact on more abstract lifestyle factors (what could be called social capital, for example), creating barriers to interaction. Life in Atlanta can consist of a series of isolated and isolating experiences;

solo commuting, houses on individual lots, and no opportunity for passing neighbours in the street. It is often racially and economically polarised, exacerbated by the creation of communities where car ownership is essential.

The most striking effects of Atlanta's sprawl aren't even the lifestyle problems it creates for residents, but rather the resulting environmental and public health issues. In 1998, 13 counties in the metro Atlanta region were deemed to have violated the Clean Air Act of 1990, failing to meet national air quality standards on ground-level ozone and particulate matter, and the city lost out on $1.7 billion of federal money to pay for new road building programmes. The summer of 1999 still saw the city shrouded in smog, with a record 69 smog alerts issued (where individuals with respiratory sensitivity to pollution are advised to stay indoors). Recent studies have started to link obesity, hypertension and back problems to a protracted commute and its associated sedentary lifestyle like that encouraged by Atlanta's urban form. The city's unchecked expansion has resulted in the destruction of wildlife habitats, soil erosion and water pollution and shortages, and—according to

Aerial view of the
roadways and gridded
streets in downtown
Atlanta, Georgia.

Computer rendering
of a high-rise area
in Atlanta, Georgia.
Image courtesy
of NASA.

NASA—fewer trees and more asphalt. Air conditioners have created a significant 'heat island' effect around the metro Atlanta area which is visible on geothermal satellite images and has the potential to alter local weather patterns. The metro region can have temperatures of up to 10°C higher than the surrounding areas which often causes thunderstorms.

Atlanta has ended up in this position for a number of different reasons. Its topology is a major factor, as the city's surroundings lack any natural boundaries—rivers, mountains, a coastline—to limit its growth. Its system

of administration has not helped, as heavily decentralised local governments struggled to form a coherent regional strategy and were free to give in to the temptation of increased tax revenue from new mall developments. Individual counties could reject mass transit plans passing through their jurisdiction, which would scupper the entire plan. The metro region does have a subway system, MARTA, but it only operates across two counties; bus services tend to be ad hoc and operate independently rather than in any co-ordinated way. This political disorganisation came to a head in 1999 with the creation of the Georgia Regional Transport Authority

(or Greta); a unilateral agency charged with providing firm control over growth and transport planning where successive local governments had failed. Empowered to build or veto roads and transit systems, the Authority must approve developers' plans for new sub-divisions, office parks and malls, and can effectively veto them by withholding permission for tying them into the road network. It is the Authority's mission to improve Georgia's mobility, air quality and land use practices.

Greta's approach is realistic; they realise that Atlantans are not going to abandon their cars completely and move into high-density developments closer to the city. A recent 25 year plan intended to reduce ozone emissions still forecasted that the region would grow by a million more people by 2025, most of whom will still choose to live in suburban areas and continue to drive. However, by reassessing and co-ordinating public transport provision, Greta hope to provide alternative choices for the commuter. Already lanes of highway have been designated High-Occupancy Vehicle (HOV) lanes—for HOVs, or carpool users—in an attempt to get the famous gridlock moving again. Other initiatives have seen the zoning restrictions changed to promote mixed-use, high-density development. Several real-estate developers have begun to work on New Urbanism-inspired developments on brownfield sites in the city—like the Atlantic Station development on the site of an old steel mill in an inner city district—in an attempt to repopulate the hollowed-out city centre.

Big business has also played its part in beginning to rehabilitate Atlanta since *The Wall Street Journal* predicted that the city's congestion and air pollution issues would inhibit large-scale investment in the region. BellSouth, the huge telecommunications company with headquarters in Atlanta announced that it would consolidate 75 offices with 13,000 employers into three regional centres, each situated close to a subway station. The Coca-Cola Company, another home-grown Atlanta concern, moved 2,500 members of staff from its suburban bases to their headquarters downtown.

But for sprawl-inhibiting policies to really succeed, it is the people of Atlanta who need to be convinced. Consumers remain firmly attached to what suburban sprawl can offer them; more space, a sense of safety, lower house prices. As Robert Bruegmann,

the writer of *Sprawl: A Compact History*, points out, we are used to seeing sprawl as an intrinsically bad thing, but it has also given us "privacy, mobility and choice".[1] Atlanta's growth pattern, he argues, is merely the same pattern already set down by cities worldwide, and people are rightly put out when this unrestricted development is curbed by city authorities. Homebuyers still prefer larger, cheaper houses in suburban districts like Cumming and Alpharetta to small, expensive properties in the city, and it seems they are willing to reconcile themselves to the ever-growing commute, the smog alerts and traffic jams that still characterise twenty-first century Atlanta.

1. Robert Bruegmann quoted in Halicks, Richard, "Q&A/Robert Bruegmann, Architecture Historian: In Defense of Sprawl", *The Atlanta Journal Constitution*, 27 November 2005.

An image of the Russia Tower, due for completion in 2011. It is situated in the Moscow International Business Center, and when complete will be 612.2 metres high.

MOSCOW CITY

Moscow City, or the Moscow International Business Centre, is a new commercial development under construction in the Krasnopresnensky district of western Moscow, four kilometres west of the Kremlin. Occupying approximately one square kilometre of land on the left bank of the Moskva River the £6 billion Moscow City development is anticipated to be a thriving new business and leisure district and the home of Europe's tallest skyscraper—the Russia Tower—by 2010. The Moscow City development was initiated by Moscow's City Hall in 1992 to relieve the heavy congestion and air pollution in the historic city centre, and to help re-energise foreign investment through a stand-alone business area along the lines of La Défense in Paris or Lower Manhattan in New York. The project has since grown to become the centrepiece of a new Russian commercial confidence in the twenty-first century, attracting investment from around the world. Moscow City has been under the special supervision of Moscow's mayor, Yury Luzhkov, since its inception and, more recently, he has helped create appealing economic conditions for foreign investment by implementing the model favoured by new business districts the world over: the designation of the area as a free economic zone. In 1999 the City Duma passed a law that gave preferential tax rates to all businesses renting office space in the area (no small incentive, with Moscow being the fourth most expensive location in the world to rent office space after London's West End, Mumbai and the City of London). Foreigners are also allowed to buy land within the zone and, so long as they fulfil planning regulations imposed by the Moscow government, they are free to build on it.

The development has not been universally welcomed, with many fearing that an ultra-modern high-rise business district situated just across the river from the old city centre's historic landmarks and low-rise buildings would be too out of keeping with the spirit of the city. The government has been at pains to demonstrate Moscow City's self-sufficiency in this regard, and the benefits to the historical city centre in terms of reduced traffic. It also allows developers to experiment with forms and materials very different to those which would be acceptable in the preservation-focused old city, and a chance to establish contemporary Russian architectural emblems.

When complete in 2015, the Moscow City project is estimated to include around 2.5 million square metres of office, shopping and residential space, hotels, parking for 30,000 cars and state-of-the-art sports and leisure facilities. It will also be the new home of the local Moscow government, with a new 230,000 square metre City Hall and City Duma complex. Three new subway stations and a high-speed transit system are planned, which will eventually link the development with the city centre and three of Moscow's airports. The city itself will only finance the construction of the new administrative buildings and the area's infrastructure, while the other complexes on the site will be financed by outside investment.

The site is divided into 20 'parcels', or building plots, filled by 18 buildings from 13 different developers in various stages of planning and completion. The first two structures to be completed were Tower 2000, a 34-storey office building begun in 1996 on the opposite bank of the Moskva River to the rest of the development, and the Bagration pedestrian bridge which links it to the main Moscow City site on the left bank. Many of the proposed structures will be towers, causing the development to be dubbed by some 'Moscow's Manhattan', and two of its skyscrapers—the Federation Tower and the Russia Tower—will be the tallest buildings in Europe when completed in 2009 and 2011; one superseding the other at 506 metres and 612 metres, respectively.

Construction began on the Federation Tower in 2003. Designed by German architects, Sergei Tchoban and Peter Schweger, it will be Europe's first 'supertall' building, comprising two towers of 243 metres, and 360 metres, and a spire of 506 metres tall. Glass elevators will run up the core of the tallest section, offering panoramic views, and the towers will house 420,000 square metres of high-end office space; luxury apartments, shops, restaurants and a 44-storey Grand Hyatt Hotel. The developer of the Federation Tower, ZAO Mirax-City of Moscow, has little experience of building supertall structures; they erected the smaller of the building's constituent towers first, to "test [their] technology", according to Mirax's chief of construction.[1]

The Russia Tower has been designed by Foster+Partners as a mixed-use, super-dense 'vertical city' to accommodate 25,000 people. The tower rises as an elongated pyramidal form from a triangular footprint, and will utilise sustainable technology, such as a natural ventilation and heat recovery system to regulate the building's temperature and heat its water, and a rainwater and snow harvesting water recovery system. Retail and office clients will occupy the wider base of the tower, with residential and hotel accommodation located higher up on smaller floorplates, to maximise daylight. To resist the wind and spread the building's load, the tower features a geometric lattice-like facade made up of sloped fan columns. The building's outer shell will be triple-glazed, and will feature photovoltaic cells to harness solar energy. Construction began in September 2007.

The massive scale of the production of visible symbols of Russia's new wealth and optimism shows no sign of ending with the Moscow City development. City Hall have announced their plan to build around 200 new skyscrapers in the Moscow region by 2015, and work has already begun on a further vast development project, Moscow City-2, or the 'Big City', in the area surrounding Moscow City.

1. Quoted in Forrest, Brett, "Manhattan on the Moskva", *The New York Times*, 10 September 2006.

Suburban housing
in Stapleton.

STAPLETON

Occupying the 19,020 hectare site of the former Stapleton International Airport east of downtown Denver, Stapleton is one of the largest urban redevelopment projects in America. Construction of the mixed-use community began in 2001 after a lengthy planning and consultation process, and is currently estimated to be around 25 per cent complete with more than 7,000 residents having moved in.

The development is ultimately expected to have a population of around 30,000 people in 12,000 households when completed in 2020. The housing stock will be a mix of 8,000 houses and 4,000 apartments, served by four schools, numerous neighbourhood 'centres' with public amenities and two million square feet of retail space. The project aims to generate a new employment base of around 30,000–35,000 jobs, with 54 per cent of the developable land earmarked for employment use.

The plan adheres largely to the so-called New Urbanist model of development, whose 13 key tenets for creating successful urban communities—as set out in the 1993 Charter of the New Urbanism—could be pared

down in Stapleton's case to co-founder Peter Calthorpe's pithy summation: New Urbanism aims to create communities that are "walkable and diverse".[1] New Urbanism came about as a response to the increasing environmental and social impact of suburban sprawl, a result of badly planned and managed growth. Urban development, which rigorously zones usage into low density, isolated mono-functional residential areas and strip mall and 'big box'-type commercial developments creates a high impact, auto-dependent, commuter-focused lifestyle. New Urbanist communities are, instead, higher density and pedestrian-centred, with definable and walkable town centres, sufficient public transport options, and mixed-use residential and commercial areas. They aspire to integrate development with its surrounding natural environment, to surround it with as much open space as possible, and to respect local traditional materials and building practices germane to the area being developed. As the Stapleton developers put it, "less Sub, more Urb"; nuclear good, distribution bad.[2]

Although the Stapleton marketing department have chosen to represent their development less as a social experiment and more as

the logical conclusion of a common sense approach ("there is a reason neighbourhoods were built this way for hundreds of years: it works"), the thinking behind developments like this one has a larger theoretical point to make about the capacity of the physical form of the urban environment to shape and enhance the human communities that populate it.[3] Despite the slightly vacant-sounding platitudes of the marketing website ("It's good. It's fresh. It's Stapleton. And it just feels different.") and a fondness for non-quantifiable abstract nouns—lots of 'vision' and 'desire'—Stapleton does offer a markedly different experience than the average US urban infill development.[4] Its social, economic and environmental aims set it apart from the cookie-cutter sprawl estates currently colonising previously-undeveloped US land.

Planning began in 1989 when the decision was taken to close Stapleton International Airport. After a two year community and industry consultation process, the creation of jobs and the inclusion of open space emerged as priorities. In 1995, the Airport closed and the Stapleton Development Plan was adopted, known affectionately as the "Green Book". In 1998, Forest City Enterprises were selected by competition to be the overall developers of the Stapleton site and, in 1999, they hired Calthorpe Associates—Calthorpe's practice—to masterplan the town, with particular emphasis on the Town Center area. Construction began in 2001 and, in 2002, the first residents began to move in.

The Stapleton Development Plan guides the broad physical, social, environmental, and economic framework of the transformation of the Airport site. A degree of flexibility is written in, with its aim being to establish the basic community infrastructure—character, density and mix—while remaining flexible as consumer and market needs change in the future. Stapleton aims to be a model of 'smart growth'.

The overall plan for Stapleton organises development into eight distinct districts, "a network of urban villages", as the developers put it, each with its own definable neighbourhood centre with transport links and its own amenities. In each district, employment, commercial and residential areas are integrated, and approximately 65 per cent of the available land is assigned to urban development, and 35 per cent to mixed-use open space. The average density of the residential areas is around 12 units per .4 hectares, sufficient to sustain a public transport service, and this density increases closer to the neighbourhood centres. Its compact scale means that walking and cycling are preferred modes of transport, and the town has a continuous network of cycle paths. Schools are within walking distance of all residential areas, and function—like all community buildings—as multi-use facilities. A light rail service linking Stapleton and downtown Denver was approved in 2005.

Diversity is written into the plan in several ways: areas are mixed-use, for a start. Aesthetically, too, the developers have tried to ensure variety; homebuyers can choose between around 20 housebuilders, and inspiration for the architecture of Stapleton's housing stock has come from a variety of sources, from traditional Denver neighbourhoods to ultra-modern city-centre living. A variety of housing types also caters for a range of income levels, encouraging social diversity.

The unique heritage of the Stapleton site has focused some of the developer's environmental aims. Once the brownfield site had been cleaned up and made safe for habitation, there was the issue of how to dispose of the Airport's infrastructure. Six million tons of concrete runways have been recycled into 'Staplestone' aggregate for use on road surfaces and cycle paths; converted airport buildings now house a variety of organisations including local sports clubs and a police training academy. This drive towards recycling and environmental sustainability is evident throughout the planning of the development: in addition to a full domestic and commercial recycling programme, all homes completed since 2006 are Energy-Star certified, and the 647.5 hectares of parks, trails and recreation areas serve a functional purpose in managing the development's stormwater and irrigation needs.

So far, so good, but the Stapleton development has not been without its problems. Despite its commitment to social equity, a weak point in its offer has been the condominium housing intended for low-income families. Sales have not been as high as hoped, and it has been speculated that the homes are just too small and too expensive to appeal to their target market. A concurrent strand of criticism for the wider New Urbanism project is that it often prices socially disadvantaged groups out of the market. Social diversity has arguably not yet been achieved.

The Stapleton development also requires vast amount of financing, far above and beyond what could be generated by residential taxes. In addition to schemes negotiated with the City of Denver, much of the revenue needed has come from retail taxes generated the Quebec Square shopping mall, a conventional 'big-box' style 750,000 square feet retail development which is seen as distinctly out of kilter with the Stapleton ethos. The developers have commented that they anticipate that the Quebec Square mall will be replaced by something more in keeping at a later date, when Stapleton's financial state has had time to mature. The 58,000 square foot East 29th Avenue Town Center, with its mixture of local and national tenants, offers more of a model for the project's ideal retail development.

Stapleton's original projection of ten million square feet of office space is also on the back burner, with only 34,000 square feet having been built so far. It may be walkable and diverse, but a relatively high vacancy rate in downtown Denver has meant that the live-work non-commuter dream is some way off becoming a reality.

Aerial view of
Stapleton town.

1. Peter Calthorpe quoted in Rebchook, John, "New Urbanism Founder Guiding Stapleton Redevelopment", *Denver Rocky Mountain News*, 12 March 2000.

2. See: http://stapleton.cciconstellation.net/Redefine-Community.aspx

3. See: http://stapleton.cciconstellation.net/Redefine-Community.aspx

4. See: http://stapleton.cciconstellation.net/Redefine-Community.aspx

EXOPOLIS: THE RESTRUCTURING OF THE URBAN FORM

Edward Soja

EXOPOLIS AS SYNTHESIS

In trying to weave together the various strands of the discourse on the restructuring of urban form, I have decided to enter the naming game with my own preferred choice: Exopolis. The prefix exo- (outside) is a direct reference to the growth of 'outer' cities, and also suggests the increasing importance of exogenous forces shaping cityspace in an age of globalisation. Perhaps never before, short of military invasion, has endogenous development and localised synekism been as intensely affected by global constraints and opportunities.[1] The prefix can also be seen as denoting a hint of the 'end of', as in the ex-city, the rise of cities without the traditional traits of cityness as we have come to define them in the past. Hence, there are implications of a significantly reconstituted cityspace, urbanism, and polis/civitas.

I also use the term "Exopolis" to signify a recombinant synthesis and extension, a critical thirding, of the many oppositional processes and dualised arguments that have shaped the general discourse on urban form. The new geography of post-metropolitan urbanism is thus seen as the product of both a decentering and a recentering, deterritorialisation and reterritorialisation, continuing sprawl and intensified urban nucleation, increasing homogeneity and heterogeneity, socio-spatial integration and disintegration, and more. The composite Exopolis can be metaphorically described as 'the city turned inside-out', as in the urbanisation of the suburbs and the rise of the 'outer city'. But it also represents 'the city turned outside-in', a globalisation of the 'inner city' that brings all the world's peripheries into the centre, drawing in what was once considered "elsewhere" to its own symbolic zone (to refer back to Iain Chambers' allusive phrase). This redefines the outer and the inner city simultaneously, while making each of these terms more and more difficult to delineate and map with any clarity or confidence. In the spatially reconstituted post-metropolis, there is room for optimism and pessimism, nostalgia and exuberance, despair and hope for the future.

There are complex utopian and dystopian ramifications for social justice and economic development, and for the amelioration of ethnic, class, and gender inequalities. And as a new form of lived space, it is open to a multiplicity of interpretive approaches, challenging all attempts to reduce explanation to narrowed causes and consequences. Hence the need to keep the scope of critical interpretation radically open to many different perspectives, while at the same time being guided by a political project, by interpretations of the post-metropolis that can best assist in the praxis of achieving greater social and spatial justice. Continuing this political project, I turn next to the exemplary geography of Los Angeles to illustrate some of the more concrete expressions of the exopolitan restructuring of urban form.

REPRESENTING THE EXOPOLIS IN LOS ANGELES

The maelstrom of globalisation, economic restructuring, and mass regional urbanisation in Southern California has produced a cartography of everyday urban functions and spatial practices that is filled not just with social polarisations of increasing magnitude, but also with intensified 'spatial polarisations' and a growing multiplicity of what have been called 'spatial mismatches'. Receiving the most attention from local planners and urbanists has been the 'jobs-housing imbalance', a mismatched geography of affordable housing and available employment opportunities that has always been a part of urban life but has grown to unusual proportions in the increasingly kaleidoscopic geography of the Exopolis. More than just a matter of reducing the journey to work or simply adding more housing, the challenges raised by such spatial discordance reach deeply into questions of transportation planning, industrial policy, environmental regulation, regional governance, community development, social welfare, urban politics, and the wider struggle for social and spatial justice. The unbalanced geography of jobs and housing thus forms a revealing window through which to explore a few representative sites in the restructured geography of post-metropolitan Los Angeles.

STARTING IN THE NEW DOWNTOWN

30 years of globalisation and economic restructuring have recentered the Los Angeles post-metropolis, as well as the local urban imaginary, around a materially and symbolically assertive downtown. Superseding the Hollywood sign and the palm-fronded

beach as the most popular postcard icons, the new downtown skyline symbolises Los Angeles as never before. Viewed from the air, its skyscrapers, government offices, and corporate complexes seems to float above the urban flatlands surrounding it, like volcanic Hasan Dag above the ancient settlement of Çatal Hüyük. But viewed from below, it takes on a different character and flavour.

On the ground, competing territorialities position themselves in the microgeography of the downtown core, creating an assemblage of enclaves that materialise and make visible all that has been happening in the past three decades. With regard to jobs and housing in particular, this enclaved downtown is the site of two striking agglomerations representing the extremes of presence and absence. In the western half, consisting of the civic centre complex of city, county, state, and federal offices, and the corporate towers of the central business district and its southern extension around the Convention Centre, is the densest single cluster of jobs in the polycentric post-metropolis. In the middle of the tiered enclaves that comprise the eastern half is Skid Row, on any given night the largest concentration of homeless people in the region if not the whole of America. With cruel irony, the homeless, with neither good jobs nor housing, probably outnumber the housed and employed residential population in the downtown core, despite concerted public efforts to induce middle class residents to live in the area and to control, if not erase, Skid Row.

The streetscape and daily life downtown take on some distinctive rhythms as a result of these peculiar presences and absences of jobs and housing. For five days a week during the daytime working hours, the Westside population may reach above 100,000, counting tourists and visitors as well as workers. In the evening and on most weekends, the Westside empties out into a virtual urban desert. Audiences rush in and out of the Music Centre and the Museum of Contemporary Art without appearing in any significant numbers on the streets or in the very few public spaces. When all is most quiet, usually at night but also in the daylight on Sundays, the homeless move out of their eastside shelters to reoccupy the abandoned west, at least as far as the sparse local police will allow them to roam.

Meanwhile, beyond the wall of high-rise apartment blocks that separates the two halves of downtown, the eastside bustles all week long, especially on Broadway, the busiest and, according to some estimates, the most profitable commercial street in the region. Broadway serves as the central commercial and cultural

axis of Latin American LA, connecting on the north to the old Plaza and El Pueblo area where the city was born more than 200 years ago, and stretching south to the Garment District, where thousands of Latin Americans work in what has become the core of the largest apparel manufacturing industry in America. Few Latin Americans actually live in the downtown core, although they form an increasing proportion of the homeless, especially women and children. But to the east, south, and west of downtown, just beyond the triangle of freeways that defines its borders, are the most densely populated barrios, where at least one million Mexican and Central American immigrants have clustered over the past 30 years in low- to mid-rise buildings that are now among the most overcrowded in the country. On bustling Broadway, one is aware of another re-occupation of the most central place of the Los Angeles conurbation.

There is also a significant and growing Asian presence on the eastside of downtown. Although there are relatively few Asians in Skid Row, they shop on Broadway, work and own establishments in the Garment and Jewellery Districts, and occupy their own residential and commercial enclaves in Chinatown and Little Tokyo. The most unusual Asian enclave, however, is Toy Town, a zone of warehouses for toys and other cheap consumer goods from mainland China, Hong Kong, Taiwan, Thailand, and other East Asian countries. Located between the upscale Little Tokyo to the north and down-and-out Skid Row to the south, Toy Town has its own peculiar rhythms linked to the microgeography of jobs and housing. It acts as a buffer against the northward spread of the homeless into Little Tokyo, with its tourist attractions and hotels and other services for visiting Japanese businessmen. Several of the warehouses, for example, have water sprinkling systems at the entrances which work only at night, to prevent the homeless from finding a dry niche to sleep. But the aim is not to repel the homeless entirely, for there is need for their cheap and timely labour during peak moments of loading and unloading. Here the jobs-housing imbalance takes on a very different spin.

There is no better way to enter the globalised exopolis of Los Angeles than through a walking tour of its downtown archipelago of enclaves. Despite its sprawling polycentricity, the urban region has always been centered here and this centrality continues to hold as both a pole of attraction and a node of dispersal. Few other downtowns today contain such a distillation of contrasts and extremes in so small a space, so much evidence of centrifugal and centripetal forces, the city turned inside out and outside in, the core and the periphery entwined together in the same time and place.

Opposite: The outlying suburbs of Los Angeles.

Left: The city of Los Angeles from space, showing its situation between mountain ranges and the Pacific Ocean.

Right: The Tiro district of Los Angeles. The inhabitants of this area are primarily of Latin American descent.

INNER CITY BLUES

Sweeping outward from the new downtown in a half circle that runs from East Los Angeles around the south of downtown to Korea Town and the primarily Central American barrio of Pico-Union to the west, is what might be described as the 'new inner city'. At its geographical and symbolic core is South Central Los Angeles, located astride the old industrial zone that once stretched from downtown to the twin ports of San Pedro and Long Beach. Over the past 30 years, plant closures and white flight have emptied this area of its manufacturing jobs and resident Anglo population, devastating many neighbourhoods and creating the formative conditions for what the neo Chicago School sociologist William Julius Wilson described as the welfare-dependent "permanent urban underclass". Wilson locates the underclass in primarily African American communities geographically stranded in de-industrialised inner cities, epitomised in Chicago and repeated in many other major cities in eastern America. The problem in these "new American ghettoes", as Camilo Vergara calls them, is not so much a jobs-housing imbalance but the relative absence of both decent jobs and adequate housing conditions, as well as the vicious circle of poverty this produces.[2] Just such a process of deepening impoverishment has affected the African American community of Los Angeles over the past 30 years, creating conditions that in some areas have significantly worsened since the Watts Rebellion of 1965.

In terms of statistical measures of job accessibility, Watts was once in a highly favourable location, adjacent to (although often racially excluded from) the region's largest concentration of unionised manufacturing jobs. Most of these high-paying jobs have disappeared, resulting in the outmigration of most of the once job-secure white working class and many African American families as well. This has reshaped the iconic 'black ghetto' of South Central Los Angeles in at least two ways. It has pumped large numbers of the most destitute and welfare-dependent African Americans into downtown's expansive Skid Row. In addition, Latin American populations have not only replaced the predominantly southern white working class that occupied much of the southeastern quadrant of Los Angeles County, but have spilled over to become the majority in Watts and other South Central communities. This has pushed the core of African American Los Angeles westward, further compacting the ghetto and bringing the poorest and wealthiest African Americans into even closer proximity than they were before.[3]

The eastern formulations of spatial mismatch theories and the welfare-dependent urban underclass thus have some resonance in Los Angeles, but the metropolitan geography of jobs and housing has always been more complex and poly-nucleated than in eastern cities. For example, the westward shift of the core African American residential area has brought the population closer to the major job concentrations of the LAX airport complex and the rapidly growing multimedia entertainment centres of Santa Monica and Culver City. Although racial job discrimination is still intense, it cannot be argued empirically that African American job seekers are geographically stranded from available opportunities to the degree they are in other post-metropolitan areas. Simple models of inner versus outer city employment patterns do not work as well in Los Angeles as they might do in Chicago.

Complicating the picture further has been the Latinisation of poverty in Los Angeles and the emergence of what local scholars have called, in contrast to the welfare-dependent underclass, the 'working poor'. Far from welfare-dependent, jobless, or homeless, the mainly immigrant and largely Latin American working poor have grown on the massive expansion of low-wage and/or part-time jobs that have traditionally been unattractive to most African American, Anglo, and Chicano/a workers. Combined with the underclass and joined by other immigrant entrepreneurs, they have created an extraordinary milieu of adaptive survival in the new inner city. Attempting to make the best of the 'surge of inequality' and deepening poverty that has been so characteristic a part of the post-metropolitan transition, the working poor and others have become part of a vast and growing informal or underground economy of swap meets, bartered personal services, street vending, day labour, drug distribution, and other specialised legal and illegal activities. And here too, in these peak population densities of the "gritty city", as Thomas Bender called it, innovative new strategies for community-based struggles for a better life are emerging, evoking another variation on the theme of synekism, the stimulus of urban agglomeration.

The survival economy of the new inner city, despite deepening poverty and the absence of a sufficiently responsive public realm, has produced in the real and imagined space of South Central Los Angeles a paradigmatic post-metropolitan icon of the contemporary urban condition. At once the epitome of despair and the source of creative energy in nearly all aspects of contemporary popular culture, the gritty spaces of South Central, along with the barrios of East Los Angeles and Pico-Union, have become the focal points for a growing public discourse and concerted community activism aimed at increasing political empowerment for the expanded and multi-cultural underclasses. And what has been developing in this real and imagined realm of 'greater' South Central affects more than Los Angeles. If only for a fleeting moment, all the world heard the resounding demand that emanated from these lived spaces in 1992: no justice—no peace. As much as in any other place in the post-metropolis today, it is here where, to recall Lewis Mumford un-nostalgically, "time becomes visible" to invigorate new sources of solidarity and new strategies in the struggle for social and spatial justice.

Exemplifying the creative solidarities of the working poor are a number of post-1992 coalitions that have consciously used the specific geography of the post-metropolis as a staging point for renewed political struggles over explicitly spatial justice, especially with respect to the far-reaching implications of the jobs-housing imbalance. Although beginning well before 1992, community struggles over the siting of noxious facilities and the geographical distribution of environmental hazards with respect to the location of minorities and the poor have generated a particularly vigorous environmental justice movement in Los Angeles. Increasingly allied with other movements, such as those for a living wage and for growth-with-equity, the now regionalised environmental justice movement is richly conscious of the restructured post-metropolitan geography, and uses its discordant inequities as a mobilisation strategy. From the siting of hazardous facilities to the geographical distribution of the worst health effects of air pollution, it is being made clear that (a) poor and immigrant communities suffer disproportionately; (b) these environmental effects are, to a significant degree, socially constructed; and (c) therefore the conditions can be changed through concerted social action.

There are also signs that the environmental justice movement is expanding into a wider collective struggle over explicitly

spatial justice and what can be called regional democracy. One particularly important example that creatively illustrates the potential public power that can arise from a critical geographical consciousness and new forms of urban cultural politics is the recent court case involving a new alliance of the working poor called the Bus Riders Union (Labour/Community Strategy Center v Los Angeles Metropolitan Transit Authority). The Bus Riders Union (BRU) was created under the leadership of Eric Mann and the Labour/Community Strategy Centre (LCSC), a broad-based and multiracial organisation that grew out of struggles against factory closures in the 1980s. The LCSC has used its labour-organising base to reach into a wider variety of community issues revolving around class, race, and gender, and more general questions of social and spatial justice.[4] In the mid-1990s, Mann and the LCSC, through the newly created BRU, turned specifically to the needs of the 'transit-dependent', consisting primarily of poor immigrant populations concentrated most heavily in the new inner city.

In a lawsuit against the Metropolitan Transit Authority, the BRU and its lead counsel, the NAACP Legal Defense Fund, linked civil rights legislation to the geography of transit use in Los Angeles to argue that a particular population of transit-dependent bus riders were being discriminated against by the policies and investment patterns of the MTA, which clearly favoured wealthy, white, and predominantly male suburban users of the expensive new fixed-rail system being constructed, as well as by existing bus services, which studies showed subsidised wealthy bus riders more than the poor. Certified as a class action suit on behalf of 350,000 bus riders, the case was resolved in late 1996 through a Consent Decree that, while still being worked out in detail, has contributed

A cluster of skyscrapers typical of Downtown, Los Angeles.

significantly to forcing a dramatic shift of attention and resources in the MTA from fixed-rail construction to the improvement of bus services, especially for the transit-dependent.[5]

The impact of this still tentative victory is difficult to gauge, but in combination with many other events it has (temporarily) stopped the multi-billion dollar construction of the planned fixed-rail transit system and induced a potentially massive re-allocation of funds to serve the primarily poor, minority, immigrant, female, and inner city transit-dependent population. The BRU has committed itself to "the fight against racism, class oppression, sexism, and the oppression of immigrants" and to an ambitious programme, Billions for Buses, that could play a significant role in the economic development of the new inner city in the future. Never shy in proclaiming his victories, Eric Mann is completing a book entitled *Driving the Bus of History: The Los Angeles Bus Riders Union Models a New Theory of Urban Insurgency in the Age of Transnational Capitalism.*

At the very least, the BRU represents an important example of coalition-based movements arising at the spatially specific intersections of race, class, and gender, and having a socially beneficial effect on the geography of the post-metropolis. Viewed more ambitiously, it can be seen as opening traditional notions of civil rights to a more specifically spatial politics revolving around new visions of democratic citizenship and the rights to the city, the rights—and responsibilities—of all urban dwellers to participate effectively in the social production of their lived city spaces.

THE MIDDLE LANDSCAPE

Tucked away in the affluent Westside outer city, just east of the LAX airport complex, is Lennox, a tiny residual plot of unincorporated county land with a population of 23,000 and an area of 1.6 square kilometres. Nearly 90 per cent of the population is Latin American and more than 60 per cent are foreign-born (as against around 40 per cent for Los Angeles County). Unemployment rates are not particularly high but household income is well below surrounding areas, for Lennox has become a highly specialised outer city enclave of the immigrant working poor, a ghetto of hotel and restaurant workers cheaply servicing the three 'Edge Cities' Garreau defines for this area: Marina Del Rey-Culver City, Los Angeles International Airport-El Segundo, and the South Bay-Torrance-Carson-San Diego Freeway area. The problem here is not so much a mismatch between jobs and housing but an immiserating concentration of the worst of both. And the problems are compounded by globalisation. The recent devaluation of the Mexican peso and the general decline of the Mexican economy has had a particularly devastating effect on Lennox, where much of the population maintains bi-national households. Such specialised pockets of poverty are embedded in, and play a key role in sustaining, the expansive development of the outer cities.

48 kilometres east is another example of what Mike Davis, the noirest of the local explorers of the dark side of the Exopolis, calls "the suburban nightmare" that is nestled in the "political middle landscape", the in-between zone of older and newer urbanised suburbs where inner and outer city mix together. He looks in particular at Pomona, a municipality of around 150,000 residents on the eastern edge of Los Angeles County and the gateway to the Inland Empire, the name given to the 'anticipatory' outer city of San Bernardino and Riverside counties.

A nighttime view of Los Angeles' city sprawl.

Once upon a time a placid town basked in the golden glow of its orchards. In the 1920s, it was renowned as the 'Queen of the Citrus Belt'. In the 1940s, it served as one of Hollywood's models for Andy Hardy's hometown. In the 1950s, it became a commuter suburb for thousands of father-knows-bests in their starched white shirts. Now, its nearly abandoned downtown is surrounded by hectares of vacant lots and derelict homes. Its major employer, an aerospace corporation, pulled up stakes and moved to Tucson. The 4-H Club has been replaced by local franchises of the Crips and Bloods. Since 1970, nearly one per cent of its population has been murdered. This town is, of course, Pomona, Los Angeles County's fourth largest city.

Although geographically a suburb, Pomona now displays pathologies typically associated with a battered inner city. Its incidence of poverty, for example, exceeds Los Angeles' and its murder rate, in bad years, approaches Detroit's. Its density of gang membership, as a percentage of the teenage male population, is one of the nation's highest. Unfortunately, Pomona is not unique. Across the nation, hundreds of aging suburbs are trapped in the same downward trajectory, from garden city to crabgrass slum. This silent, pervasive crisis dominates the political middle landscape.... [America] seems to be unravelling its traditional moral centre: suburbia.[6]

In his own reclassification of Garreau's Edge Cities, Davis devises a geographical class war between the "new pariahs", older suburban cities such as Pomona and those around Minneapolis, Chicago, and in the Bay Area; against the "predatory" edge cities "further out on the spiral arms of the metropolitan galaxy". What results, he contends, is "an unstable mosaic" of new polarisations, an emerging second round of urban crises, expressed in Southern California in "the widening divides between northern and southern Orange County, the upper and lower tiers of the San Gabriel Valley, the east and west sides of the San Fernando Valley or the San Fernando Valley as a whole and its 'suburbs-of-a-suburb'—like Simi Valley and Santa Clarita".

Davis adds to his darkside revisioning of the Exopolis an almost apocalyptic picture of the environmental devastation that arises from the unbalanced geography of well-paying jobs, affordable housing, and shorter and less automobile-dependent journeys to work. In his view, Los Angeles has become a "Cannibal City", a fountainhead of "ecocide" that continues insatiably to devour natural and human landscapes, especially in this middle zone. In "How Eden Lost Its Garden", Davis lists the "lost landscapes" of Los Angeles, from the nineteenth century destruction of native grasslands and the oak savannah to the late twentieth century elimination of the remaining tidal marshes and coastal sage scrub, an intentional reference to the Playa Vista project of the New Urbanists.[7] Although framed by historical continuities, there is a clear intimation that recent developments have accelerated these processes, adding a potent environmental critique to the discourse on the restructuring of urban form, one that is sure to expand in the future.[8]

OFF-THE-EDGE CITIES

Further out, on the distant borderlands of the megacity, the jobs-housing imbalance takes on still another distinctive form. Flushed by the success of Orange County, the Westside, and more recently the West San Fernando Valley, and intensified by fear

of the new inner city, a remarkable anticipatory building boom has taken place in the outer fringes of the Los Angeles Exopolis over the past two decades. In the 1990 census, more than half of the fastest-growing small cities in America were found in this region. Where jobs were relatively abundant and accessible, such as in Irvine and Mission Viejo in Orange County, and somewhat later in places such as Thousand Oaks, Westlake Village, and Simi Valley straddling the Los Angeles-Ventura county border, thriving middle class communities were formed. In other areas, where outer city industrialisation and job growth stalled, whole cities were left stranded, creating a socio-spatial crisis of outlandish proportions. Two of these areas, Moreno Valley east of Riverside and Palmdale and Lancaster in the Antelope Valley in the high desert of northern Los Angeles County, deserve special attention, for they illustrate well an argument that underlies and spins off from all the discourses on the post-metropolis, that 30 years of crisis-generated restructuring are currently leading to the onset of a period of restructuring-generated crises that are not located only in the ghettoes and barrios of the old inner city.

In Moreno Valley, located about 95 kilometres east of downtown Los Angeles and almost as distant from Irvine, the jobs-housing mix has become disastrously out of whack. The 1990 census listed Moreno Valley as the fastest-growing city over 100,000 in the entire country. Attracted by affordable housing, mainly young lower-middle working class families flocked to the area, in part also to escape the real and imagined problems of the old and new, inner city. Population boomed from 45,000 at the time of incorporation in 1984 to almost 120,000 in 1990. Today, the city is described as "solidly middle class" with a population of about 135,000, a median family income close to $45,000, and a racial mix of 57 per cent Anglo, 23 per cent Latin American, 13 per cent Africa American, and six per cent Asian and Pacific Islanders. Beneath the appearances of comfortable suburban life, however, there are unforeseen problems of social pathology and personal despair as intense and disruptive as those seemingly left behind.

With local employment growth far below what was promised by the optimistic community developers greedily driven by the development of adjacent Orange County, the journey to work (as well as an unemployment rate higher than 12 per cent) has become an unusual burden. Many working residents are forced to rise well before dawn to drive or to be taken by a fleet of vans and buses, often for more than two hours, to the places of employment they held before moving to their affordable housing. Without a large commercial or industrial tax base, public services are poor, schools are overcrowded, free ways are gridlocked, and family life is deeply stressed as residents contend with their location in a wannabe Edge City.

Advertised as "A City of Promise.... Poised for the Twenty-First Century", Moreno Valley boomed on what a local observer likened to a Ponzi scheme, based on the flow of developers' permit fees. Aggravated by the closure of the nearby March Air Force Base and reductions in the flow of permit fees, Moreno Valley recently elicited other headline descriptions—"Bad Time for a Boom Town" and "Boom Town Going Bust"—as it plunged into a budget crisis, unable to maintain basic police, fire, and even school crossing guard services without a substantial increase in local taxes.[9] The plight of Moreno Valley reached national attention in leading eastern newspapers and on television's multiplying "newsmagazine" programmes, where the remarks of happy valley residents were contrasted with demoralising stories of broken marriages, delinquent children, disruptive van romances, and spousal abuse, further evidence for many of the California dream-become-nightmare.

Locally, as is typical in these off-the-edge cities, all problems were blamed on incompetent municipal leadership and the failures of planning, ignoring the inherent dynamics of exopolitan restructuring and the need for effective regional coalition-building among similarly affected areas. Both views are seriously short-sighted, for such enclaves of 'invisible' middle class immiseration are a characteristic feature of post-suburban landscapes all over the country, as much a part of the Exopolis as the new American ghettoes of the underclass and the working poor or the burgeoning technopoles and successful edge cities. The restructuring of urban form, in combination with mass movements against increasing taxes and for smaller government, is creating a new round of fiscal crises in post-suburbia, leading an increasing number of the constellation of local governments that comprise the post-metropolis to the edge of bankruptcy, and beyond, as occurred in Orange County in 1994. But the crises that are affecting the off-the-edge cities are even deeper and more difficult to address.

The 100 Mile City and the notion of spatial polarity take on a new meaning in places such as Moreno Valley, located roughly 160 kilometres east of its post-suburban antipode at Malibu, also recently incorporated as a municipality. Located a similar distance apart, but north-south rather than east-west, is another pairing of even more extreme socio-spatial polarities: the peninsula of Palos Verdes, where the tiny incorporated and gated community of Rolling Hills recently topped *Worth* magazine's list of the most wealthy communities in America (with an average household income of more than $300,000), and Palmdale, located in the high desert of northern Los Angeles County. The development of Palmdale and the entire Antelope Valley was given an even greater push to excess than Moreno Valley, as the area contained both the site for a proposed international airport and a cluster of big aerospace firms associated with sprawling Edwards Air Force Base, a major cog in the NASA network of space stations.[10] In the 1980s, the rolling brown hills and sage-brushed sands of the Antelope Valley, pictured at the Palmdale freeway exit by David Hockney in one of his most famous photo-collages became covered by a sea of peach and beige stucco houses with red-tiled roofs selling at bargain basement prices, at least in comparison to the city far away to the south.

With the end of the Cold War and the steep decline of the region's aerospace industry, as well as the ensuing real estate crisis and economic recession of the early 1990s, the booming Antelope Valley became the site of what one reporter called a "middle class implosion". In a pair of richly detailed articles, *Los Angeles Times* reporter Sonia Nazario painted an agonising picture of road-blocked dreams and the unfolding of what she described as a new "class struggle".[11] Even more so than in Moreno Valley, excessively long journeys to work were having pathological effects on family life and personal health. In the mid-1990s, nearly 40 per cent of work commutes in Palmdale and 30 per cent in the entire Antelope Valley took two hours or more, compared with 15–17 per cent in LA, Ventura, and Orange Counties, 25 per cent in Riverside and San Bernardino Counties, and six per cent for America as a whole. Many workers spend more than five hours a day in their cars and young children are often left for more than 12 hours in day-care centres that open before dawn. Suicide rates are unusually high in Palmdale and nearby Lancaster; the local Sheriff's Office reports that domestic violence felony arrests are above those of any of their other 16 stations, and there are more child abuse reports than most anywhere in California. The Antelope Valley psychological centre that specialises in domestic violence is reputed to be the largest in America. The number of violent juvenile crimes and gang membership has increased precipitously and some shopping malls have prohibited entry to anyone wearing a baseball cap backward or to one side. In one recent period, over 100 teenagers a day were arrested for truancy.

With plummeting land values, mortgage foreclosure rates (at around ten per cent) are now among the highest anywhere in the country, and many of the empty homes are becoming filled with underclass squatters from the inner city, still another example of the metropolis inverted. In recent years, Nazario reports, 25,000 public assistance cases have been transferred from the City of Los Angeles to the Antelope Valley. She also states that nearly 50 per cent of those receiving public assistance are white, 32 per cent Latin American, 17 per cent African American, and two per cent Asian. Sweatshops have been set up in the area and crackhouses have been raided by police battering rams. There are some who still maintain their middle class dreams amidst this implosion. "Here we are really content", says one resident, an LAPD officer, but most would agree with the conclusion of a local Lutheran priest: "This way of life is destructive." Some academic analysts might argue that these conditions are only temporary growing pains, but temporary or not, the present day reality of the Antelope Valley stands out as one of the darkest outcomes of exopolitan restructuring.

1. The term "synekism" derives from "an Ancient Greek word that appears from time to time in the archeological and historical literature on cities and urbanism in its English form, 'synoecism' (pronounced 'sin-ee-sism').... Synekism is directly derived from synoikismos, literally the condition arising from dwelling together in one house, or oikos, and used by Aristotle in his Politics to describe the formation of the Athenian polis or city-state." Soja, Edward, *Post-metropolis: Critical Studies of Cities and Regions*, Oxford: Blackwell Publishing, 2000, p. 12.

2. Vergara, Camilo, *The New American Ghetto*, New Brunswick, NJ: Rutgers University Press, 1995. Vergara is a photo-sociologist whose photography traces the transformation of the built environment in the ghettoes of New York, Newark, Detroit, Chicago, and LA over the past 30 years.

3. Los Angeles County is reputed to have the wealthiest and the poorest predominantly African American municipalities in America.

4. The LCSC publication, *Los Angeles' Lethal Air: New Strategies for Policy, Organising, and Action*, Mann et al., 1991, remains a key document in the growing environmental justice movement, and its comparative analysis of service workers' wages helped to spur one of the most effective labour struggles affecting poor and minority communities, Jobs for Janitors.

5. Eric Mann et al., *A New Vision for Urban Transportation: The Bus Riders Union Makes History at the Intersection of Mass Transit, Civil Rights, and the Environment*, a report of the Labour/Community Strategy Centre, 1996. For another view of the BRU case, see Brown, Jeffrey, "Race, Class, Gender and Public Transportation: Lesson from the Bus Riders Union Lawsuit", *Critical Planning* (Journal of the UCLA Department of Urban Planning) No. 5, 1998, pp. 3–20.

6. Davis, Mike, "The Suburban Nightmare: While Older Suburbs Experience Many Problems of the Inner City, 'Edge Cities' Now Offer a New Escape", *Los Angeles Times*, 23 October 1994.

7. See Davis, Mike, "Cannibal City: Los Angeles and the Destruction of Nature", *Urban Revisions*, R Ferguson ed., 1994; and "How Eden Lost its Garden: A Political History of the Los Angeles Landscape", *The City: Los Angeles and Urban Theory at the End of the Twentieth Century*, Scott and Soja eds., 1996, pp. 160–185. For another look at the "Apocalypse Themepark" of LA, see Davis, "Los Angeles After the Storm: The Dialectic of Ordinary Disaster", *Antipode*, No. 27, 1995, pp. 221–241.

8. For a compilation and expansion of this apocalyptic environmental critique, see Davis' most recent work, *Ecology of Fear: Los Angeles and the Imagination of Disaster*, New York: Metropolitan Books, Henry Holt, 1998.

9. See German, Tom, "Moreno Valley: Boom Town Going Bust Turns to Voters", *Los Angeles Times*, 28 October 1996, and "Bad Times for a Boom Town", *Los Angeles Times*, 12 January 1994.

10. The area also contains the barely visible ruins of Llano del Rio, the socialist utopian community founded in the early decades of the century and celebrated by Mike Davis in the introduction to his *City of Quartz*, 1990.

11. Nazario, Sonia, "Suburban Dreams Hit Roadblock", *Los Angeles Times*, 23 June 1996, and "Class Struggle Unfolds in Antelope Valley Tracts", *Los Angeles Times*, 24 June 1996.

NOMADIC

| ROOTED

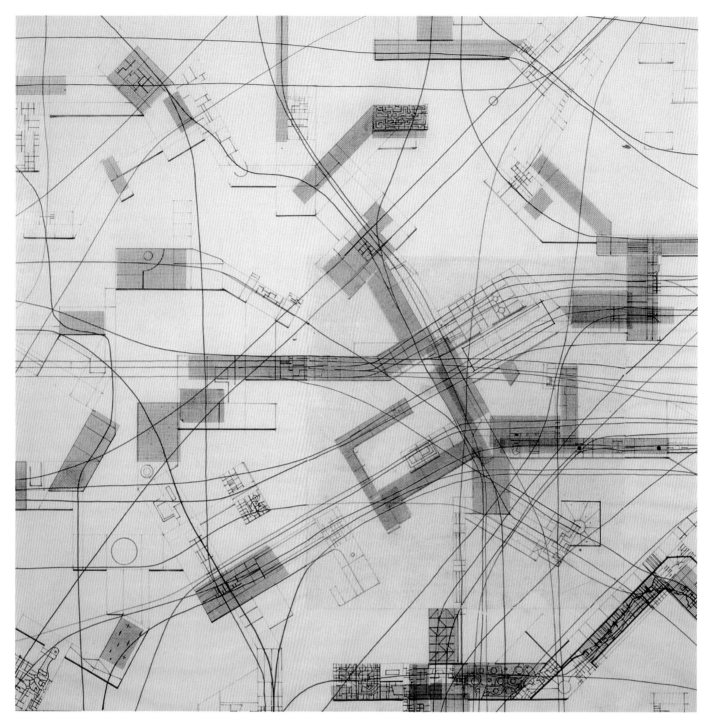

Constant Nieuwenhuys,
New Babylon,
1959. Inspired by
a temporary gypsy
settlement in Alba,
Italy, Constant's *New
Babylon* is a nomadic
city without borders;
a camp for nomads on
a planetary scale. As
a nomadic urbanity,
it presented a radical
alternative to the
modernist city.

Movement is at the heart of the city's existence. Historically, towns and cities sprung up at the junctions of trade routes and transit corridors, generally as a marketplace for the goods and for the traders that peddled them. The cities of today function in much the same fashion, but in a global context. Cities change and evolve, grow and decay and at the heart of this change is the evolution of transport infrastructure; as a means to get in, around and out of the city. The ongoing development of road, rail and air facilities serves to keep the lifeblood of commerce flowing around the city. The habitation of cities might be said to be secondary; it happens as a direct response to the needs of commercial travellers and in turn, offers commercial opportunity. As a result, settlement occurs when the promise of work and security attracts migratory populations, whether non-urban or foreign. However, the creation of instant settlements is not always purely economic. Factors such as government intervention or armed conflict can themselves create new, artificially sustained settlements such as refugee or internment camps.

DESERT TENTS

Early humans were nomads, indeed recent DNA evidence suggests that a single group left Africa about 70,000 years ago and started to spread around the world by migrating along coastlines. While the great majority of communities today are rooted, there are some modern examples of nomadic peoples worth elaborating on, for example the Bedouin in the Middle East. They travel the deserts stretching from the Arabian Peninisula, across the Sinai desert and deep into the Sahara in Libya. The scarcity of water and vegetation has made their lifestyle one based on movement, herding sheep and goats as they make their way across the desert landscape. Interestingly, the word for a family unit in Bedouin Arabic is *bayt*, which also means tent, reflecting the rootless nature of their existence. Traditionally, Bedouins retreat deeper into the desert in winter and settle at oases in the summer. When they stop, often for months at a time, they build houses of stone, which take the same structure as their tents; rectangular in plan and divided into gendered sections, often with a third area for sick family members and animals. The Amsterdam-based anthropologist Zbigniew Kosc has studied the life of the Ababda, a Bedouin tribe who live between the Red Sea and the Nile. In 2001, he noted that their settlements were made of plywood, cardboard and salvaged materials—often sections of oil drums are used to hold water. In other words, these are settlements much like the shanty towns of the developing world—a semi-permanent environment created from whatever materials are close to hand. In the 1960s, the Egyptian government resettled many of the Ababda in newly built villages, as the creation of a vast reservoir alongside the Nile had flooded much of their traditional territory.

This is not the only example of the forced rooting of the Bedouin people, In the Negev Desert, the Israeli government has restricted the movement of Bedouins, and since the 1950s, half of this nomadic population have been forcibly settled in villages. While they are restricted from expressing their traditional migratory lifestyle, the Bedouins are also prohibited from building permanent structures, which have been known to be bulldozed by the Israeli government when they do crop up. According to the Israeli Union for Environmental Defence, some of these 'instant' villages are even located on toxic dumping grounds, and often take on the characteristics of an internment camp. Governments across the world from Mauritania to Mongolia have tried to root nomadic people in permanent settlements, which invariably suffer from deprivation and a lack of facilities needed for an adequate quality of life, such as schools or hospitals.

Worse than the internment camp, is the refugee camp. This is the end of the line for communities forced to become nomadic through war and internal conflict. In Darfur, the Sudanese-armed, Janjaweed militia, have been at war with non-Arab groups since 2003. The Janjaweed are famous for using murder, rape and looting as weapons to terrorise the civilian population, driving nearly two million non-Arabs from their villages and into refugee camps adjacent to Darfur towns or across the border in neighbouring Chad. These camps are not much more than vast open fields of makeshift dwellings, constructed using branches covered with

Top: Wigwam Villages, which are motels for travellers, were built between 1936 through to the 1950s along Route 66, in California. © Thomas Barnard, 2002.

Bottom: A service station on Route 66, which originally ran from Chicago, Illinois, to Los Angeles, California.

Opposite: The Bullring, a commercial area in the centre of Birmingham, England. The Bullring shopping centre is currently one of the largest in Britain, and its redevelopment is a prime example of how shopping has promoted a change in lifestyle from the city's inhabitants as they demand more commodities which in turn needs more storage space.

cloth and whatever other materials are available. Rudimentary guidelines for constructing refugee camps, such as siting them on slopes to provide drainage, or limiting their size to 20,000 inhabitants in order control fire risks and the spread of disease, have frequently been impossible to implement. That is not the only threat to the safety of refugee camp populations. In October 2007, Reuters reported Sudan-backed attacks within the Kalma camp, which houses 90,000 refugees. This was sadly not an isolated incident and is a problem faced by many displaced populations.

Nomadic settlements and refugee camps in the Sahara present a stark contrast to the modern, urban environment: from the seasonal settlements of the Bedouin, driven on by hardship and scarcity of resources, to the deprivations of the Darfur refugee camps, living with and driven on by the reality and threat of violence. These are not cities, but instant settlements of the rootless and provide a vivid contrast to more traditionally rooted urban developments shaped by modern transport and the global economy.

THE DRIVE FROM MAIN STREET TO THE NAKED STREET

The car has had a big impact on the urban landscape. This is manifest in two ways—the instant city of purpose-built infrastructure; created to accommodate and support the widespread use of motor vehicles and the damage road vehicles inflict upon the urban and wider environment.

One of the single biggest issues facing modern cities and indeed, humanity in general, is the environmental consequence and 'carbon footprint' brought about by the proliferation of the car. Not only do cars represent the most polluting form of transport per capita, but they have also been the catalyst behind 'urban sprawl', a phenomenon particularly prevalent in America. This low-rise, low-density urban expansion outwards from cities vastly increases the per capita energy use of its citizens. In the suburbs, aside from commuting, the car is essential for access to shopping and leisure, whereas in the compact city (a high-density urban settlement) everything is most easily reached by walking and public transport.

Suburban expansion has largely been a post-war phenomenon, however long before this the city had started to adapt to the internal combustion engine. The first car-entrance to a building was built in Chicago in 1908, which is also the site of the first multi-storey car park, a five-storey structure, built at the Hotel LaSalle in 1918. By 1931 the multi-storey car park had really taken off, with the Carew-Netherland garage in Cincinnati reaching an astonishing 104 metres high. The first underground car park was built beneath Union Square in San Francisco in 1942. Needless to say, the main thrust behind this auto-friendly development was economically, not socially driven: in the 1930s, General Motors pursued an aggressive campaign to buy up tram companies operating in American cities, so that they could sell more buses. However, with roads clear of trams and their infrastructure and parking entering the built environment, why ride a bus when you could drive a car? Aside from practicality, car ownership and the burgeoning commercial highway culture became synonymous with the American Dream. In the 1930s, Route 66 (the 'Mother Road' or the American 'Main Street') was built to take travellers from Chicago to California, where new dreams and the New America was being built in the west. Its 3,862 kilometres were paved by 1938 and along it, a strung-out 24-hour instant city emerged; an endless line of roadside advertising, gas-stations, motels, diners and drive-in cinemas. The first McDonalds restaurant opened in 1940 on Route 66 in San Bernardino, California, employing 'carhops' on roller-skates who brought food out to parked customers so that they would not have to leave their cars. Here, as at Holbrook, Arizona, Route 66 hosted clusters of wigwam-shaped guest-houses called the Wigwam Motels, where rooms were available by the hour in the 1950s, complete with signage encouraging travellers to "do it in a tee-pee". The bizarre, kitsch architecture produced many other mimetic structures, for example, diners shaped like pies, sombrero hats or soda fountains to advertise their offerings. As the traveller descended west into Los Angeles' hinterland, juice stands shaped as giant oranges dotted the route. In 1985, Route 66 was replaced by Interstate 40, however these examples demonstrate something of its importance as an 'instant highway city', a phenomena that now occurs in some form along major highways in America, as well as elsewhere.

The vehicle-centric society was a cultural export Europe was hungry for, but it arrived without the romance and dazzle of the American highway. In Britain, as elsewhere in Europe, road schemes became the basis of much urban planning from the 1950s onwards. The urban fabric was scarred with motorways and the inner city, an inconvenience to the driver between the centre and the home or distribution centre, was bypassed with flyovers and isolated with ring roads. The Bullring, the city centre of Birmingham was turned into Europe's largest shopping centre development in the 1960s, and was surrounded by a ring road that isolated it from the rest of the city so tightly that in 1999, Theresa Stewart, the City Council leader, described it as "a concrete collar". (The redeveloped Bullring now stands as a vibrant, pedestrian-friendly example of downtown renewal.) As new urban road space was built in an effort to relieve congestion, so traffic increased to fill it, rarely moving any faster than it had before.

The economic cost of the car culture hit the West in the oil recession of the 1970s. By this time, pollution and congestion were tangibly degrading the urban environment. Jon Savage documented the bleak cityscape of London's North Kensington under the new Westway flyover in photographs; all desolation, graffiti and empty blocks sealed off by corrugated iron. When prosperity returned, the American-style suburban shopping mall grew to take advantage of consumers' new liquidity, their success dependant upon and to an extent responsible for the ubiquity of the car. These huge new structures cast their shadow on the high street, which weakened, was then colonised by the chain outlets. Even when the inner city revived, the children who had played in its streets had been replaced by cars; either parked or whizzing past. Social housing projects may take the blame for destroying the social cohesion of the inner city, but the car has certainly played its part.

Currently, the refashioning of the city for the driver's convenience is in full force and nowhere less than in the developing world, where millions aspire to own a car and can increasingly afford them. In China, for example, there has been a rapid and exponential escalation in urban vehicular traffic. Soviet planners first proposed a layout for Beijing with ring roads in the 1950s, during a period in which the USSR offered wide economic and political support to China, then its ally. There was a second ring road built in the 1980s, mainly along the path of an old moat by the ancient city walls. Between 2001 and 2003, the Fifth Ring Road, ten kilometres outside the centre, was the first orbital toll-road expressway, a sixth ring road, another expressway up to 20 kilometres out, was subsequently built. Radial expressways started to penetrate the city from outside in 1993 with 20 kilometres linking Capital Airport to the Third Ring Road and there are now nine of them. With these roads comes a plethora of overpasses, junctions, gas stations, service areas and road signs, although Beijing does not have elevated highways as Shanghai does, nor as yet the billboards that mark America's highways. These roads are like European motorways or American freeways; traffic light-free and often with many lanes. "Vehicles entering into the freeway system from any point in the urban area will find a thoroughfare without intersections and be able to reach any other point with no red light ahead" enthused Wang Guangtao, Beijing's vice mayor in 2001, promising that no city trip would take more than an hour. The reality is different. Official figures reported in 2005 indicate that 47 per cent of Beijing's traffic is within the Second Ring Road, which is just six per cent of the capital's area, and contains the rapidly vanishing traditional *hutongs* with their narrow lanes and tight housing. Gridlock can last for 11 hours a day. In 2007, Beijing experimented with a four-day ban on odd or even numbered private vehicles, each about 1.3 million of the city's three million vehicles. Traffic was still heavy but air pollution fell to officially acceptable levels. Pollution, congestion, and the uprooting of low or no-traffic neighbourhoods for traffic-orientated expansion looks like another urban export from the developed to the developing world.

Congestion charging, which Singapore pioneered in 1975, is one means to tackle downtown traffic jams and it has since been taken up by Rome (2001), London (2003), and Stockholm (2007). However, these schemes have been shown to reduce traffic by less than a third, with traffic levels soon rising again after their introduction. Naturally, the single most effective way to win back the city from the car is to ban them from city streets. Copenhagen's main central thoroughfare, Strøget, was first pedestrianised in the 1960s by urban planner Jan Gehl. This was a pioneering project that has influenced pedestrianised downtown zones both in Europe and North America. While an American backlash against the car is implicit within the pedestrian-friendly aspects of New Urbanist ideas from the 1980s, and postmodern urbanist thinking elsewhere, such as Richard Rogers' ideal of the compact city, the reality is that the car is here to stay.

TRANSPORTING MASSES RAPIDLY

Before cars were so prevalent, public transport was the main driver of urban sprawl. Local railways led to the radial expansion of cities like Chicago in the early twentieth century. Opening in 1848, the Galena and Chicago Union Railroad was the city's first and served to provide transportation links between the eastern and western states of America. This new system, along with a flourishing economy and the opportunity for work, attracted and fostered both people from rural communities and beyond. Such was the city's economic growth in its first century, it was ranked as one of the most rapidly-expanding cities in the world. Today, urban rail is usually built to serve urban development rather than perpetrating it. Within a city, by far the most effective way of moving people is by underground railway.

New metro systems not only relieve congestion and drive regeneration, they also create an underground city that is as busy as the streets above. The architecture of stations becomes part of an urban identity and redefines local

Top: Munich's Westfriedhof Station has bare industrial concrete walls and an intricate lighting concept by Ingo Maurer.

Bottom: One of Rome's spaghetti junctions is congested despite the ban of unauthorised traffic from the central part of the city during the week. Rome's traffic congestion is an unsolved problem despite a series of drastic measures. Image courtesy of Olivo Barbieri.

Opposite top: Shanghai's widespread road transportation system is largely based on buses. This rapidly expanding metro system is conveyed here in the work of Italian photographer Olivo Barbieri. Image courtesy of Olivo Barbieri.

Opposite bottom: The Galena and Chicago Union Railroad was the first railroad in Chicago. As a result Chicago became the largest railroad centre in the world.

geography. For example, many underground stations in Bilbao, Spain, were designed by Foster+Partners in 1995 and these rise to the street in curvy, accordion-like canopies known as "Fosteritos". The signage for both the Paris Metro and the London Underground have become key parts of their respective cities' iconography. Below ground, entirely new environments are fashioned— the concourse of Los Angeles' Hollywood/Vine station is a rich evocation of early Hollywood glamour mounted with early film projectors, designed by the artist Gilbert Lujan and architect Adolfo Miralles. Platforms themselves are stages for mounting art—Stockholm has been commissioning subway art since 1950. At Brussels' Zwarte Vijvers, a 1981 painting by Jan Burssens above the tunnel entrances evokes the 'black springs' of the station's name. At Munich's Westfriedhof station, opened in 1998, huge light-shades designed by Ingo Maurer evoke film noir. Even the tunnels themselves can be adorned; for example the coloured light installations in the Shanghai subway section beneath the Bund.

The biggest problem with metro systems is that they are very expensive to build. Across China, the cost was estimated at $50 million per kilometre in 2001, however New York's Second Avenue line is costing US$4 billion just for the 2.4 kilometres of the first stage between 63rd and 96th Streets. Light rail systems, which can be anything from street trams to lightweight short trains running on elevated tracks, are a lot cheaper—in 2002, American Light Rail systems were reckoned to cost on average US$22 million per kilometre. Consequently, cities scrambling to modernise public transport often choose such systems. Phoenix, Arizona, provides an example, where the new light railway is seen as the solution to problems ranging from a lack of downtown parking places to recruiting knowledge workers who, according to a local employer, "don't like to drive". The long-awaited Metro in Mumbai; vital to its ambition to become a world city, started construction in 2008 with an elevated light rail from Versova to Ghatkopar. Such systems will transform not just local travel patterns, but will act as economic drivers and transform the built environment, creating the instant city of the future.

LOST IN SPACE

As climate change continues to escalate, vast migrationary activity is likely to occur, and the city will have to find new environments to take root in. If the majority of the planet is uninhabitable, where else do we go? Space is the obvious answer, however feasibility is clearly an issue. The energy and cost involved in transporting the entire mass of building materials for a city is enormous. In 2008, the International Space Station orbiting at around 340 kilometres from Earth had taken ten years to build and housed a permanent crew of just three. This is clearly no instant city. The total cost of the station by 2010 may be as much as US$130 billion—a prohibitive cost.

The idea of space colonies was explored at length during the 1970s and the two most serious projects relied, like Arthur C Clarke's space station in *2001: A Space Odyssey*, on rotating structures to create artificial gravity. In 1975, NASA proposed the Stanford Torus, a ring, 1.6 kilometres in diameter, spinning once a minute with mirrors positioned to reflect sunlight onto the inside of the outer ring of the structure, which would be the space station's habitable surface. This construction was envisioned to house as many as 160,000 people. The physicist Gerard O'Neill, along with his Princeton students, had earlier developed the idea of building cylinders in space and in 1977 he published *The High Frontier: Colonies in Space*, explaining them in detail. Broadly, In Island Three, paired cylinders each 30 kilometres long and six kilometres in diameter are divided lengthwise into six solid strips for colonisation. Farming takes place on a 15 kilometre ring attached to the head of the space structure, thereby enabling Island Three to theoretically support a population of 10 million. More recent visions such as Forrest Bishop's Ring World illuminated by an artificial star (a 'luminaire'), or Tom McKendree's multi-layered cylinders, are based on using carbon nanotube material technology to create spinning structures with thousands of kilometres of internal distance.

The question of sustainability is crucial to creating a city in space, and a local source of building materials and water would make the idea a lot more feasible.

Opposite top: The Earth, as viewed from the International Space Station. Its construction is a major endeavour of aerospace engineering. Image courtesy of Nasa.

Opposite bottom: An artist's impression of a space colony. Image courtesy of Nasa.

Above: Nils Norman, *Ideal City*, 2007. Installation view at Picadilly Circus Image courtesy of the artist and London Undergound. Photograph by Andy Keate. Norman's project for Transport for London's Art on the Underground consisted of an installation and a series of laminate maps in all Picadilly line trains.

Rocks can supply structural and organic material, so an existing organic structure is the most likely proposition. Water is difficult to find but hopes persist that it is frozen and accessible on the Moon and on Mars. The largest asteroid, Ceres, may harbour more water frozen beneath its surface than the Earth's oceans. Because of processes that took place in the early formation of the Solar System, smaller asteroids are less likely to contain water, but if some did, they could, theoretically, be hollowed out, to create vast new cities to live in.

BIOSPHERES

The key to the possibility of sustainable cities in space, is the self-sufficient artificial biosphere, where everything including oxygen and water is recycled and energy is produced entirely from renewable sources. Biosphere Two was the first serious attempt to build and monitor a sealed biosphere. Designed by the Biosphere Design Corporation and occupying over a hectare in the Arizona desert, near Tucson. Inside, a rainforest was cultivated and the ocean was simulated in a large water installation. The first occupant entered in 1988 and a crew of eight lived there for two years in the early 1990s. There were significant problems however—food grown never staved off hunger, animal life introduced subsequently died and carbon dioxide levels fluctuated wildly. A second crew of inhabitants were so stressed that they began to vandalise the facility and the mission was called off after just six months. This experiment has highlighted the difficulty of completely isolated sustainability and the problem of maintaining an isolated eco-system.

Although not intended to be sealed or self-sufficient, enclosed environmental projects continue, reproducing natural habitats in enclosed spaces. The geodesic dome invented by Buckminster Fuller is an efficient, robust structure to enclose space. Montreal's 62 metre high Biosphere recycles one designed for Expo 67 as a living exhibition about local water and ecosystems. The Eden Project nestling in disused clay pits in Cornwall, England, designed by Nicholas Grimshaw, was opened in 2000 and continues to expand, aiming to provide a self-sustaining

Above: A panoramic view of the geodesic domes at the Eden Project, Cornwall.

Opposite: View of the Biosphere in Montreal, whose geodesic dome was designed by Buckminster Fuller.

natural environment to use as a model for biospeheric human habitats. Here, a number of geodesic domes house different ecologies—the 1.55 hectare Humid Tropics Biome at 55 metres high, is the largest greenhouse in the world. Already, there are 5,000 plant species being cultivated in the Eden Project

These examples show where work on biospheres has taken us so far and serve to remind us that the ecosystems within them are microcosms of the largest and most complex biosphere of all—the Earth. It supports millions of plant species, as well as animals, humans—and their cities—and its upkeep is immeasurably more complex than any artificial biosphere. For the moment, we are rooted on it and the most pressing challenge in the coming century is to adapt the city in order to allow the survival of this original biosphere.

DUBAI METRO

The Dubai Metro project is an automated, driverless rapid transit system currently under construction in the United Arab Emirates city of Dubai. The £2 billion, 70 kilometre long, first phase consists of two 'Lines', Red and Green, linking Jebel Ali Port and the Airport Free Zone via the American University and the city centre, and the Festival City and Rashidiya via the city and Terminals 1 and 3 of Dubai International Aiprort respectively. It is anticipated that these first Lines will be fully operational by September 2009, and Dubai Road and Transport Authority estimates that they will carry 1.2 million passengers on an average day between them. Two additional Lines—Blue and Purple—will follow at a later date, extending the network further. When completed, the Dubai Metro will be the world's longest fully automated metro system at a proposed 319 kilometres by 2020. Groundworks began on the Red Line in February 2006, with a Japanese-Turkish consortium—Dubai Rapid Link—undertaking the work on the first phase.

The plan for a high-tech urban rail system in Dubai was begun under the leadership of Sheikh Mohammed bin Rashid Al Maktoum, who had set a target to increase Dubai's visitor numbers to 15 million by 2010. Increased tourism, the city's growth as a hub for international business activity and relentless property development have since made this figure a realistic possibility. Combined with Dubai's growing resident population—the city had 1.9 million inhabitants in 2006 and forecasts have put the population at around 5.25 million by 2020—it was obvious that Dubai's transport infrastructure would have to be overhauled in order to cope. A particularly car-centric city, Dubai has suffered severe congestion and air pollution as its ever-growing population takes to the roads. In order to relieve traffic problems, increase capacity and facilitate future development, an urban rail system—running on a combination of city centre underground tunnels and suburban elevated viaducts—was identified as the most suitable solution, a bold and costly undertaking for a city where the surface development becomes more dense every month. In this era of transit oriented development (TOD), where transport networks are integrated from a development's inception, it is relatively

DUBAI METRO AND BEIJING AIRPORT

Artist's rendering of
the elevated tracks of
the Dubai Metro.

rare to find such an infrastructure being retrofitted wholesale.

Unusually for a retrofitted transit infrastructure, the Dubai Metro system will be fully integrated with other public and private means of transport. Bus routes and taxi ranks will be organised around Metro stations and, at suburban stations, there will be park and ride facilities for travel into the city centre. An integrated smart card ticketing system will be introduced to allow passengers problem-free transition between different modes of transport. The rail system is either elevated or below ground—at no point do the Metro rails run across roads—and this segregation will ensure the smooth flow of traffic across all transport modes. Eventually, it is hoped that a 268 kilometre network of light rail 'feeder' lines will make the Metro system accessible to areas even further outside the city. The Red Line will have 29 stations in total, four of which will be underground, and the Green Line will have 14, with six underground; there will be interchange stations at Al Ittihad Square and Burjuman for passengers to connect between lines. The viaducts for the network's elevated sections have been designed specifically to enhance the urban architectural aesthetics of their surroundings.

In May 2007 the 49 kilometre Purple Line received official approval. This express, eight-station Line will link the current international airport with the new Dubai World Central International Airport which is being built at Jebel Ali, part of a 140 square kilometre multi-mode transport hub.

The network's rolling stock is equally impressive. In order to minimise both the visual and environmental impact of the new system the Red and Green Line trains will operate on a 'third rail' electrical collection system, which removes the need for intrusive overhead power lines. Each line will utilise almost 100 five-car, 75 metre long trains, with seats for up to 400 passengers on each train and standing room for many more. Trains have been designed to meet Dubai's specific climatic and cultural needs: each fully air conditioned train will offer standard and first class accommodation, along with a women and children only section. Long, panoramic windows will allow passengers to make the most of the view of the city through the elevated sections of the network, and although the trains are driverless, passengers will be accompanied by trained wardens to assist them. In January 2008 the Road and Transport Authority delegation witnessed the

technical trial run of a Dubai Metro train on the test track at Mistubishi Heavy Industries, Mihara City, Japan, and the first trains are expected to arrive in Dubai by late 2008. For many, the Dubai Metro represents a shift in the city authorities' priorities. Dubai has built a reputation on its commitment to facilitating a high luxury lifestyle well out of the reach of most ordinary citizens, and its car culture was just another aspect of this. In planning and building a rapid transit system as a municipal project which will, in theory, be accessible to everyone (the planned fare for a single journey is around 2.75 UAE dirham, about 40p) the Metro could represent a new 'democratising' of the Dubai authorities' vision. In full operation the Red and Green Lines will carry 355 million passengers per year, and the Road and Transport Authority claim that the Metro's operating costs (including staff, maintenance and power) will be easily met through fares and advertising revenue. They do not, however, see Dubai's populace abandoning their personal vehicles altogether; estimating that Metro journeys will eventually account for a modest 12 per cent of total journeys in Dubai.

Beijing Capital
International Airport,
Terminal 3, opened in
2008 and designed by
Foster+Partners.

BEIJING AIRPORT TERMINAL 3

One of the most impressive of the many multi-billion pound constructions ready to greet visitors to the twenty-ninth Olympic Games is the new Beijing Airport Terminal 3, designed and built in just four years at a cost of £1.8 billion and with an approximated 50,000 construction workers on site at its height. With ground first broken in March 2004, the Foster+Partners-designed terminal building opened on 29 February 2008, in effect doubling the capacity of the airport (it is estimated that the facility will handle 580,000 flights per year by 2015). The first six airlines moved in to begin operations a week after opening.

The terminal building is the world's largest and arguably most advanced airport building, both in terms of the sustainable technology it utilises and the quality of passenger experience it provides. The anticipated sharp increase in passengers travelling to Beijing for the 2008 Olympics was the catalyst for its construction and the new terminal will be capable of processing— via 120 gates—an estimated 60 million passengers per year by 2015. It measures 800 metres across at its widest point, and encloses a total floor area of 1.3 million square metres; 17 per cent larger than all of London Heathrow's five terminals put together and the first building ever to exceed the one million square metre mark.

Foster+Partners—in partnership with Dutch airport planners NACO and engineers Arup— were awarded the contract in November 2003 after a competitive tender process which attracted submissions from a number of leading architectural practices and design teams. The collaborators' previous experience in contemporary 'flagship' airport design recommended them to the job, having previously worked on the then groundbreaking 1991 Stansted airport redesign (which re-oriented airport design for a new era of large-plan terminal buildings of lightweight construction and underground services and infrastructure) and on Hong Kong's Chep Lap Kok airport, 1998, one of whose many design challenges included the formation of an island to accommodate part of the terminal.

The form of the Beijing terminal building takes its lead from these previous designs in terms of its lightweight above-ground construction, floating roof, integrated services and use of natural lighting, but its scale and the minutely detailed thinking behind its features is unprecedented. It is not merely a functional and sustainable design, but one that is intended to be culturally meaningful and passenger experience-focused; a welcoming, uplifting and aesthetically pleasing—as well as efficient—space. Using the concept of 'spatial clarity' as a guiding design principle, the terminal is formed by two curved Y-shaped lightweight structures topped by a unifying soaring roof canopy, creating a vast, cathedral-like space open to outside views and natural light to both elevations. As it is a deep plan building, the penetration of natural light to the centre of the terminal is aided by a central line of skylights running the length of the building along the north-south axis, and this subconsciously aids passengers' orientation as they move through the building. These rooflights— themselves angled southeast—also efficiently capture thermal energy to warm the air and minimise the terminal's heating load, but are small enough to mean it does not require much cooling in the summer months. The building makes use throughout of such passive environmental technology in a sophisticated, sustainable building management system. The roof is clad with uneven raised triangular 'scales', which aid cooling in summer and heat retention in winter and which echo the aesthetic of Foster+Partners' other works based on repeated geometric elements.

The form of this cladding has been likened to the scales on a dragon's back, and comprises part of the design team's attempts to instil a distinctly Chinese aesthetic in the terminal building. Even the colour scheme—red, gold and green—has been carefully selected to evoke Chinese tradition and positive symbolism; echoing Beijing's Forbidden City, the Ming Dynasty palace in the centre of the city. As passengers move through the building, tints on the skylights change from yellow to red. Foster+Partners also consulted a Feng Shui expert on the ideal shape and layout of the arrival area, in order to create a space as calming and inviting for passengers as possible. To ensure an impeccable standard of passenger care, the terminal features 'barrier free' facilities for the disabled floor tracking for the visually impaired and multi-denominational prayer rooms. 26 designated smoking rooms are fitted out with advanced filtering systems.

On a larger scale, the entire building had to be as efficient as possible while also retaining the potential for future expansion and modification. The chosen form and configuration of the buildings maximises the perimeter available for aircraft stands, while maintaining a compact footprint. Bringing everything closer together under a single roof aids communication and simplifies the passenger experience and airport services. Rapid transport within the terminal itself and public transport connections are fully integrated, walking distances for passengers are short with few level changes, and transfer times between flights are minimised. This configuration also allows maximum flexibility in the future; the modular construction allows for easy expansion should passenger number exceed predictions.

The expansion project, though passing into service almost completely without hitch, has not been without its controversies. In common with many other large, state-planned construction projects in China the location of the new Beijing terminal has been rumoured to have required the compulsory relocation of around 10,000 people from nine nearby villages, and the working conditions and rates of pay endured by the local Chinese construction workers on the project are said to have been far from acceptable by Western standards. Its completion in less than four years has inevitably invited comparisons with Heathrow's Terminal 5, opened in complete disarray a few weeks later after more than 20 years in the pipeline. As Norman Foster pointed out to the BBC, it took the same length of time to complete the entire Beijing Terminal 3 building as it did to complete a public enquiry into the viability of a Heathrow expansion, let alone design and build it. To bring an airport in on time and on budget, as *The Times* architecture critic Tom Dyckhoff recently put it, it seems "you can't beat a one-party state".[1]

1. Dyckhoff, Tom, "Cattle Queues at last give way to Civil Aviation", *The Times*, 15 March 2008.

Interior of Terminal
3 at Beijing Capital
International Airport.
The many windows in
the terminal roof allow
the building to be filled
with daylight, and can
be adjusted to ensure
appropriate lighting.
Image courtesy
of Nigel Young/
Foster+Partners.

SOMALI REFUGEES IN EASTLEIGH, NAIROBI

Manuel Herz

Refugees often represent one of the weakest and most vulnerable members of a society. They are conceived of as a unanimous mass, warehoused in refugee camps and more often than not can't decide upon the context and circumstances of their lives. Their physical location is a key factor for this powerlessness (refugee camps are usually located in remote areas). The distance to a social, cultural or economical context limits the possibilities of refugees and creates a dependency on humanitarian aid. Cities and urban regions, on the other hand, could provide refugees with the potential of exchange on various level and therefore with a certain level of independence. It is exactly because of this reason, though—seen as unfair competition by a local population and politicians—that many countries deny refugees their rights to settle in urban regions and a consciously controlled impotence is created, which only strengthens the image of the refugee as a passive recipient of assistance and charity.

Urban refugees represent a minority amongst displaced people. Especially in Africa—the continent currently most affected by forced migration—only about ten per cent of refugees and internally displaced people are settled in an urban context. The few examples of urban refugee communities, however, paint a different picture to the one of the refugee as parasitical profiteer. Arising from the pressure of self-sustainability, their (at times existential) willingness to occupy niches and the international network that refugees are often embedded in are complex and lively urban conditions which are of benefit to the local population as well as to the refugees themselves.

EASTLEIGH

It had been raining throughout the night. The (still wet) air is saturated with the smell of rotting food and human sweat. Thousands of minibuses and trucks force themselves through narrow streets. Diesel exhaust flows as thick black pulp from the exhaust pipes and fills the air with a nauseating stench. The streets are covered ankle deep in mud. Dense masses of people move and push themselves in a perpetual flow through the narrow gaps left by the cars. Hawkers sell plastic buckets and coat hangers, t-shirts and jeans. Somali street vendors offer household goods or plastic jewellery. The few existing pavements are filled with parking minibuses and pick-up trucks unloading goods or packing them in adventurous constructions on top of the vehicles' roofs. A continuous strip of shopping plazas flanks both sides of the roads.

'1st Avenue' is the main street of Eastleigh, an area of Nairobi located two kilometres east of the city centre. Shaped by the

dominating presence of Somali refugees, it is one of the most intense and striking places in the Kenyan capital and, at the same time, a centre of a global trade network. Also coined 'Small-Mogadishu' for being a dislocated proxy seat of government of a disintegrated country, Eastleigh—with its approximately 100,000 inhabitants—represents one of the largest Somali cities, and the second largest contiguous Somali community outside of Somalia itself. Because of the relatively well-established infrastructure in Nairobi, it is assuming administrative functions of the barely operating capital of Mogadishu. A major part of Somali trade is coordinated via Eastleigh, one of the few operating Somali banks has its headquarters located there, it is a centre of the Somali finance network and location for meetings of Somali ministers and politicians of various fractions to discuss the future of a tragic country. Populated predominantly by non-registered refugees who

are not in possession of legal documents—living there informally or illegally—it is a part of Nairobi, located in its very heart, but ignored by the administration of the Kenyan capital, its population "hidden in plain view".

FROM AN ASIAN TOWN TO AN AFRICAN CITY

Nairobi started off as an Asian city. A few years after it was founded in 1896, as a station of the East African Railway half way between Mombasa on the Indian Ocean and Kisumu on Lake Victoria, Indian traders started settling in the city. At that time hardly any local Kenyan population was living in Nairobi. Kenyans were only allowed to live within the boundary of the city as bachelors and if they had a formal job employed by one of the white settlers or by one of the companies of the city. Their families had to reside beyond the city limits in other parts of the country.

Indian and Arabic traders who had dominated trade along the east African coast played an essential part in the construction of the train line and were moving with it to Nairobi, especially to Eastleigh. The neighbourhoods of the few white settlers in the west of the city—located at a higher altitude, marked by forests, winding roads and an abundance of little streams and rivulets— profit from a good climate and fresh air. Eastleigh, located in the dusty east of the city, was laid out in a chessboard-like street pattern, with six avenues in north-south orientation, intersected by 15 streets in east-west orientation. The Indians settling there developed efficient trading structures and quickly dominated most of the trade in the city. A policy change in the 1940s allowed Kenyan families to join their husbands and fathers in Nairobi. This coincided with the growing wealth of the Asian trading community, which was moving to the better neighbourhoods of Westlands and Parklands in the west of the city. Eastleigh was thus again to become an 'immigrant's' neighbourhood, this time for a population of local Kenyans, all moving into the colonial capital for the first time. With the political independence of Kenya in 1963, segregation of residential spaces along ethnic lines were abolished, and the population of Nairobi increased considerably. Along with the Kenyans from villages and rural areas, some Somali traders move to Eastleigh and settled there.

With the toppling of the Somali president, Siad Barre, in 1991 civil war broke out in the country at the Horn of Africa. Somalia suffered from famine, lack of basic needs, the destruction of its infrastructure, and slid into a condition of anarchy and lawlessness. Within a short period of time hundreds of thousands of Somalis fled into Kenya. They were placed into refugee camps near the Kenyan city of Dadaab, and eked out a dismal existence in this disconnected part of the country. The Kenyan government which, during the 1980s and 90s, had practiced liberal and generous refugee policies and had granted refugees full mobility within the whole country, now opted for more restricted regulations when facing the increase of the refugee flow. From this point on all refugees had to reside in the camps and were not allowed to take on work. The refugee camps in the east of the country became virtual prisons.

Considerable numbers of those fleeing from Somalia are well-off traders from Mogadishu. They come from an urban background and are not used to the 'rural' way of life in the camps. Having sold off their goods and real estate before their escape to Kenya, they arrive with gold and cash. With the lack of trading possibilities in the refugee camps, they move to Nairobi. Based on the pre-existing contact with the Somalis who have lived in Kenya's

capital for longer, they situate themselves in Eastleigh. Thus, for its third time, Eastleigh becomes an immigrant's quarter for Somali refugees who are settling there illegitimately. Initially Somali refugees travelled to Nairobi with the aim of settling administrative affairs so as to move on quickly to London, Dubai or America. Guesthouses and other kinds of lodgings are constructed where they pass the time waiting to receive their exit visas. One of these guesthouses is 'Garissa Lodge' located on 1st Avenue. The refugees—arriving with considerable amounts of money and often lingering for months before finishing their administrative affairs— begin to spend their time trading and, as they cannot set up their own infrastructure, they run such businesses from their hotel rooms. As a result, Garissa Lodge has slowly changed from an accommodation space into a trading place (it was recently bought by a—now legendary—Somali refugee and business woman who

MANUEL HERZ

has completely transformed it into a shopping mall). This nucleus of Somali trading centres in Eastleigh has multiplied quickly, many of which have sprung up along Eastleigh's central road. This proliferation of trading has attracted an even greater number of Somali refugees to Eastleigh; an estimated 100,000 people now live in the streets of 'Small-Mogadishu'.

SHOPPING MALLS

The Amal Shopping Plaza currently represents the most developed and sophisticated standard of shopping mall in Eastleigh. Located next to the former Garissa Lodge, recently renamed 'Bangkok Shopping Mall', it is the highlight of retail environments in this urban refugee settlement. Over four floors, products from all over the world are sold for the lowest prices. The distribution of merchandise within the building follows a specific curatorial

Opposite: 1st Avenue, the main trade centre for the Somali community in Eastleigh, Nairobi.

Above: The population of Somali refugees has increased due to the possibilities for trade in Eastleigh, and the area has fast developed an economic hub despite its illegitimate nature.

concept. On the ground floor cheap textiles are sold in bulk. The individual shop units, each having a size of approximately six square metres, are completely filled from floor to ceiling. Trading usually takes place either in a small niche within the merchandise itself or in the corridors in front of the store; a functional separation between storage and shopping does not exist. More than 160 stores are offering commodities in this condensed way. Higher quality clothing is sold on the first floor. For 500 to 1,000 Kenyan Shilling (approximately £5–7) one can buy Jeans from China, or t-shirts for a fraction of the price. On the second floor, two or three single units are joined into larger stores selling shoes, sneakers, dresses or suits. Electronic stores sell televisions, hi-fi systems and mobile phones. The more service-oriented businesses are located on the third floor. Travel agents offer flights to any destination world wide, a Western-Union branch and offices of the global Islamic money banking system—Hawala—can transmit money within minutes to places all over the world and an Afghan fast food restaurant serves excellent lunch next to a local mosque. At the other end of the floor a clinic run by the Aga Khan Trust offers medical services to the local population. The offices of Amal's general management are located one floor higher, separated from the main shopping centre.

The individual levels of the Amal Shopping Plaza are connected by a sequence of intersecting, cascading and spiral staircases, ramps, bridges, elevators, galleries and access corridors. Various internal voids and atriums bring daylight down to the lowest floors creating a complex three-dimensional structure of shopping areas, circulation spaces and communication zones. It is an architecture that simultaneously merges aspects of the informal and vernacular with the highly formalised and conventional. Elements of a standardised repertoire of shopping malls such as galleries and atriums are compressed and densified, and then combined with functions such as mosques, money trading or bulk shopping. Three separate circulation systems exist in parallel and within each other: a complex system of stairways, with intermediate landings and connected bridges that are used as the main circulation system by the majority of visitors; ramps which are used to roll, carry or push the commodities to the individual shops, though also used by the general public; and two elevators installed mostly for representational reasons as they were the first elevators to be built in Eastleigh (symbolising modernity and comfort) though are hardly used on a daily basis. All three systems of circulation are folded into each other, linked and connected, sometimes changing directions, leading upwards and then downwards again. Together with the atriums and galleries, they create a complex

Right and left: Street scenes in Eastleigh, Nairobi, showing the shops and stalls that line the area.

Opposite: Shopfronts in Eastleigh, Nairobi.

space of seemingly free movement in any direction and in all three dimensions where shopping, trade, delivery, supply, storage, bargaining, dealing and transactions take place simultaneously.

The Amal Shopping Plaza was constructed in 2003. Since then a number of additional shopping malls have been built and more are in planning phase or undergoing construction. Shopping malls have identified architecture as a medium of identification and a means to achieve a notion of uniqueness with their customers. They compete with the most expressive facades, shapes of windows, systems of stairs and ramps, as well as with their size, in order to attract more customers.

A GLOBAL TRADING NETWORK

The civil war that broke out in 1991 (which has continued more or less unabatedly) has created a Somali diaspora that extends over the whole world. Somali refugees live all over Africa, on the Arabian Peninsula, in North America, Europe, Australia and East Asia. This Somali Diaspora has, amongst other things, developed a global trading network whose center is in Eastleigh. Transactions are prepared and conducted via Somali middlemen and contact persons in Dubai, Hong Kong, Minneapolis or London. The merchandise reaches the Somali neighbourhood mostly via Dubai and Mombasa, Kenya's port on the Indian Ocean. Scores of trucks enter Eastleigh daily to supply the individual shops with goods. Neither central distribution points nor storage facilities exist in the neighbourhood. As is the case in the shops themselves, there is no separation between retail, wholesale, trade, storage or warehousing. Semi-trailer trucks and 18-wheelers with huge containers squeeze themselves through the narrow streets of Eastleigh, stop in front of a shopping mall, and unload the goods by hand which are then carried through its main entrance and stuffed into the small shop units. Streets are blocked for hours and the traffic repeatedly comes to a complete standstill.

It is not only the merchandise that reaches Eastleigh from all over the world. Because they are able to take advantage of global price differences in their wholesale purchases, due to the low transport costs and the fact that they are often able to evade import taxes, the Somali traders can offer their merchandise at very competitive prices. What started as a local market, whose relevance hardly went beyond the extent of the neighbourhood itself, quickly gained influence over trade of the whole region. By now the group of people who take advantage of the low prices offered by the Somali refugees come from all over Nairobi, and has even grown far beyond. Customers, middlemen and other shop owners come from all of Kenya, Uganda, Tanzania and Rwanda into the Somali neighbourhood to purchase goods in bulk, which they then resell in their home regions. Eastleigh, this dirty, dense, intense and most striking neighbourhood of Somali refugees has become one of the main trading centres of East Africa.

REFUGEES AS SPATIAL ACTORS

Somali refugees in Kenya are consciously acting on a spatial level. They have set up a matrix of places, both inside and outside of this host country, and are able to take advantage of the different potentials these locations offer. Structural interrelations exist especially between Eastleigh and the refugee camps near Dadaab, with their 180,000 inhabitants roughly twice the size of the Somali community in Nairobi. Refugee families living in the camps usually send their sons to several places—the town of Garissa located near the camps, to Nairobi and, if possible, to Dubai—in order to explore their potentials. Their task is to investigate the financial possibilities, conditions of personal security and general quality of life as well as support the family back in the camps financially. On a monthly basis, sums in the range of $50 to a few hundred dollars—so-called remittances—are transferred from Nairobi back to the families in the refugee camps. Even though their temporary residence might transform into a permanent settlement, for many inhabitants Eastleigh is a place where they can earn money as 'foreign workers' to support their families and eventually to return to their home country. As the Somali refugees living in Eastleigh are often registered in one of the refugee camps, they have to return there on a recurrent basis. In regular intervals, UNHCR registers the refugees and performs headcounts in the camps. They are usually announced a few days prior and are of importance to the refugees as entitlements to food rations and

other material support is distributed based on this registration. A headcount in Dadaab means big business for the travel and bus companies that are based in Eastleigh offering daily connections to the refugee camps and to many other places all over East Africa. The night before, the streets of Eastleigh are even more congested with people and their luggage, when hundreds, if not thousands, of refugees set out to travel through the whole country to be registered by UNHCR in Ifo, Dagahaley and Hagadera, and then drive back again the following day. Even though being one of the most vibrant parts of Nairobi, on a certain level Eastleigh represents a mere outpost of the refugee camps in the east of the country.

With all the urban qualities, the intensity and the vibrancy that Eastleigh exhibits its quality of life is problematic. The air is heavily polluted by the countless cars, minibuses and trucks. Playing fields for children do not exist, just as there are no parks or recreational areas. Most of the buildings are in bad condition and their sanitary facilities are inadequate. Nevertheless the rent levels have risen sharply in the last few years. Even though occupied almost exclusively by Somalis, many of the residential buildings are not in Somali hands. Today, they acknowledge their mistake of having invested predominantly in trade and not in real estate. Because of the high population density and the fact that living closely together in one neighbourhood has a priority for the refugee community, Kenyan landlords can charge almost arbitrary rental fees without relation to the quality of the residential spaces.

As the density is ever increasing, rental fees continue to climb, the quality of life remains unsatisfactory and the lack of expansion area within the neighbourhood is becoming more and more obvious, urging the question: how will Eastleigh develop in the

coming years? It is ever more apparent that the neighbourhood and its residents have to develop new spatial strategies, because the pressure of the rising population cannot be accommodated and a further increase of trading facilities is not possible locally. Due to lack of suitable sites additional shopping centres cannot be built along 1st Avenue. Somali refugees and investors have realised these tendencies and have started a process of creating satellites of their neighbourhood on three scales.

Within Nairobi, Somali traders start developing areas and individual streets outside of Eastleigh. Taking over individual shops in streets near the central business district, they expand rapidly, controlling those streets in no time. A dislocated piece of Eastleigh, with all its density, distinctive sounds, smells and visual qualities swiftly moves into an area previously held by other trading communities.

The investors and owners of the shopping centres, who are experiencing the limits of growth in Eastleigh first-hand, are developing even larger scale strategies of expansion. Once again Amal Shopping Plaza, despite the limits of its 4,000 square metre plot size, is at the forefront of formulating new business strategies for Eastleigh's shopping malls. Two years ago this Somali trading centre opened a brand new mall in Johannesburg. Currently the management is in the process of establishing itself in cities of their home country. A branch of Amal Shopping Plaza has just opened in Mogadishu and two further malls are currently under construction in the Somali cities of Bosaso and Galkaio. In a strange reversal of the principle of dislocation, it is now Somali refugees in Nairobi that have started economically settling and colonising their home country, and establishing some of the few operating infrastructures and businesses on home territory: a dislocation of the dislocated, a 'diasporisation' on domestic ground.

In the meantime the Eastleigh Business Community is considering how smaller cities in the periphery of Nairobi can be identified as new areas of settlement for Somali refugee traders, and how development of trading infrastructures in these towns can be started. The focus lies on the cities of Thika and Athi River, each lying approximately 30 kilometres northeast and southeast of Nairobi's centre. Somalian refugees will be pioneers in a process of metropolitanisation that the Nairobi City Council has been planning for years, but has been unsuccessful in implementing. Having grown beyond the relatively small-scale administrative borders of the city, Nairobi is attempting to formulate a coherent scenario of urbanisation and growth in coordination with the surrounding towns and communities. The cooperation of the individual communities has, so far, been less than satisfactory, and any steps towards implementation have repeatedly been delayed. One cannot deny the irony when Somali refugees, unwelcomed and unwanted by state institutions and the city administration, are pursuing this process of metropolitanisation more constructively and with a better understanding of the urban fabric than the Nairobi City Council seems to be capable of.

Somali refugees have developed a fascinating neighbourhood with urban qualities—but also pronounced problems and deficiencies—that can hardly be found in any other part of Nairobi. As the centre of a hectic, efficient and very professionally run global trading network, providing all of East Africa with goods, developed and built by residents with no legal status, and exhibiting an intense urban culture, Eastleigh is probably unique in its current form.

It exhibits a conscious understanding of urban operations and spatial practices. Different places within the city are strategically selected and occupied. The relationships between Nairobi and the neighbouring countries, as well as those between Eastleigh and the refugee camps, are utilised and taken advantage of, and the services of the neighbourhood, and the neighbourhood itself is outsourced, dislocated and replicated elsewhere. Faster than the Nairobi City Council the Somali refugees have realised the benefits of a large-scale metropolitan region and are being implemented long before the apathetic and self-obstructing local administration can develop concrete ideas or plans. Born of a need, a financial interest and a well-connected network of different players, they are practitioners of spatial planning.

Housing typical of the
refugees that live in
Eastleigh, Nairobi.

GLOBAL | LOCAL

At the beginning of 2008, an architectural competition to regenerate a run-down square in Zürich was won by an entry that featured a reproduction of a recently demolished house in Chongqing, China. Rejuvenating Escher-Wyss-Platz into an attractive built environment had presented a challenge, not least because a highway overpass runs along one side of the Swiss square. In the scheme by architect Caruso St John and the artist Thomas Demand, a line of old Chongqing shops is reproduced, and next to them, jutting just above the level of the overpass, a replica is planned of the Nail House, which rose to international fame in 2007. Its owners, unlike all their neighbours in Chongqing, refused the bullying of a local developer who had acquired and cleared the rest of the site to make way for a shopping mall. The Nail House was left standing on a finger of land surrounded by a ten metre deep hole, until the developers eventually increased their offer and the owners finally acquiesced.

Escher-Wyss-Platz tells us many things about the way cities operate at both local and global levels. First, some cities are of global significance, but whatever mix of criteria provide for that state of affairs, it is clear that size alone is relatively insignificant. For example, Zurich is a world financial city, but it only has a population of 370,000 (in a conurbation of one million). Chongqing, on the other hand, is a conurbation estimated to have anywhere from 3.3 to ten million inhabitants (in a municipality of 31 million), with the city populated by those displaced from the Three Gorges Dam project, and the rural poor seeking employment and opportunity in line with a trend prevalent throughout the developing world. Chongqing is China's largest inland metropolis, and by some estimates the fastest growing metropolis in the world, but isn't well-known outside of China's borders.

Despite their obvious differences and their approach to urban planning—Zürich's success is already well-established while Chongqing's is still very much developing, Zürich can afford to commission a unique civic scheme, while Chongqing is more concerned with establishing itself as a 'modern' city through the construction of buildings that communicate modernity—in the main, both settlements refer to a global aesthetic, rather than a vernacular culture.

THE SPREAD OF HOMOTOPIA
It can be said that Far Eastern cities build themselves up as heterotopias of Western cities, and the built environments in Zurich and Las Vegas indicate that a similar trend extends to Western locales as well. But what if elements were not just transposed from one place to another, but entire urban environments, and the activities that went along within them? Such places could be called "Homotopia", and, in certain light industry sectors (retail, for example), they are spreading so rapidly they are in some sense instant cities in their own right.

In Britain, the expression "clone town" has been coined to describe high streets in disparate geographical locales that are all lined with the same shops, branded with the same signage and express the same physical characteristics. The international version of the clone town street is now the clone mall, ubiquitous across Europe, North America, China, Japan, the United Arab Emirates and elsewhere. When the new Chongqiang mall opens, it is likely to be occupied by Western retail and food outlets, increasingly familiar to the Chinese population. Fast food restaurants such as Subway, Starbucks, Haagen Dazs, KFC and Pizza Hut have long since made their home in malls and high streets of the developing world. McDonalds expect to have 1,000 branches in 2008, while KFC already have more than 1,700 Chinese outlets. All of these franchises are marked with the same signage and logos that pepper the streets and malls of the Western world, creating an eerie similarity between geographically distinct cities.

There are new shopping centres that are exceptions to these homotopic trends in architecture and shop decor. A good example is the thriving Lehel Market in Budapest, designed by László Rajk. Here, the architecture is exuberantly deconstructivist, offering a postmodernist re-interpretation of the city's nineteenth century architectural styles. In Lehel, the traders themselves are strictly local, and there are no "anchor tenants", as chain retailers leasing large floorspaces (usually over multiple floors) are termed.

Opposite and above:
The Continuous Monument is a concept proposed the radical Italian architectural group Superstudio, founded in 1966. Wrapping itself around the globe, destroying natural landscapes and eroding cultural diversity, the *Monument* would swallow all in a vast, generic, Western-style urban superstructure; Superstudio's comment on the way in which globalisation was taking over the world.

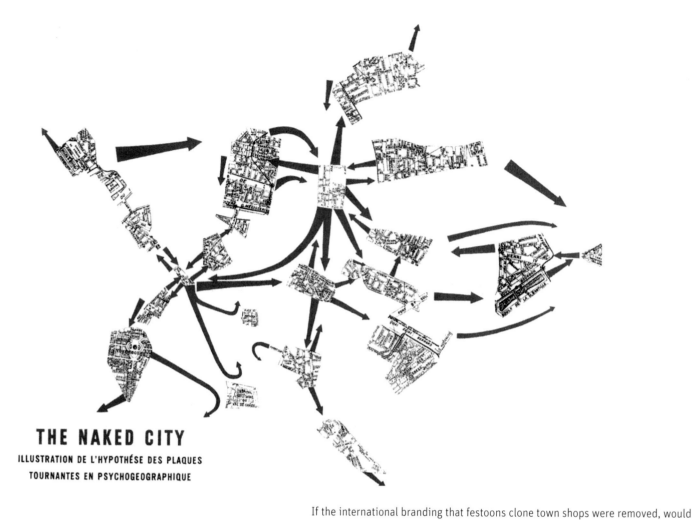

THE NAKED CITY
ILLUSTRATION DE L'HYPOTHÉSE DES PLAQUES TOURNANTES EN PSYCHOGEOGRAPHIQUE

Above: *The Naked City* psychogeographical map, Guy Debord, 1958. This map summerises the attitudes and concepts of the Situationists in abstract form. Notions such as the *dérive*, and *détournment* come into play here, evidenced by the arrows that depict movement and the details of specific cities.

Opposite top:
Situation 1 from the series *Hidden*

Town, 2004–2007, Linz-Warsaw-London. In his exploration of the urban landscape, Gregor Graf reduces images of the city to generic urban scenes by removing any textual or visual information that might give clues as to identity or locality.

Opposite bottom:
Illustration from the *Situationist Internationale*, No. 3, Constant Niueweneys, 1959.

Following pages: *The Descriptive Map of London Poverty*, 1889, Charles Booth. Booth's map was the first of its kind to document the 'geography' of social groups within the city. After the 1889 there was fierce competition to produce new, and more complex, maps aiming to show similar such socially-directed data.

If the international branding that festoons clone town shops were removed, would a sense of the local return? In his 2006 photographic project *Hidden Town*, the Austrian artist Gregor Graf manipulated photos of London, Linz and Warsaw to strip them of not just brand shop-signs, but all people and signage as well. The result of this, in an image of London's Oxford Street, is a restoration of the original facades lurking behind the commercial veneer, but it also strips the street of its big-city atmosphere. The Victorian jumble of buildings could belong to any British medium-sized town. This suggests that at a national level at least, clone street shops are merely the most obvious and superficial of factors that have been eroding local urban identities for hundreds of years. The geographical spread of vernacular architectural styles is another such factor. Gothic architecture, for example, spread across Europe in Medieval times, with relatively subtle variations between countries and regions. Homotopia, therefore, is not a uniquely modern phenomenon.

Nevertheless, there are other modern phenomena that simultaneously represent the globalisation of the local in any city, and the localisation of the global at a particular spot. Examples include CBDs marked by skyscrapers (in the 1960s and 70s, these were even built in the 'international style') or system-built public housing projects, or the swathes of expressways and junctions with their curving multi-level patterns of access roads.

PSYCHOGEOGRAPHICAL NEIGHBOURHOOD TRANSFORMATIONS
Despite globalisation, cities maintain local identities—a person beamed randomly into Amsterdam or Lhasa or Cairo would instantly be able to tell that they were in one of those cities and not the others just by looking around. The architecture and activities seen in different parts of the world go a long way to ensure that the world's cities will not all blend into one indistinguishable main street arcade. Psychogeography is a concept devised to account for these and other cultural markers of the physical environment. Psychogeography first came to prominence

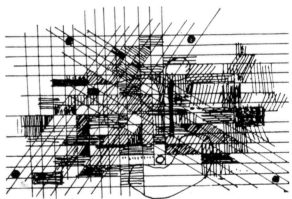

as a concept when leading theorist, Guy Debord, coined and defined the term in 1955. In putting forth this framework, Debord was primarily interested in the emotional and behavioural effects of a specific location. In order to determine the psychogeographical map of a particular location, Debord proposed the *dérive*, a walk through local streets guided only by impulse and observation. Debord noted:

> The sudden change of ambiance in a street within the space of a few metres; the evident division of a city into zones of distinct psychic atmospheres; the path of least resistance which is automatically followed in aimless strolls (and which has no relation to the physical contour of the ground); the appealing or repelling character of certain places—all this seems to be neglected.[1]

In this century, psychogeography has experienced a modest revival in literature (for example, Iain Sinclair's 2002 book *London Orbital* explores the literal edge of the city lurking around the M25 orbital motorway) and in group activities (for example, the New York festival Psy.Geo.Conflux in which artistic events, games and new variations of dérive were organised). Psychogeographical maps themselves may seem rare, but many urban maps of sociological interest have psychogeographical elements to them. When Charles Booth published the *Descriptive Map of London Poverty* in 1889, marking each street both geographically and by the social characteristics of their inhabitants, has arrived at a psychogeographical survey of London. Booth's map aimed to highlight, through colour-coding, how poverty could be geographically mapped throughout the capital, quantified household by household. It was one of the first of its kind to succinctly identify socio-economic patterns in map form and to distinguish between one locale and another on sociological, rather than geographical, criteria. The neighbourhood maps in guide books and estate agents valuations are both derived from psychogeographical principles, mapping a built environment using social—rather than physical—criteria, and thereby revealing the fundamentally local characteristics of a site.

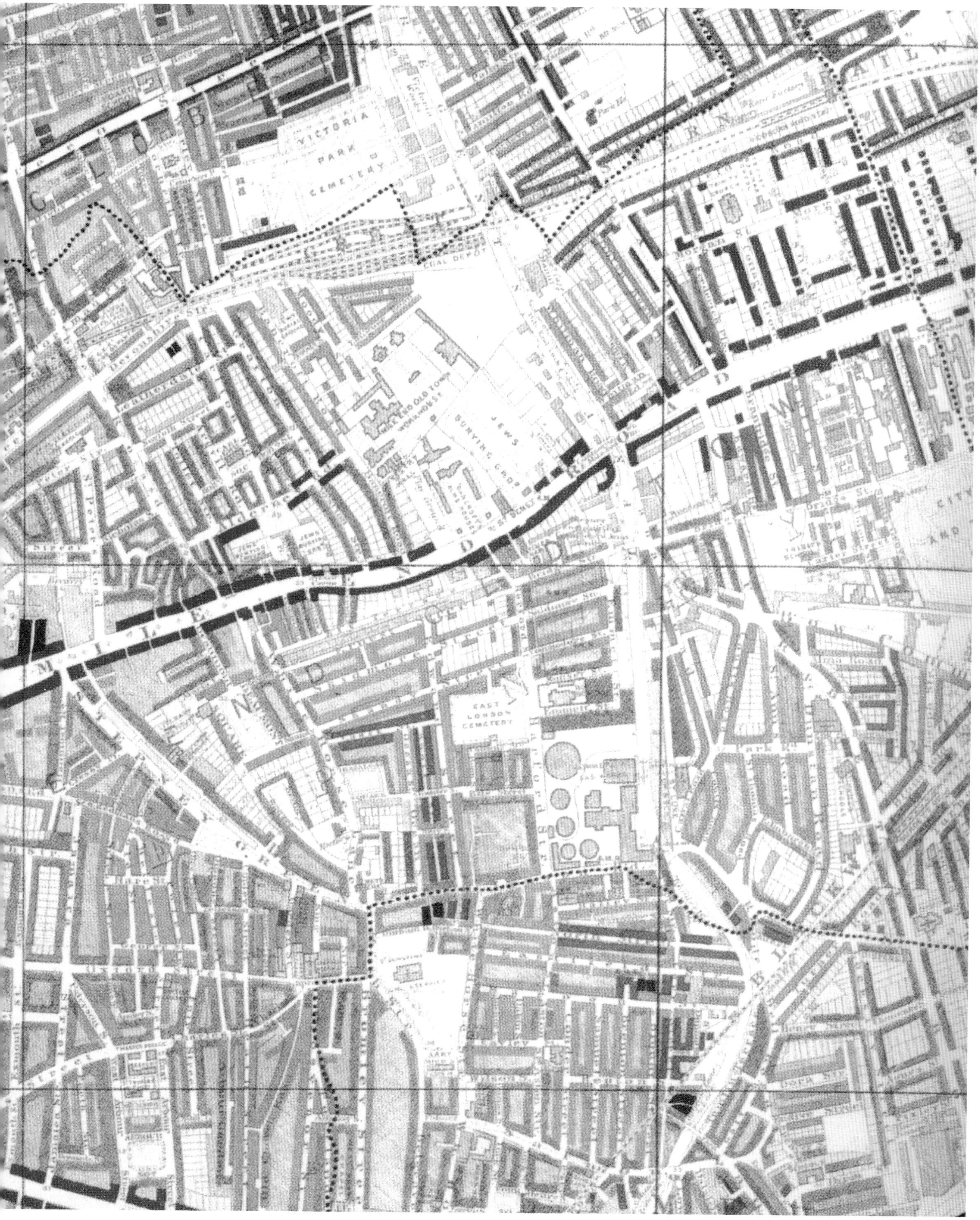
VICTORIA PARK CEMETERY
COAL DEPOT
EAST LONDON CEMETERY

Above: For three days in the summer of 1969, a dairy farm near Bethel in New York became a living, breathing, working city as around 500,000 people congregated for the Woodstock Festival.

Opposite: This structure is typical of the housing that can be found in Christiania, Copenhagen. Spread over 34 hectares, the partially self-governed borough has a population of approximately 900 inhabitants. The people of the town have devised their own laws (independent of Danish law) that require consensus before they can be passed—quite possibly as a result of the area's history as a haven for drugs and crime. Image courtesy of Jens Kristian Seier.

Local neighbourhoods change. Particular nationalities, or cultural communities tend to cluster in an area of a city, because pioneering immigrants from their country have already established property ownership and enterprise there, leading to an ethnic 'instant city' of facilities serving that community's cultural needs. For example, by locating in culturally discreet areas, specialist food outlets or religious buildings create a positive feedback loop which attracts more of a specific cultural community to the area. The American sociologist, Alejandro Portes, is credited with coining the term "ethnic cluster" to refer to these areas. They can gain leverage in the wider community politically and economically, and even become widely known internationally, as seen in many of the modern Chinatowns or Little Tokyo and Little Korea in Los Angeles. This process is not restricted to ethnic groups. In San Francisco, hippies congregated in the Haight-Ashbury neighbourhood of San Francisco during the 'Summer of Love' in 1967. This is the prime example of an 'alternative' urban community, which today range from the parallel society of Christiana in Copenhagen, to merely casual-alternative urban zones, such as Camden Town in London or Wicker Park in Chicago. Other examples of rapidly forming cultural settlements can be described by events or festivals—such as Woodstock or Glastonbury Festival—that create an 'instant' infrastructure to service a temporary population. San Francisco was also the site of another cultural cluster, the rise of the gay neighbourhood. Gays settled in Castro, and 'came out' in the wake of the free thinking climate in adjacent Haight-Ashbury. The important common feature between all of these phenomena is that when a distinct cultural group differentiates a neighbourhood from the wider city, it increases the 'localness' of that neighbourhood. This localised rebranding, especially when there is a 'cultural' aspect to it, is an important modern tool in urban revival. Alternative neighbourhoods become desirable, driving up property prices, eventually driving out the very communities that pioneered their renewal.

When neighbourhood redevelopment is planned by government agencies or developers, new Lefebrian 'constructed space' replaces old urban fabric. This

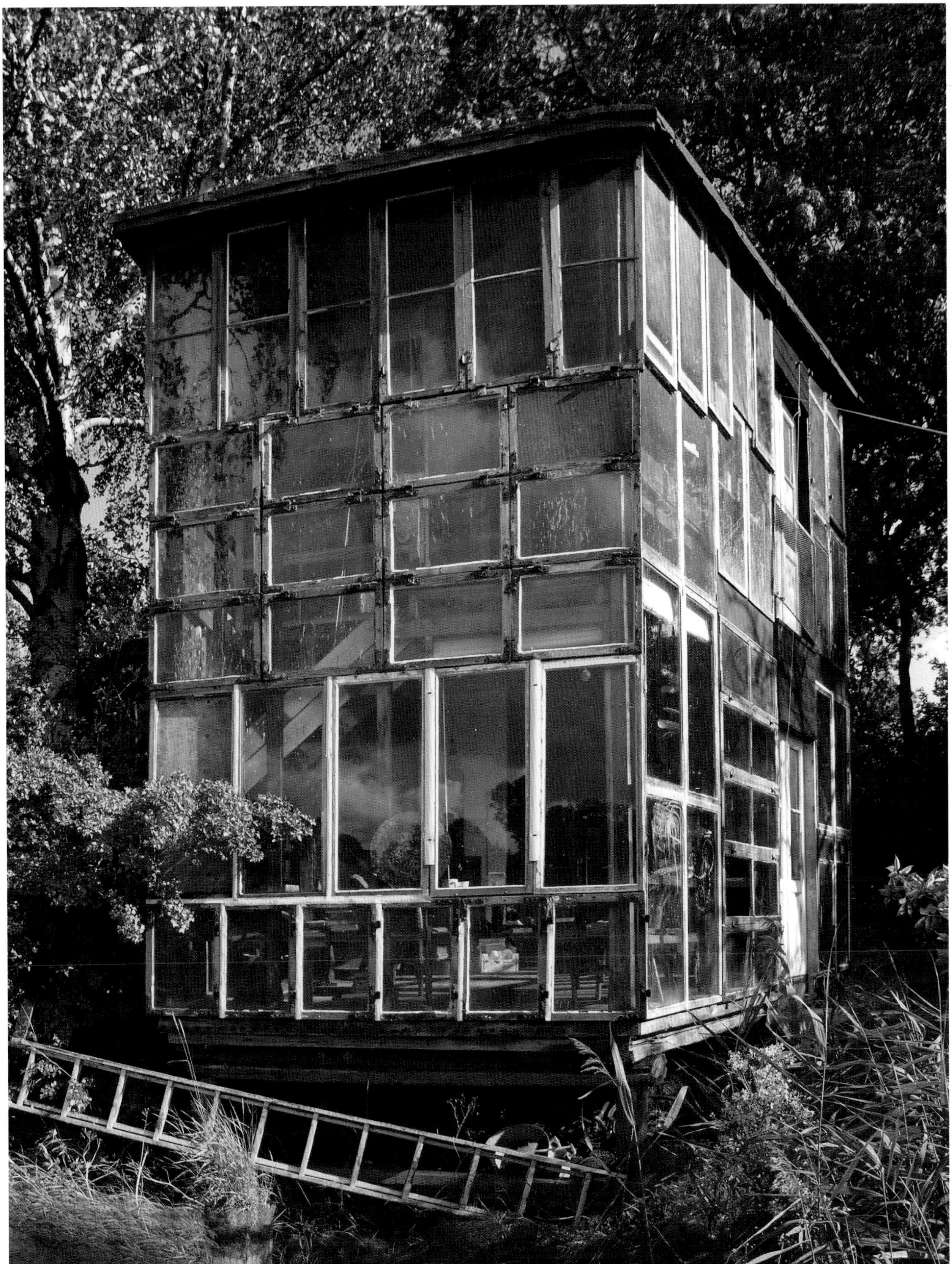

process is called regeneration in the West. New Urbanism is one strategy to incorporate a sense of localness into regeneration by encouraging community-building through design, but the new built environment it produces follows plans and formulae that are not local, and could be applied anywhere. The regeneration of waterfronts where docks have fallen into disuse is another non-local formula, including big new builds, mixed-use sites and the introduction of private urban marinas. New skyscrapers often feature large in such schemes, for example Yokohama's declining docks became the Minato Mirai 21 district, marked by Japan's tallest structure—the Landmark Tower—designed by Hugh Stubbins. Similarly, London's abandoned East India Docks became the site of the Canary Wharf development, whose tallest skyscraper is based closely on the office skyscrapers designed by the same architect, Cesar Pelli, in New York's Battery Park City, a landfill extending from disused Hudson River piers. Such developments are local in that they are geographically discreet areas, but simultaneously employ global architectural and usage principles.

GLOBAL STATUS

The destruction of the older locales in Shanghai, Beijing and Mumbai stems from their aspiration to global city status, in an effort to join the likes of London, New York and Tokyo. In a debate between London mayoral candidates televised by the BBC in April 2008, the mayor Ken Livingstone claimed that London was no longer under threat of losing its status to New York or Paris, but now had to face up to the challenge of competing with Mumbai, Shanghai and Dubai, all of which are widely perceived as up-and-coming world cities. What do the labels "world city" or "global city" mean? British planner, Peter Hall, introduced the expression "world cities" in a book of that name published in 1966, which examined diverse functions operating in major cities across the globe, and how those functions have strengthened the importance of such cities over time. The term "Global City" originated in a book of the same name published in 1991 by the American sociologist Saskia Sassen, who (since the 1980s) has been leading research into the urban impact of international migration of people and capital. What are the criteria by which qualification for these statuses might be judged?

In 2007, the London newspaper *The Independent* published the results of what was claimed to be the most exhaustive survey of world cities ever conducted, based on a wide range of economic and cultural factors. The survey included conurbation population, financial sector markers such as stock exchange trading volumes and number of international corporation headquarters, transport data such as airline departures, and cultural statistics, including symphony orchestras and Michelin-rated restaurants, in addition to factors related to tourism and sport. The international ranking that resulted had London, New York, Paris, Tokyo and Chicago in the top five, with Mexico City the highest ranking city outside the EU, America or Japan at number ten. The hubs of the rising super-economies figure across the top 50 cities in the ranking, with Beijing at 15, Hong Kong at 18, Shanghai at 21, Delhi at 28, Mumbai at 31 and Kolkata at 49, while the rising city-states of Singapore and Dubai came in at 22 and 42 respectively. Chongqing does not feature in the top 60, but Zürich ranks 47.

Has *The Independent's* 'exhaustive' process of ranking cities produced the same results as a more strictly economic assessment of those same locales? At the top, these rankings are similar to the gross domestic products of conurbations—figures for 2005 collated from sources including the UN, OECD and World Bank by London-based global accountants PricewaterhouseCoopers rank Tokyo first with a GDP of US$1.191 trillion, followed by New York, Los Angeles (number eight in *The Independent* survey), Chicago, Paris and, at number six, London (with a GDP of US$452 billion).[2] This ranking reveals that the top 20 most dollar-productive cities are found mainly in America, with 11 American cities, and only Mexico, São Paulo and Seoul ranking from outside North America, the EU or Japan. Shanghai and Mumbai figure at position 32 and 37, respectively. The same survey restores London to second position in GDP/capita, following New York and followed by Chicago, LA, Paris and Tokyo. Interestingly, when PricewaterhouseCoopers project urban GDPs to 2020, the top six biggest GDP

cities remain the same, with London rising to four and Paris dropping to six. However, the highest annual GDP growth rate is the Manchurian Chinese city of Changchun, while Chongqing comes in at just 22.

With its implications for the globalisation of culture, the connectivity of cities doing business has given rise to the global economy. Cities that were once connected by trade routes carrying goods, are now linked by connections carrying data that may define or allocate capital and intellectual property. The geographer, PJ Taylor, has led analysis on the relative power of various cities around the world in the context of a global city network. This power is analysed both in terms of capacity through connections and command through resources, and an evaluation of the network that arises in these cities to exchange information. Taylor concludes that rather than trying to emulate the global city by acquiring more service functions, it is better to strengthen the connections in the network, and occupying niches enables this strengthening and increases diversity. Cities can therefore take their place in the network as gateways to emerging markets. Interestingly, Zürich ranks along with the regional command centres of Moscow, Beijing, Seoul, Caracas and São Paulo as a top emerging centre, because of the special nature of its banking sector.

Naturally, financial or connective criteria are measures of success in the global economy, but the same cities do not come out on top in quality-of-life surveys. The American-based Mercer Human Resources Consulting surveyed cities on criteria including health, sanitation, transport, crime, education and recreation, enabling advice on relocating expatriate workers based on the local 'quality of life'.[3] With such wide-ranging criteria, results might be expected to reflect *The Independent's* survey, but in this survey Zürich ranks number one, followed by Geneva and Vancouver, while Paris, Tokyo, London and New York languish at 33, 35, 39 and 48 respectively. While these social criteria seem to reliably reproduce the same results across various surveys, cultural criteria are prone to subjectivity, and the more specific they are, the more varied the

The Fraser Canyon Gold Rush of the 1860s gave the impetus to the initial settling of Vancouver. After the arrival of the Transcontinental Railway in 1887, the small lumber mill town rapidly developed into a metropolitan centre. Now the largest metropolitan area in Western Canada, Vancouver is consistently ranked as one of the most pleasant of the world's cities to live in.

results. Religion is one such example; a survey based on pilgrimage to a city would doubtless propel Mecca, Varanasi and Rome into the top. Millions of people travel across the world to these cities because they are focal locations of their religions, and the rankings would change little over hundreds of years. Cities with a significant religious role have an interest in preserving the past because that is where religion is rooted, and religious sites are literally sacred and protected from development, so the local identity is unlikely to change. But beyond the religious sites, the adjacent cities respond to fresher forces. A strange consequence of the fanatical Wahhabi religious regime in Saudi Arabia is that their paranoia about sites becoming the subject of idolatry has resulted in the destruction of 95 per cent of Mecca's ancient artefacts (according to the American-based Gulf Institute). A cluster of towers designed by Dar al-Handasah Architects is rising directly opposite the Masjid al Haram, one of Islam's holiest sites. In an odd parallel to Las Vegas' New York New York, the Abraj Al Bait Towers evoke neo classical Manhattan skyscrapers at Battery Park City, but the tallest element is a hotel with a clocktower topped with a crescent rising 577 metres which, when completed, will stand as the second highest skyscraper in the world—where ranking cities by their highest skyscraper is a significant measure, as it reflects prestige and perceived economic power. Mecca would, then, have an instant skyscraper city status on a height list for 2009, just behind Dubai.

The factors that give urban environments local identity (such as markets, the urban fabric, culture or ethnicity) can only remain if economic, spatial, cultural and demographic change is frozen—an unlikely proposition. Almost all change points in the direction of global homogeneity. Even rapidly-expanding developing world megacities incorporate global features into their slums, for example international languages left by the colonial period like English and French in Africa, or consumer items (even if second hand) like Chinese clothing or plastic goods, or connections to mobile telecom nets or the worldwide web.

The diversity of urban environments that is local is gradually and inexorably being eroded by the global. If cities survive into another century, Chongqing could be a global hub and Zürich a quiet backwater, but the chances are that you would be able to have the same meal in a similar building in either location. Race, religion and local language will always distinguish discreet societies, but step out into the world city, and increasingly you are entering a Homotopia, where the streets of numerous geographical locations are refined to express the same architectural and cultural characteristics.

Above: Venezuela's capital, Caracas is a regional centre and part of the global economy network, offering a gateway to emerging South American markets.

Opposite: Looking like New York in microcosm, the New York New York Hotel and Casino, on the Las Vegas Strip in Paradise, Nevada, draws on numerous of its alter ego's architectural icons, including the Statue of Liberty, the Empire State and Chrysler Buildings and the Brooklyn Bridge. Image courtesy of MGM Mirage.

1. Debord, Guy, "Introduction to a Critique of Urban Geography", *Les Lèvres Nues*, No. 6, September 1955.

2. PriceWaterhouseCoopers, British Economic Outlook, March 2007.

3. 2007 Worldwide Quality of Living Survey by Mercer Human Resource Consulting.

NEW SONGDO CITY

65 kilometres south of Seoul, South Korea, a new corporate hub city is rising out of six square kilmometres of reclaimed land on Incheon's Yellow Sea waterfront. Costing an estimated £17 billion in private finance (on top of the city of Incheon's estimated £5 billion spend on municipal infrastructure) and with a completion date set for 2014, New Songdo City will be one of Asia's largest, entirely for-profit, masterplanned developments. By completion, the developers estimate the project will be home to 65,000 people and that 300,000 will work in its 60 million square feet of brand new office space. New Songdo's management and the Korean authorities hope to entice multi-national firms to locate their Asian bases there rather than Pudong, for example, and are doing everything they can to ease Western commerce's hoped-for influx. By 2008, a six lane, 12.3 kilometre bridge will connect Songdo with Incheon International Airport, a gateway airport with direct flights to hundreds of cities worldwide. New Songdo is designated as a free economic zone, where foreign companies are afforded special relief from Korea's traditionally off-putting taxation system and the land and business ownership restrictions which favour Korean businesses,

and will have an officially bilingual English-Korean city administration. Ashok Raiji of Arup Associates, who are engineering part of the project, told *The New York Times* that Songdo will provide "a comfort zone in a foreign land" for Western businesses.[1] The first phase of New Songdo's development is scheduled to be up and running by 2009.

Lying strategically between China and Japan, the driver behind New Songdo's development is pure business potential. The planners estimate that 51 cities, with a population of one million people or more, are within a three and a half hour flight o the time was right to exploit its position and challenge Shanghai and Hong Kong's monopoly on Asia's slice of global business, and approached Gale International with the idea of a Korean hub city. Gale took the project on, buying up the land which was still underwater by this point, and—in conjunction with South Korea's POSCO Engineering and Construction—hired the New York office of architects Kohn Pedersen Fox Associates to create the masterplan for New Songdo. Its development and financing is truly multi-national; Morgan Stanley Real Estate has invested around £175 million and Gale

have secured £1.4 billion in financing led by Shinhan Bank.

New Songdo will offer a well-planned and modern physical environment for global businesses and their employees to move in to. Its development has been planned pragmatically rather than according to any grand overarching scheme; the planners say they have tried to create what they term a "synergy city", drawing on elements from successful cities around the world and synthesising them to make this new business-oriented community a pleasant place to both work and live. So there will be a central park *à la* New York and neighbourhood gardens resembling those of Savannah, Georgia; distinctive features of Paris, Sydney and Marrakesh make appearances too. Buildings have been commissioned from world famous architects, including a shopping centre by Daniel Libeskind and a museum by Peter Zumthor, and other landmark high-rise buildings in the commercial district such as Songdo's signature 68-storey Northeast Asian Trade Tower further add to the mixture of densities, uses and influences. This technique has been deployed, in part, to try to avoid the sense of sterility and

NEW SONGDO CITY AND TOKYO

New Songdo City
development near
Seoul, South Korea.
Due to be completed
in 2014, the area is
hoped to become one
of the most successful
economic hubs in Asia.

artificiality that besets many Asian new
towns and cities, giving the illusion of
a diversity and texture that could have
possibly come about through organic
development. (The Songdo developers
seem to have resisted the temptation to
compete in the race for the world's tallest
building as a signifier of prestige; their
high-rises—like HOK's six mixed-use and
one hotel tower—are more modest than
those planned for other Asian 'hub' cities,
and will be overshadowed by the 151-storey,
610 metre-high Incheon Tower in the city
centre.) Gale and the masterplanners,

Kohn Pedersen Fox, originally encountered
clashes between Western urbanism and
Korean preferences, such as the local
favouring of large buildings with small
footprints linked via wide expressways, as
opposed to more human-scale development,
but were able to convincingly demonstrate
that the latter would be more in tune with
Songdo's ambitions.

What most sets New Songdo apart from its
Asian new town contemporaries, however,
is not even strictly part of its physical
fabric. When complete, New Songdo will

be the world's largest 'ubiquitous city', or 'U-city'; a high technology, completely wirelessly networked space where all major information systems are integrated and share data, and computers form part of the city's very infrastructure. Residents and businesses will enjoy high speed wireless web access from anywhere in the city, but this barely scratches the surface of what New Songdo City Development (NSCD) call 'U-life'. John Kim, vice president for strategy at NSCD, told *The New York Times*: "U-life will become its own brand, its own lifestyle." Residents' smart house key will give them access to digital services all over the city. "The same key can be used to get on the subway, pay a parking metre, see a movie, borrow a free public bicycle, and so on. It'll be anonymous, won't be linked to your identity and, if lost, you can quickly cancel the card and reset your door lock."[2] In time, the spectrum of U-life's applications could be extended almost limitlessly. The technology infrastructure will be built and managed by Songdo U-Life, a division of NSCD, and Korean network integrator LG CNS. Songdo will be the largest development where such technology has been integrated from the planning stages and, as such, will act as a test bed for new technologies. It

will offer the unique chance to study the way that people use—and are comfortable with using—smart card, sensor-based and radio frequency identification (RFID) technology on a daily basis and on a large-scale. Western societies, while often occupying the forefront of technological development, are much more reluctant to adopt ubiquitous computing technologies, seeing them as very much the thin end of the wedge of a surveillance society. This suspicious and paranoid sensibility is not one shared by governments in east Asia who tend to see ubiquitous computing as an example of prestige technology; Korea, Singapore and Japan all have national level ubiquitous initiatives in place, and RFID is already in use in South Korea. South Korea's Ministry of Information and Communication has earmarked £150 million to build an RFID research centre in New Songdo, and the city's infrastructure will enable foreign businesses to test technologies for market without having to invest outright themselves.

Although the Songdo project is decisively for-profit, its technological aspect extends to making environmental considerations a priority. Water is recycled citywide, and

energy is produced locally and conserved wherever possible. Unusually for an Asian new town, 40 per cent of the city's area is reserved for parks and green space, and the city will be fully accessible to cyclists and pedestrians. All of Songdo's buildings will be designed to meet the LEED (Leadership in Energy and Environmental Design) standards set by the American Green Building Council, according to Gale International, and the LEED for Neighbourhood Development—a standard for community design—is being applied to the whole city.

Whether Songdo achieves its ambitions won't be clear for some time, but all the signs are good. Residential units are selling well, and marketing has begun in earnest to fill its office space. Though numerous cities all over Asia are vying to become business hubs, there is arguably room in the current market for them all. What does make Songdo distinctive is its unique investment in integrated high technology, and this may prove to be its USP in a competitive market.

1. Cortese, Amy, "An Asian Hub in the Making", *The New York Times*, 30 December 2007.
2. Quoted in Licalzi O'Connell, Pamela, "Korea's High-Tech Utopia, Where Everything is Observed", *The New York Times*, 5 October 2005.

TOKYO 2016

In January 2008, Tokyo became one of seven cities worldwide to submit a bid to host the 2016 summer Olympic and Paralympic Games. Along with Chicago (Anerica), Prague (Czech Republic), Rio de Janeiro (Brazil), Baku (Azerbaijan), Doha (Qatar) and Madrid (Spain), the Japanese capital's bid team submitted an application file to the International Olympic Committee outlining their vision for the twenty-ninth Olympiad.

Winning out over two other Japanese contenders—Sapporo and Fukuoka—the

Tokyo 2016 concept lays out the blueprint for a uniquely compact, green, and distinctly urban Games: 'The City is the Games', as the application puts it. Central Tokyo itself will become the Olympic Park, home to 95 per cent of the Games venues, all within an eight kilometre radius of the proposed new Olympic Stadium on the Tokyo Bay waterfront. The Tokyo Games plan would, if successful, provide a new model for world sporting events to be delivered sustainably right in the centre of a mature contemporary metropolis. It aims

to integrate Tokyo's vibrant city life—with its projected 8.9 million population, in the city centre, by 2016—with the Games for mutual benefit, into an "integrated, dynamic and seamless experience".[1] The bid benefits from an already existing ten year city development and sustainability initiative, 'Tokyo's Big Change', launched in 2006 with building to commence in 2016. This plan already commits Tokyo to renewing much of the city's ageing infrastructure—roads, public transport and so on—and achieving a greener urban environment in perfect time for the Games.

Tokyo last hosted the Olympic Games in 1964 and an important factor in the bid for 2016 is the re-use of many of the venues built for the earlier event in the city. 21 of the proposal's 31 venues are pre-existing, and include the iconic 1964 Olympic Stadium and the Nippon Budokan. The bid team have phrased this as a clear demonstration of Tokyo's unique commitment to the spirit of the Games (many of the 1964 venues having gone on to become "a treasured part" of the city's history) and of its capacity for efficient, innovative and sensitive management of the Olympic legacy.[2] Of the ten new venues proposed for 2016, five will be permanent

Above: The Tokyo skyline including the Tokyo Tower, the city's Eiffel Tower-like telecommunications tower. Photograph by Jackson Chu.

Following pages: Aerial photograph showing the Tokyo Bay area of the city.

structures to continue this legacy project, and five will be temporary.

The Olympic Park, in the city centre, will be divided into two highly compact and overlapping zones, the Heritage venue zone and the Tokyo Bay venue zone. These zones will contain venue 'clusters', which will be themed around and integrated with major urban features and landmarks. The Heritage zone will contain the Palace Cluster, based around the Imperial Palace, and the Yoyogi Cluster, based around the famous 1964 stadium and venues. The Tokyo Bay zone is to be entirely based on reclaimed land in the waterfront area of central Tokyo, an area which is currently in desperate need of regeneration and reconnection to the city. Its two venue clusters—Dream Island and Sea Forest—will occupy land formed on landfill sites in the Bay, and will be used for equestrian, canoeing, cycling, swimming and other events. Part of this cluster's development would see the planting of an 'umi-no-mori', or 'forest on the sea', with 480,000 trees planted on the .88 square kilometre Yumenoshima landfill site, composted with waste vegetable matter gathered from the public parks of Tokyo. This zone will, the bid states, be a showcase for Tokyo's ecological ambitions.

The two venue zones overlap to form the central Musubi Cluster, the centre of the Games plan, and this area will be home to the Olympic Stadium, the Olympic Village and main Media Centre. This cluster takes its name from a traditional Japanese knot, symbolising harmony, a device which is also depicted in the bid team's proposed logo. The Olympic Village will be built in the Ariake area bordering Tokyo Bay, and will be constructed to utilise a number of eco-friendly systems like solar energy. Designed to accommodate 17,000 people, the Village would be made available to Tokyo residents after the Games as waterfront, ecologically-sound, new homes as part of the regeneration of Tokyo Bay. The Media Centre would later be converted into offices, commercial facilities and a conference hall.

As Tokyo has billed itself as the compact and green choice for 2016, it has heavily emphasised its existing efficient public transport infrastructure and road system as a distinct advantage over other cities. Travel times between venues within the eight kilometre Olympic Park will be 20 minutes or less by Olympic shuttle bus, and the government is planning the introduction of more low-emissions buses

to curb carbon pollution. Some road lanes will be designated for official Olympic use only, and all official transport will be low- or zero-emission. The successful host city will be announced by the International Olympic Committee in Copenhagen in October 2009.

1. Dr Ichiro Kono quoted in TOKYO 2016 press release, 15 January 2008. See: http://www. tokyo2016.or.jp/en/press/2008/01/tokyo_2016_ reveals_concept_gam.html
2. See: www.tokyo2016.or.jp/en

(DE)CONSTRUCTION IN (POST)SOCIALIST EUROPE: CONTINUOUS AND VARIABLE USE OF SPACES AND METHODS

Laszló Rajk

EMOTIONAL ANALYSIS OF THE VELVET REVOLUTION

Nobody questions the importance of the political changes that started in socialist Europe 20 years ago or that half of Europe was imprisoned by stereotypes for many decades. As happens during long bouts of captivity, the prisoner slowly adapts to his circumstances, believing them to be natural, albeit in a postmodern sort of way. This postmodern interpretation of everyday dictatorship led to the postmodern revolution: no street fights, no victims, no bloodshed, the wall simply falls.

Since Heinrich Schliemann discovered Troy in the 1870s (one of seven layers that he excavated) we know that civilisations, cultures, cities and buildings are layered, one above another and that cities incorporate and swallowed their predecessors. Often such conflations are seamless but parts of the original city are still

To what extent should spontaneous processes be allowed to influence the life of a city, and how far should planning be extended? This issue flares up especially at times of revolution, during dictatorship, and in periods of historical change and political transition.

In Budapest, the capital of Hungary, the political and social revolution of post-socialism has already wrought visible changes in the use of the city's public and private spaces. Of course, this is not the first time that a city has undergone such a change. A chemically pure, artificial town is not an inviting one and even planned cities—cities from which spontaneous building and development have been banished altogether—begin to show signs of humanisation. In the former Soviet Union or in Brazil, for example, trees eventually took root in the concrete mazes

prevalent, albeit in a new guise (when walking in Piazza Navona in Rome, for example, one can clearly recognise the shape of the old stadium, where the deadly quadriga races took place).

Most European languages reflect such development in European cities. The world 'boulevard' (originating from 'bulwark', a wall-like structure built to protect) shows that, long after the demolition of exterior fortifications, such structures can still be traced linguistically. While new cities or districts might consume older ones, the older always emerge in some incarnation. Sometimes these areas, such as the Tower of London, the Kremlin in Moscow or the Wawel in Krakow, for examples, are left in tact while urban sprawl proliferates around them. (Such examples are not only found in Europe but also the Forbidden City, in Beijing, and the pyramids of Giza, Cairo)

dreamed up by urban planners and people planted shrubs in loggias and balconies. Architectural structures themselves can become sites for re-appropriation, such as the housing estates of Tirana, Albania, whose ruined facades were transformed into canvases of three dimensions by the former dissident painter, Edi Rama, in the late 1990s. Going further, improvised constructions and pavilions could be perceived as anarchic additions to the high-end architecture they accompany, while rice paddies and vegetables and flower gardens lend an organic air to the high-tech skyscrapers they surround. Entire cities have been and are built without the input of architects. The products of spontaneous architecture can be detected at first glance, and not necessarily because they are ugly. Most cities, of course, exhibit both architectural planning and chaotic sprawl. At times of historical turns and political transitions, these spontaneous processes gather momentum and significance.

In post-socialist Europe, with the change of the political system over the last two decades, spontaneous processes have erupted once again with great force, radically altering the life and the face of the city. Many European cities changed almost overnight, and their various elements were reinterpreted. Quite frequently, these deconstructivist processes emerged on a small-scale and proceeded toward large-scale reinterpretations.

A typical example of such 'deconstruction' is the unorthodox and imaginative use of the inner courtyards in the apartment buildings of Budapest. In the early 1990s such spaces graduated from their traditional purpose—for parking cars—to encompass the commercial area out on the street. This extension of public space into private became a two-way process; as the opening of new communal areas as offset by the tendency of closing down courtyards to public access. Later, at the turn of the Millennium, a new profile of courtyard architecture occurred in the city. These dystopian gardens and courtyards became very important elements of Budapest's cultural and touristic life. They became transitory spaces as squatters and civic groups spontaneously adopted them for commercial/political reasons, and became shells as they changed location.

RADICAL ECLECTICISM

Eclectic architecture, synonymous with the city of Budapest, allows for a conflation of a myriad of styles: neo Renaissance, neo Gothic, neo Baroque and so on. The result is a seemingly ad hoc montage of styles, one that the modernists were not largely fond of. (In this context, the word 'eclectic', only had detrimental connotations.) If one was discussing eclecticism in relation to the strata of architecture I referred to earlier it would certainly come at the bottom of the pile. Eclectic architecture in many other European cities has almost completely disappeared which is why the example of Budapest is such an important one when discussing this style.

In Budapest eclecticism became the personification of conceited power, especially for the post-war modernists of the Soviet Empire. Communists adopted eclecticism as the grounding of their new style; Social Realism. (In 1994 in Bucharest, Romania's former dictator, Nicolae Ceausescu, decided to build an enormous palace, called the House of the People. This is probably one of the last examples of eclectic architecture employed for socialist means and also one that demonstrates how an architectural product by a dictator could be transformed. The palace now houses the Romanian Parliament as well as many other organisations; and one part of it is now a museum for contemporary art.)

Eclecticism presents us with the classic post-socialist European dilemma. In any examination of the eclectic method, we must recognise that it employs deconstructivism with almost chemical purity. It appropriates and conflates diverse elements and removes them from their original context. This detachment from context is often so extreme that individual architectural elements are created which are divested of meaning. This jumble of semiotically incomprehensible elements are not legible separately but rather emerge as a new form of semiotic meaning specific to the juxtaposition of the variables in question. (I honestly believe that every building designed in this way by a talented architect represents a unique style, but for the sake of simplicity I accept eclecticism as a definition.)

Opposite left:
The pyramids
at Giza, Egypt.

Opposite right:
One of Edi Rama's
many painted facades
of the estates in
Tirana, Albania.
Photograph by
David Dufresne.

Top: The Palace
of the Pariament,
Bucharest, Romania,
was designed during
the rule of Nicolae
Ceausescu. When he
was overthrown in
1989, the building was
unfinished, and parts
of it remain so
to this day. Image
courtesy of Romanian
National Tourist
Office—UK and Ireland.

Bottom: The Lehel
market in Budapest,
Hungary, designed
by Laszlo Rajk.
Photograph by
Lenke Szilagyi.

Not long ago, I put forward a proposal that would work to transform the Collegium Hungaricum, Vienna, a building typical of 1960s architecture in the country. The project was theoretical as it was one that would allow the building to disintegrate over time. In so doing it would be transformed into a temporal rather than static structure, were time was embraced, rather than resisted, in its creation and maintenance. The Collegium Hungaricum is twisted in form; its upper corner leans outwards, while the lower corner curves out (therefore the upper part is protected, while the lower part is more exposed to the weather). If my experiment were to be successfully carried out, the lower part of the building—its mouldings, painted walls and sub-structures—would be degraded by time and the load bearing structure exposed. The vertical wall would start peeling away (although only after a period of many years), while the upper part would remain intact. This concept not only serves as a built example of the partnership between architects and time, but also brings to the fore the crucial question: when does building become complete. In the case of the Collegium Hungaricum, a building is never complete if we take time seriously.

Naturally the techniques of re-assembling different elements in architecture are not unique to socialist Europe. Such techniques are customary to the postmodern world. These were my methods while working on the Lehel Market in Budapest, from 1998–2002. When I first saw the slave sculptures of Michelangelo in the Louvre, I was struck by their similarity to those statues that support the balconies of eclectic buildings in Budapest. This tradition (of using art as a blueprint for making structures that we encounter in everyday life) was something I wanted to further explore. The question I posed was: What happens if we continue this technique, of borrowing and re-interpreting symbols and making them into objects/structures—in peoples' houses, churches, spontaneously-constructed balconies, loggias, backyard tool-sheds or hovels, all elements that have their own peculiar aesthetics—that become familiar to all occupants of the city? Lehel Market contains as many layers of eclectic, modernist or deconstructive signifiers as it does personal environments. Here was a building whose constituent parts I took apart and reassembled to create an altogether new context; a structure, like Troy, comprised by layering, both conceptually and literally. Lehel Market's internal working order has changed little from the former open-air market that occupied the site, with its circulatory system. It now occupies multiple levels and, while it mimics the dimensions of retail outlets, an old market remains at the epicentre. With its interior entirely renovated, the market reflects the original precisely. The pavilion is ensconced in its

1960s casing, all of which is incorporated into the steel-framed, industrial revolution-era, vault and surrounded, in turn, by the reinforced concrete building of the modern period. The outer layer is of postmodern inspiration: large pillars (tree-trunks) support an enormous plant holder (crown), in memory of the perished sycamores of the streets framing the site; an assembly of colourful constructivist and deconstructivist structural elements are suspended in-between, playfully echoing one another.

ECLECTIC SPACES

Although the 'small is beautiful' movement, and those advocating liberation from centralisation, began to emerge in Europe in the twentieth century, efforts within the Soviet Union differed cardinally from them. Movements in socialist Europe not only looked for independence, but also forced those in power into dialogue.

Between 1992 and 1993 in Tbilisi, Georgia, refugees of the Abkhazia war took control of and squatted in the formerly elegant, five-star Hotel Iveria, built in 1967 during the Soviet era. The hotel towers over Tbilisi's city centre—a modern symbol of the town. It was a home to roughly 800 internally-displaced persons who transformed it into a 'little town' of sorts. On one floor a market was situated, on another 'authority' offices installed; while residents constructed built-in balconies in order to expand their living quarters. The hotel was closed down in the summer of 2004, and is now still awaiting its future fate.

Post-socialist cities are now witnessing a profusion of 'reclaimed' spaces that were previously ordered and proscribed in nature. All of a sudden, cities encompass something of which we had previously been unaware, or forgotten. Tradesmen, street hustlers and smugglers took the city structure apart—deconstructed it—and rearranged it differently. Such processes have now proceeded toward large-scale re-interpretations of city structures.

Emblematic examples of such re-interpretation are the border towns of the Czech Republic, whose sex industry is rife, with prostitution largely concentrated along the country's borders with Austria and Germany. The small, belle époque town of Dubí—on the E55 highway on northern Bohemia's Czech-German border—for example, was originally famous for its mineral springs. Now, however, it is a site whose physical atributes became signifiers for sex. Such a vocabulary extends to the city of Saigon during the Vietnam War in the late 1960s and in Amsterdam, for example, where even bus stops have taken on the colour red, a linguistic referral to the term "red light district" and all that it implies.

Another, but very different example, is the conquest of a real symbol of the centralised power: the transformation of the All-Russia Exhibition Centre (VDNKh) in Moscow in 1992. This crystal clear, social-realistic complex was built in 1935 for the All-Union Agricultural Exhibition, comprising 2,375,000 square metres and 400 buildings in total. From the early 1990s all kinds of shops and stalls could be found, one could buy anything from underwear to Kalashnikovs.

Eclectic techniques are well known methods for architects—not only in a technical sense but especially in the free handling of different 'elements'. There is no harm in deconstruction being a general method rather than a style, however, it is clear from the discussion laid out in this essay that deconstruction (at least in the relation to the examples I have cited) as a term is outmoded and not necessarily correct.

Above: Detail of the exterior of the Collegium Hungaricum in Vienna. © Lugo.

Opposite: The Collegium Hungaricum in Vienna. © Judit Rajk.

HUMANITY

| ENVIRONMENT

Cities are like huge living, organisms spread across the surface of the Earth, drawing in water and nourishment and churning out organic and inorganic solids, liquids, airborne pollutants and excess energy into the environment. Major climate change is already a matter of observation and empirical evidence, and its future effects are predicted by constantly improving models. The possible consequences of rising global temperature this century include the conversion of the Amazon, which supplies a fifth of the world's oxygen, and other rainforests to savannah and scrubland, the drying up of the great rivers that flow from the Himalayas to nourish China and Northern India, and the disruption of deep ocean currents that distribute thermal energy around the planet. The changes will hit the poorest regions the hardest. Any solutions to climate change must involve the city—meaning changes to our urban environment that will inextricably result in new forms of the city.

Above: Cappadocia is probably one of the earliest examples of eco-cities to date. Located in Turkey, records of its existence date back as far as the Bronze Age. Like the pueblos of southwest America, this is an entire city literally carved out from the natural environment. Cappadocia is constituted not only by a number of villages but also over 30 rock-carved churches. While the city may be 'sustainable' in its design, this did not translate to the quality of life of its inhabitants. In 1975 a study from three small villages in central Cappadocia—Tuzköy, Karain and Sarhd—found that nearly 50 per cent of all deaths were caused by properties in the rocks. Photograph by Mila Zinkova.

Opposite: Working with Kuwait-based KEO Consultants, CRJA, the architectural design and environmental planning firm, have proposed a new headquarters for the Kuwait Investment Authority in the guise of the KIA Tower, Kuwait. Organic in shape, it proposes to incorporate green space in a seamless progression from the foot of the building to its top, while sustainability comes in the form of wind turbines and photovoltaic panels.

Climate change is already a prime suspect in major urban catastrophes. In Paris, deaths in 2003 were 50 per cent higher than normal, exacerbated by the traditional tin roofs of the city's buildings, turning them into virtual ovens. But globally, 2003 was only the third hottest to date since the 1880s—1998 and 2002 were even hotter. When Hurricane Katrina devastated New Orleans in 2005, it may have seemed a random event, but a rise in sea surface temperatures promote hurricane formations and with global warming models predicting increasingly frequent extreme weather conditions we are only experiencing the first of such major disturbances. In 2007, residents in the Turkish capital Ankara had up to ten days without water, because mismanagement of reservoirs was exacerbated by extreme drought. As these events become commonplace, global warming emerges as not so much coincidence, but as something held in common. Such dramatic changes inevitably effect the way cities are structured and planned, provoking architects and planners to make work that not only acts to defend ourselves from the elements but that, in theory, may help subvert the more hostile effects of climate change.

NEW-LOOK GREEN CITY

If things go well, what will the thriving city look like in 25 years time? Much of the built environment may be the same as now, but there should be a palpably cleaner, brighter veneer to the city. From the air, cities may look like a quilt of living and hard surfaces, the green of vegetation vying for dominance against the subdued hues of stone and brick and glints of glass and steel. Buildings will be variegated by dark solar collection surfaces and plants, including agricultural crops. New eco-buildings will spread across suburbs and expand in dramatic upscale mixed-use developments downtown, where colourful assemblages of moving images play on low-energy LED displays stacked over streets cutting through high-rises like canyons. The retro-fitting of old buildings, from suburban villas to great edifices, will make them look fresh again. Traffic will move gently at levels not seen in prosperous cities for perhaps a century, and highways could even be dominated by bicycles, as in Chinese cities right up into the 1980s. Pedestrianised zones will connect across whole districts, emulating the Italian Renaissance city that inspired Richard Rogers' public realm vision. By comparison with today, the domination of space by the car will seem an aggressive aberration, and the built environment of the modern contemporary city will look as shabby as post-war housing or un-refurbished 1960s office blocks look now.

Roofs are a great unused resource that become brilliant tools to moderate local microclimates by waterproofing, laying soil and planting vegetation, which can even include fruits or vegetables. Sedum and moss species need no soil, but intensive green roofs, capable of supporting trees, require a concrete deck as well as gardeners. Such roofs insulate buildings, thus saving on cooling and heating, absorb noise, dust and pollution, provide wildlife refuge, cut rainwater run-off that contributes to the overloading of sewers and causes floods—and they even moderate microwave radiation levels. Although some 1930s Art Deco buildings incorporated roof gardens, the value of green roofs was first explored by Reinhard Bornkamm, a researcher at Berlin's Free University in 1961. And, since then,

Studio Boeri's
Bosco Verticale is
an eco-sustainable
architecture proposal
comprising of two
eco-towers. Each tower
will host a variety of
plants, such as birches
and oaks, as well as
aeolic towers and is
meant to help in
the regeneration of the
urban environment.

Germany has led the way in their increasing popularity across the world. In 1989, it had one square kilometre of such buildings, but eleven times more by 2001. Green roofs absorb the heat from the sun in such a way that they can lower the overall climate heat emissions of that building's roof by four per cent (as opposed to buildings without). Other benefits include stormwater runoff management and, as green roofs tend to retain approximately 70 per cent of rainwater, a gradual release of rainwater back into the atmosphere while pollutants remain stored in the soil. As cities have expanded in the last two decades so have the number of eco-buildings within them increased. After Chicago's mayor, Richard Daley, was introduced to Germany's green roofs, he incorporated them into city planning in 1998. Nowadays Chicago City Hall has one of the most iconic green roofs in America. Other city administrations including Atlanta, Portland and Tokyo have planning directives that require them in new developments, as does national legislation in Germany, Scandinavia and Switzerland.

Less traditional eco-buildings have also sprung up within the city. The University of Guelph in Ontario, Canada, even has a vertical green wall over four storeys, covered in diverse plant species. In 2008, Italian architects Boeri Studio unveiled concept models for a Bosco Verticale (Vertical Forest), in which towers, two at 108 metres and one at 78 metres, are topped with turbines, which could allow for the growth of 900 trees.

Skyscrapers are, in a certain way, intrinsically green, in as much as they create a lot of space on little ground. However, most post-war buildings had especially appalling environmental consequences. Environmental awareness in the energy consumption of the high-rise has taken a long time to emerge. The first eco-tower, utilising wind to drastically cut back the energy expenditure of air conditioning, was designed by Ken Yeang in Georgetown, Malaysia, in 1994. Yeang is one of the leading advocates of bio-climatic skyscrapers, with these including passive rather than active internal climate controls and incorporating greenery throughout.

Skygardens enclosed in stacked atria also appear in Foster+Partners' Commerzbank in Frankfurt, one of two German skyscrapers completed in 1997 that reduced energy consumption by about a third relative to equivalent buildings, achieved through the use of pioneering ventilated facades. The other was Ingenhoven Architects' RWE headquarters in Essen, which was also an early adopter of transmission-efficient low-iron glass. Wind is another force to harness in this regard, and the first skyscraper incorporating massive wind turbines is the Atkins-designed Bahrain World Trade Center, completed in 2007.

The ten-storey Council House 2, a city administration block in Melbourne designed by Design Inc and the City itself, uses seven-eighths less energy and gas than older council offices. Photovoltaics may only contribute a few per cent of the building's needs, but that is enough to power the external window louvres which prevent build-up of solar gain (where trapped sunshine causes interior temperatures to soar). Many of its features and those in other buildings of all heights are invisible from the outside, such as onsite CHP (co-generation combined heat and power units), or fuel cells to reduce energy draw from the grid when wind or sun may not be 'harvested'. Another alternative energy supply is the use of biomass as a fuel. Furthermore, there are reported cuts in work-related stress and sickness given the benign effects of eco-buildings.

In the suburbs, zero-net-energy developments are already a reality. The BedZED development in southwest London, designed by Bill Dunster Architects, was completed in 2002 and includes 82 homes incorporating roof gardens, photovoltaics, CHP, low-embedded energy materials and planning that encourages walking and discourages car use. The Swedes are probably the leading nation to date in developing eco-suburbs. Hammerby Sjöstad in Stockholm and Västra Hamnen in Malmö are both new waterside developments that will house tens of thousands and showcase integrated environmental systems for energy, recycling and waste. They have architecturally varied environments and impressive transport networks. Developments like these are models for larger plans, like the Thames Gateway that stretches eastwards from London.

But the bigger challenge than building low-energy is retro-fitting the existing city. Berlin has been upgrading energy efficiency in its public sector buildings since 1997, and has cut their energy costs by about a quarter. Even well-designed new buildings can benefit—in 2005, the Jin Mao Tower in Shanghai, though only seven years old, had its energy consumption cut by a fifth by altering operations and maintenance practices—and replacing sliding doors with revolving ones. In 2006, the C40 Cities Climate Leadership Group initiated the Clinton Climate Initiative to tackle carbon emissions by pooling the cities' buying power on sustainable materials and infrastructure, synchronising environmental auditing, and working with the private sector to finance retrofits. One of the first schemes announced in 2008 is a renovation of London's Canary Wharf office buildings to cut carbon by a quarter. Simultaneously in Frankfurt—not one of the C40 cities—re-engineering began on Deutsche Bank's twin skyscrapers, with a target of halving its carbon footprint. In North America, the Commission for Environmental Co-operation reckoned in 2008 that retrofitting buildings across America, Canada and Mexico could reduce their annual emissions from 2.2 billion tons to 500 million. Director, Adrian Vazquez, was quoted on the BBC saying that "green building represents some of the ripest 'low-hanging fruit' for achieving significant reductions in climate change emissions".

Big coastal cities can protect against flooding by storm surges with civil engineering, such as the construction of dykes (which protect The Netherlands) or flood barriers. Much of New York is just three metres above sea level, and as hurricanes grow more frequent, the prospect of the flooding of the subway and sewage systems gets ever more likely. Just three barriers similar to the Thames Flood Barrier would offer protection. In the Thames Gateway, an extension of wetlands is planned, with such natural features acting like massive sponges to their immediate environment.

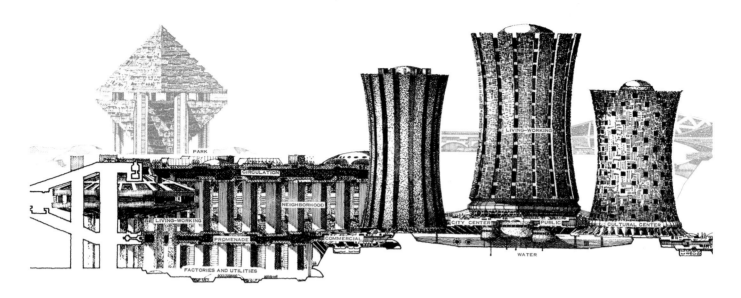

The green city of the future has parallels to the Garden City that Ebenezer Howard imagined a century ago—an integration of town and country. But it will be more vast, more compact and varied?

INSTANT ECO-CITIES

What if cities where designed from scratch with built-in sustainability? Now entire cities, rather than unique buildings, are being planned with sustainability and the environment in mind. The Italian-American architect Paolo Soleri is one of the first pioneers of such ideas. In 1955, he built himself an 'earth house' just outside Phoenix Arizona, using traditional techniques and exploiting the thermal properties of the ground in which it was submerged to keep cool in the day and warm at night. In the 1960s, he developed the concept of 'arcology'—that is, megastructures that combine ecology and architecture to house people at extreme densities with minimal use of resources (including land) and the aim of being self-sufficienct. In 1970, he started work on the trial-run desert arcology, a town called Arcosanti, projected to house 5,000. Arcosanti has been under construction since then, and is now a village occupying just a single hectare, with a few low-rise residential buildings, a visitors centre, an amphitheatre and bronze-making facilities.

Not yet a success, however, Arcosanti could soon find itself with a new and massive neighbour. One of the new generation of eco-cities is being planned by London-based Arup Associates, who are proposing a solar powered town with the capacity to accomodate 300,000 people. Another Arup-planned development—the world's first zero-energy city which will eventually house 500,000— is planned for Dongtan, which is sited on an island in the estuary of the Yangtze River, not far from downtown Shanghai. Polder embankments will provide protection against a (currently) one-in-a-millennium storm event. Carbon neutrality is achieved by a planned energy mix of 30 per cent wind, five per cent solar and anaerobic digestion, and 60 per cent from biomass—the last, it is hoped, will come largely from rice husks grown locally. The city will have town densities as well: somewhere between 200 and 240 people per hectare, representing the densities of only a third of built-up Shanghai and comparable to European cities.

Arup have taken the lead in the current proliferation of eco-cities, citing Dongtan as an "ecological demonstrator". But other designers are also exploring this area. Foster+Partners have been planning a zero-net-carbon university town in Abu Dhabi called Masdar, which will accomodate 30,000 as well as 36,000 commuters. The main driver in the masterplan is energy, and here, Masdar draws deeply on the vernacular architecture that has long given Arab urbanism equilibrium within the desert. Features such as tiered gardens, with the cool colonnaded gardens below and a hot, exposed plot above, as well as water pools

Above: Paolo Soleri's BABELNOAH Arcology, which proposes to construct a site (in a coastal flat region whose density is 333 acres by 800–1,700 metres) that could accommodate a population of up to 6,000,000. This illustration was originally published in the revered text *Arcology—City in the Image of Man*. Image courtesy of the Cosanti Foundation.

Opposite: The EDITT Tower, designed by Ken Yeang, won the 1998 competition for Ecological Design in the Tropics. The project proposes to rehabilitate a site classified as "zero-culture": a completely urban, non-organic site where the natural ecosystem has been completely devastated. The Tower's design ensures that it will be 55 per cent self-sufficient in terms of water supply (using both collection and rainwater) and will

also gain nearly 40 per cent of its energy from solar paneling. The building is designed so as to direct wind for ventilation, and uses ceiling fans to reduce the need for refrigerant-based air conditioning; providing all the comforts its occupants might expect.

and wind towers, are integrated into a compact city walled within a square in which driverless vehicles operate at ground level while pedestrians circulate above. Streets are orientated to the prevailing winds for cooling and shaded by vegetation and canopies. Energy demand will be moderated by the thermal massing of buildings and will come from a mix including photovoltaics, wind and thermal 'tubes', while water demand will be met by solar-powered facilities. In 2008, Foster+Partners are extending Masdar's ideas to the larger Blue Town project in Oman, and they are also masterplanning a set of car-free hill-towns in the Bulgarian oak forests and the valleys around Byala, Bulgaria.

FEEDING THE CITY

Transporting food costs energy and food-miles is a growing energy issue with literally global consequences. There are good reasons for bringing the farm to the city, and designs for urban skyscraper 'farms' that operates all year round are already being proposed.

The Netherlands is a small country where long-distance travel is not an issue. In 2001, Rotterdam architects MVRDV publicised a proposal called Pig City. The thesis informing Pig City follows: if all Dutch pigs were raised organically, three-quarters of the country would need to be dedicated to pig farming, and the whole country would be an extreme eco-disaster zone. Hence, Pig City houses all 15 million Dutch pigs, their feed production, biomass-recycling, slaughter facilities and even balconies with trees, in 76 towers each 622 metres high.

Pigs are one thing but there is a continuing rise in vegetarianism and demi-vegetarianism in sophisticated urban society, as well as the world at large. Furthermore, it is more efficient to 'grow' plants than animals, which are major contributors to methane production, a gas with 23 times the greenhouse effect of carbon dioxide. The Tour Vivante is a 2006 plan by Paris-based soa architects to grow tomatoes, salads and strawberries in a mixed-use tower 102 metre high,

Above: TR Hamzah and Yeang, Chongqing Tower, China. Based on ecologically sound principles, Hamzah and Yeang's Chongqing Tower in China is meant to be a low-energy building, easily adaptable to different climatic needs.

Opposite: Proposed by the Rotterdam-based architects, MVRDV, for the first Biennial of Architecture in The Netherlands, 2003, *Container City* comprises 3,500 containers (recycled from those that are traditionally used in the trade industry) which act as the floor, walls and ceiling of an immense space whose central point is a giant hall. Around this are areas for sleeping, eating, exhibiting, and performing. It also provides space for hotels, bars, galleries, a spa, conference spaces, shops, business units, ateliers, schools, and crèches. each container can be accessed by galleries, stairs and 'construction lifts'.

Following pages: MVRDV's Pig City is an innovative design consisting of giant high-rise towers dedicated to organic pig farming. The idea is to reduce the spread of diseases and avoid unnecessary transportation and distribution by concentrating production on one single area.

topped with windmills and employing a full range of eco-technologies such as photovoltaics, passive ventilation, rainwater collection, grey-water re-use and low embedded-energy materials. In 2007, another curtain-walled urban skyscraper farm using hydroponic farming techniques—also 30 storeys high—was proposed by Columbia University's Dickson Dupommier. This project was powered by a photovoltaic roof dish with biomass generated internally. Simultaneously, architect Gordon Graff produced plans for an open-air SKYfarm with 58 storeys situated in downtown Toronto, designed to feed 35,000 people with a full range of vegetables, as well as chickens and eggs which would be battery-farmed on the northern side of the 'farm'.

Agriculture is already a mechanised multi-billion dollar business, and a prime driver of deforestation. It long ago moved indoors with the invention of the greenhouse. With urban skyscraper farms, the greenhouse effect is tackled head-on, and may even allow the traditional small-scale country farm to prosper again, competing with urban produce and able to command a price premium for authenticity. In the developing world, water could be desalinated with solar energy (as in Masdar) or biomimetic techniques, which mimic the functions or even the form of living things, such as the structures planned by British architects Grimshaw in their Santa Catalina Isthmus project for the Canary Islands. Such technologies would enable coastal skyscraper farms that could revolutionise food supply. These, and other schemes elaborate the thesis that skyscrapers could be a part of the future of food production, and a powerful tool in the sustainability of our built environment.

1. World Resources Institute Climate Analysis
Indicators Tool (CAIT) on-line database for 2004.

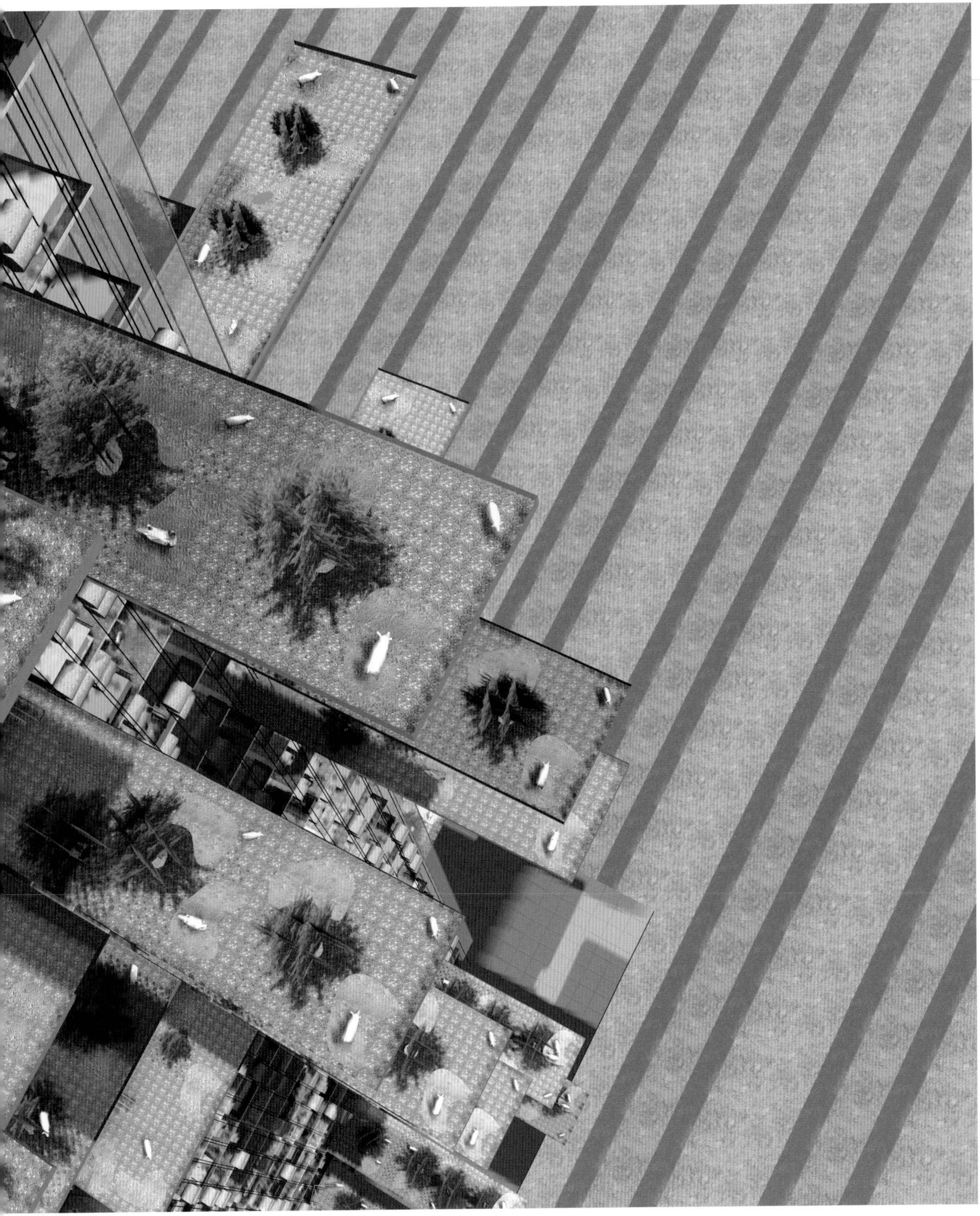

RIZHAO

Rizhao is a prefecture-level regional city on the southeastern coast of the Shandong peninsula in China, with an area of 5,310 square kilometres and a population of just less than three million people. Its name roughly translates from the Chinese as "city first to get the sunshine"; very appropriate, since Rizhao is a city which makes unusually good use of its solar resources. An incredible 99 per cent of Rizhao's urban households use solar water heaters to generate their hot water, and more than 6,000 families use solar cookers in their kitchens. Nearly all the city's traffic signals, street lighting and park illuminations are powered by photovoltaic solar cells. In June 2007, the city authorities won a World Clean Energy Award for Policy and Lawmaking, and the city was designated as an Environmental Protection Model City by the central Chinese government.

A radical municipal retrofit programme to clean up the city's energy generation and consumption begun in 2001 when the new Mayor, Li Zhaoqian, made it mandatory for all existing buildings in the city centre district to install solar water heating systems, so that new buildings could not pass new stringent planning and building regulations without their inclusion. The city now has over half a million square metres of solar water heating panels in operation, reducing conventional electricity use by 348 million kilowatts each year, and the government is working on mandating other forms of clean energy generation.

This thermo-solar strategy is part of the Rizhao municipal government's wider commitment to reducing the city's carbon emissions and air pollution, diversifying its energy generation and creating what they term a 'circular economy', where otherwise wasted energy is conserved, and industrial, agricultural and domestic waste is reduced, recycled or utilised by other industries. In Rizhao's outlying rural areas, for example, solar energy is being harnessed to increase the land temperature for agricultural production to ensure faster maturation of crops in the spring. During the fallow season, 470 million square metres of farmland is covered in biodegradable plastic film, which acts as a giant greenhouse. Also, more than 60,000 greenhouses are heated by solar panels, reducing overhead costs for farmers. Methane gas—a byproduct of agriculture and the wastewater treatment industry—is being generated and collected on both an industrial and domestic scale, fuelling generators which can produce enough energy annually to substitute for around 40,000 tons of coal. With the utilisation of solar energy across agriculture, construction, lighting and heating, 3.8 billion kilowatts of electricity can be saved every year in Rizhao, displacing 1.44 million tons of coal. By 2010, it is estimated that ten per cent of Rizhao's energy needs will be met by solar and methane-generated electricity, and these methods are just the beginning for Rizhao's development and adoption of clean energy technologies; research is currently being conducted into the local applications of geothermal and wind power.

High-impact industries which previously contributed to harmful emissions and pollution are being upgraded, and fitted out with new technology, to allow energy and water conservation, clean production practices and the comprehensive utilisation of resources. Small-scale, low density operations are being amalgamated or shut down.

In 2005, Rizhao passed the ISO14001 Environmental Management System Regional Certification audit, and was listed as an EMCP project (EU-China Environmental Management Cooperation Programme),

RIZAHO AND ARCOSANTI

One of many urbanised
areas in Rizhao,
circa 1990s.

bringing their environmental management in
line with international practice.

Air pollution in Rizhao has subsequently
dramatically improved, and the city is now
ranked one of the top ten cities in China for air
quality. Sulphur dioxide and carbon dioxide
emissions have been reduced significantly,
and it has been estimated that, through
the use of solar energy and methane gas
and the elimination of polluting industries,
Rizhao's carbon emissions can be reduced by
3,300,000 tons, sulphur by 21,600 tons, and
ash dust by 20,300 tons.

Developing a positive environmental profile
has enhanced Rizhao's economic and social
profile too. Its reputation as an eco-city has
triggered a positive cycle of an increasing
amount of direct foreign investment, and
has spurred a growth in tourism to the area.
Universities are constructing campuses in
the city, and many academics have bought
second or retirement homes there.

What is most remarkable about Rizhao's
environmental achievements is the extent
to which the commitment to clean energy
has been popularised and mainstreamed

in such a short period of time. Rizhao was,
until 2001, a relatively ordinary Chinese
city, facing the same environmental issues as
every other mid-size regional conurbation: it
was not a city designed with sustainability
and clean energy in mind, and it was rapidly
urbanising; being heavily dependent on coal
for its energy, and its economy was largely
based on inefficient low density light industry
and small-scale agriculture. Per capita income
in Rizhao is below the national average, and
it did not look at all like a candidate for a full-
scale environmental turnaround.

But the holistic and pragmatic strategy
adopted by Rizhao's government produced
startling results. First of all, they were mindful
of Rizhao's low GDP; any system which
required heavy personal investment would
not be popular. One way to get around this—
using a method often employed in Britain
to increase take-up of new environmentally
sound technologies—is to subsidise the
purchase and installation of a system. But
this can lead to stagnation in the price of the
system in the long term, and can condemn
a government to subsidise it forever. The
Rizhao government instead subsidised
industry research and development, which
quickly brought the unit cost of a solar water

heating system down to the same price as electric alternatives (to around £100). They also highlighted the money saving benefits of the system: using a solar water heater for 15 years costs around £1,000, less than a conventional electric system, and saving nearly £70 per year on utility bills. It was also made as simple and easy to adopt as possible: solar panels could be mounted directly on walls and roofs with little modification, and the government offered on-site assistance. Consequently, even in Rizhao's outlying suburban and rural areas where solar powered water heaters are not mandated, more than 30 per cent of households use them anyway. Industrially, the municipal government offered companies tax incentives to fit methane generators, exempting them from wastewater charges, for example.

In contrast to many Western governments' reticence in adopting new environmental technologies, the Rizhao government were extremely proactive in encouraging research and development, and then enshrining the new technology in mainstream policy to ensure its adoption. Where many governments make token gestures towards clean energy and sustainability, Rizhao is an example of a city where strong governance

and well-planned strategy—similar to that of Curitiba in Brazil—has yielded high adoption rates. An awareness-raising, public education initiative accompanied the introduction of the solar heater legislation, with clinics and lectures laid on alongside television adverts and guidance publications. Government officials' homes were the first to have the systems installed, projecting a positive message to the city's residents.

Rizhao offers a unique model for the retrofitting of clean energy systems which will need to take place across already-existing cities in China and the rest of the world. There is great value in the lessons to be gleaned from eco-cities, 'from-the-ground-up' developments like Dongtan, but they are of limited use in ecologically rehabilitating older urban areas. Cities like Rizhao offer a testbed for new technologies in extant settings, and an opportunity to examine the role that legislation plays in ensuring universal adoption. In terms of real, practical ways to change how we live within our current urban spaces there can be few more critical areas for development than this.

ARCOSANTI

Arcosanti is the famously unfinished experimental city 110 kilometres north of Phoenix in the Arizona desert, begun by Italian-born architect Paolo Soleri and his Cosanti Foundation in 1970. In 1976 *Newsweek* proclaimed that, "as urban architecture, Arcosanti is probably the most important experiment undertaken in our lifetime"; by 2008, it is a crumbling architectural curiosity that survives thanks to the efforts of a group of dogged disciples.[1]

Arcosanti is one of the few built examples of an 'arcology' (a portmanteau from the words 'architecture' and 'ecology'), a loose term used to describe the design of super-dense hyperstructures constituting self-contained and self-sustaining 'cities'. With their highly integrated and intensely compact and dense form, these structures are designed to minimise human environmental impact and enable the conservation of energy and resources, bringing the living and the built into harmony. Miniaturisation and densification are the guiding principles of arcologies. In contrast to organically-developed cities, which sprawl in two dimensions and are highly inefficient, arcology design aims to produce complex

and efficient constructions in three dimensions. Man and society have evolved, Soleri argues in his book *Arcology: The City in the Image of Man*, into complex and efficient organisms, and we do the societal institution of the city a fatal disservice in allowing it to evolve in this inefficient way.

An arcology requires around two per cent of the land footprint of a traditional city to house an equivalent number of people, eliminating the need for automobiles, and approximately ten per cent of the water to service it. Many arcology designs are highly speculative and represent urban 'thought experiments' in which the outer reaches of planning and architecture are explored. The ultimate in arcology design—which, as a discipline, largely remains unrealised due to its vast scale—is perhaps Soleri's 'Hyper Building', a one kilometre high construction catering to the every need of its 100,000 residents. It exists only on paper.

Arcosanti was intended to make solid this philosophy, and to do nothing less than reconfigure humanity's relationship to their dwellings, their cities and their planet. It was not designed for 100,000—in the manner of the Hyper Building—but,

rather (and more realistically), for 5,000 inhabitants. Soleri was first introduced to the Arizona desert when working on his mentor Frank Lloyd Wright's Taliesin West in the 1940s. In 1970 he deemed the 16.5 square kilometre site—a basaltic mesa overlooking the Agua Fria river north of Phoenix—the perfect environment to reveal man's folly and designed a poured-concrete megastructure, intended to occupy only .1 square kilometres of the site and, to utilise radical conservation methods. Construction was undertaken by a group of committed volunteers; despite the contemporary media is trumpeting of the project it was given no official funding, a situation which persists to this day.

Its dense three-dimensional construction incorporates many conservation features which were considered radical in the 1970s, and remain so today. Evaporative cooling pools release moisture into the arid desert air and, in winter, heat from the foundry furnace is collected and redistributed throughout the apartments above. In the future, an 'energy apron' around the perimeter of the site is proposed, whereby greenhouses trap heat and disperse it through the dwellings during the colder months. Great emphasis is placed upon

Aerial view Arcosanti, Arizona Photograph by Bruce Colbert.

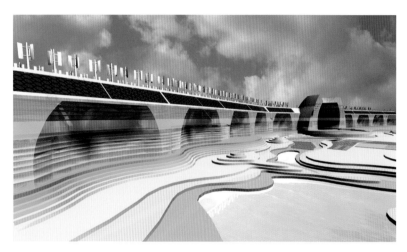

Paolo Soleri's most recent Arcology design, SOLARE The Lean Linear City. Image courtesy of 3D by Dennis Konstantin Gerigk.

communal responsibility and on-site duties are divided between residents. Residents and visitors are keen to dispel the idea that Arcosanti is any sort of commune, however, and insist that they work for one purpose only: "To make arcology work."[2]

However the skyline of modern-day Arcosanti, many visitors note, doesn't do justice to the grand ideals that underpin the project; a pair of concrete apses, a network of modular concrete dwellings, some old cranes and the other detritus of protracted construction fail to adequately illustrate the

revolutionary potential felt at its inception. Only four per cent of the proposed structure has been completed, and the resident population of Arcosanti remains at just 100. The Cosanti Foundation's website optimistically states that the project will house 5,000 when complete, but quite when this completion will occur is unclear.

Despite Arcosanti's chronic underfunding, it manages to eke an existence as an educational facility. It offers a four-week workshop programme which teaches building techniques and arcological philosophy, whilst

continuing the community's construction. Many architecture students attend these workshops, and often receive university credit for it. Soleri himself still lives near Phoenix and spends a few days a week at Arcosanti. Residents—mostly alumni of the workshop programme themselves—offer instruction in planning, computer aided design, maintenance, carpentry, metal work and ceramics. As an educational process, then, Arcosanti functions quite well with short-term interns passing through at a steady rate. Even as a tourist attraction it works to a certain extent; the Arcosanti foundry turns out bronze 'Soleri bells' to sell to the estimated 40,000–50,000 visitors passing through as a profitable sideline. As a functioning city (its raison d'être), however, it has not achieved Soleri's revolutionary aim.

There is an uncomfortable irony in the undeniable creep of the outer suburban sprawl of Phoenix ever closer to the boundary of the Arcosanti site, with cookie-cutter sub-divisions now residing just at the end of the access road, and locals suspecting the residents of Arcosanti of belonging to some sort of cult. It could be said that, even in its early days, there was an inclement historical climate for constructing a hyper-urbanised concrete megastructure in the desert. Now, it occupies prime land and its philosophy seems quaint in an era of ultra rapid low density development. What was once considered to be the future of intelligent urban design has descended into something bleaker: a stalled vision of revolutionary urban planning that was just too ahead of its time. An eternal failed prototype, or the ruins of the future, perhaps.

The physical realisation of Arcosanti as an exemplar of arcological theory may have disappointed, but the philosophy behind it is another matter. The message is finally getting through that sprawling development is detrimental to the environment and to quality of life, and organisations like Smart Growth America and movements such as the New Urbanist school of planning are emphasising the importance of densification in creating viable urban communities. Similarly 'sustainability' is a current buzzword in urban development, with many of Soleri's passive heat collection and water conservation theories being scaled up for commercial use, and even being mandated in some of the world's cities. Arcologies—self-contained cities— still preoccupy the global architectural

imagination, particularly in visionary and speculative architecture. Foster+Partners' proposed Millennium Tower—a 170-floor, 840 metre high cone-shaped arcology, to be situated two kilometres out into Tokyo Bay, and intended to accommodate and service the needs of 60,000 people—is such an example. It too remained unrealised, but we are getting closer to achieving the technology that would make a full-scale arcology a real possibility in the not-too-distant-future. Arcosanti might then be judged as the forerunner of the real cities of the future.

1. Davis, Douglas, "Arcosanti: Dream City", *Newsweek*, No. 78–79, 1976.

2. An Arcosanti student quoted in Chris Colin, "Sipping From a Utopian Well in the Desert", *The New York Times*, 16 September 2007.

ELEVATION FIVE AND THE FUTURE OF GREEN

Peter Clegg

David King, the British government's chief scientific advisor, suggests that climate change is a more significant threat than terrorism. If so, then architects need to move to the front line and adopt a carefully considered battle strategy. Their advance should be driven by an improved appreciation of conservation technology and bio-climatic design, as well as by changes in attitude and lifestyle in respect of energy use. The history of green architecture could be described as learning by experience; trial, and occasionally error. The first generation of green buildings (in Britain, at least) tended to rely on passive solar design. These failed when we realised that adding extra insulation to the building envelope simply reduced the heating season to the few months of the year when there was no solar energy to harness. The second generation preoccupied itself with thermal mass, daylight rather than sunlight, and light-time cooling. These strategies worked but, quite often, measured performance demonstrated failures in the basics of air-tightness and under-estimated the increase in internal gains from equipment. The land is now shifting beneath our feet. Climate change is beginning to kick in and has added a couple of degrees to peak summer temperatures that we need to design for. And an insatiable appetite for more power at our fingertips, in both home and office, means that electricity costs and the consequent internal gains in our buildings continue to rise.

Whereas over the last 20 years we have looked to northern Europe (and particularly Scandinavia) for innovation in reducing energy demands, we now look to the south for our precedents. The art of shading will become an even more significant part of our architectural language. As for the ever-increasing use of electricity, we can either decide that power generation is beyond our architectural remit, or we can specify highly efficient equipment and investigate turning our buildings into generators. In these circumstances, the roof plane becomes the most significant climatic moderator and, as our theoretical study showed at the National Trust, for an office building in Britain to approach carbon neutrality, providing all of its heating, cooling and power requirements on site, a low-rise solution has considerable advantages. Day lighting from roof lights is almost three times as efficient as from windows, and roof planes are the most efficient location for photovoltaics. Land values, however, may dictate that more conventional shallow-plan, high-rise solutions are more economic and may, because of the urban density they achieve, be more sustainable.

OPTIMISM—OUT FROM THE SHADOWS

As for lifestyle changes, we do need to be wary of overdosing on climate change and indulging in guilt. Real changes will only take place through a combination of education and legislation, with a recognition that a lower carbon lifestyle can provide real benefits. These include improving the urban realm, encouraging higher density living without burning unnecessary transportation energy, where the advantages of high quality open space, social space, communal facilities and employment opportunities all co-exist. There are precedents which prove that this sort of vision can work.

Curitiba in Brazil has revolutionised public transport much more successfully than countries which may think themselves more 'developed'. Freiberg in Germany has produced a new urban architecture (using local practices) and set new standards for sustainable community planning. Germany's plans for a renewable

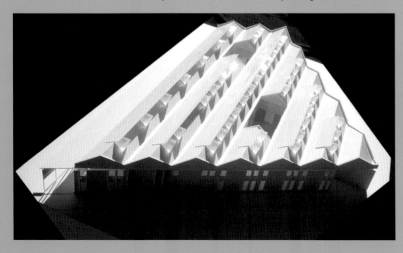

energy future are firmly rooted in projects that depend on community energy supply companies. So the next generation of real 'green' architecture and planning; is likely to focus on the urban scale, integrating transport planning, urban landscape and building communities around car sharing, food co-ops and local energy supply companies.

There is a desperate need to learn from these initiatives, and to cooperate in advancing our understanding of reducing carbon emissions. Looking to America we need to circumnavigate the White House and consider what is being done at the more grassroots level of states, cities and communities. There are 164 American cities (as of 10 June 2005) that have signed up to Kyoto principles. The American benchmarking system known as LEED (Low Energy Environmental Design) has a much higher uptake than its British counterpart BREEAM (BRE Environmental Assessment Method). Technologies of photovoltaics, hydrogen and fuel cell development are more advanced, and a combination of technology and motivation could be harnessed to slow down the gas guzzling machinery that gives the country such a bad name. But as Thorn Mayne's new government building in San Francisco proves, there is still a need for icons (or paradigms) of green design, for buildings to tell stories, to reflect the social concerns of their time and to nail colours to an environmental mast.

A QUIETER PARADIGM

We need to clarify our definition of 'green'. The familiar iconography of timber, glass and grass roofs of 20 years ago needs to be called into question. There is an argument that locking up as much timber in buildings for as long as possible helps develop forest industries which sequester carbon. However, it is easy to produce over-glazed buildings which end up on the wrong side of the equation that links daylight to heat loss—and green roofs can look great and help with rainwater attenuation but don't stand up to much greater environmental scrutiny.

It is significant that the non-domestic building in Britain with the lowest operational carbon dioxide emissions is still, as far as we know, John Miller's Elizabeth Fry building at the Universtity of East Anglia (UEA). Built ten years ago using high thermal mass and insulation, a modest amount of glazing and a heat recovery ventilation system, it is not designed to proselytise. Architectural solutions don't need to be overtly green, despite the fact that clients and users often demand that they be so. Both a new iconography and a quieter language need to be developed, in tandem with a benchmarking system that should be part of the public understanding of buildings. We are familiar with the environmental performance of our cars: we can understand the scale of kilometres per gallon and even kilograms of carbon dioxide per kilometre, how long before the profession, let alone the public, can quantify our buildings in terms of annual carbon dioxide emissions? The European directive requiring energy labelling will help, but the sooner we demand, advertise and most importantly measure those statistics, the easier it will be to expose false icons and develop a new visual understanding of 'green'.

Opposite left: Model of Heelis, the National Trust offices in Swindon, Britain, designed by Feilden Clegg Bradley Architects. Image courtesy of Feilden Clegg Bradley Architects.

Opposite right: A bus stop in Curitiba, Brazil. The city has an innovative masterplanned transportation system which consists solely of buses. Some streets are dedicated to the city's bus system, which aims to provide a high-quality service similar to that of rail transit. Image courtesy of Steven Wright.

Top: The Elizabeth Fry Building, University of East Anglia, Britain. Image courtesy of John Miller + Partners.

Bottom: The Elizabeth Fry Building at the University of East Anglia, designed by John Miller. Completed in 1995, the building has continued to achieve extremely low energy consumption and emissions through temperature regulation. Image courtesy of John Miller + Partners.

FURTHER READING

Apollonio, Umbro, *Futurist Manifestos*, Boston, MA: Museum of Fine Arts, 2001.

Augé, Marc, Non-places: *Introduction to an Anthropology of Supermodernity*, London: Verso, 1995.

Ballard, JG, *High-Rise*, New York: Henry Holt, 1975.

Banham, Reyner, *Los Angeles: The Architecture of Four Ecologie*s, London: Allen Lane, 1971.

Baudrillard, Jean, *America*, London: Verso, 1989.

Baudrillard, Jean, *Simulacra and Simulation*, Ann Arbor, MI: University of Michigan Press, 1994.

Bell, Julian, *Mirror on the World*, London: Thames & Hudson, 2007.

Benevolo, Leonardo, *The Origins of Modern Town Planning*, Judith Landry trans., London: Routledge & Kegan Paul, 1967.

Berman, Marshall, *All that is Solid Melts into Air: The Experience of Modernity*, New York: Simon & Schuster, 1982.

Bernstein, Alan, Bob DeGrasse, et al, Silicon Valley: *Paradise or Paradox? The Impact of High Technology Industry on Santa Clara County*, Mountain View, CA: Pacific Studies Center, 1977.

Bishop, Ryan, John Phillips, et al, *Postcolonial Urbanism: Southeast Asian Cities and Global Processes*, New York: Routledge, 2003.

Boddy, M, J Lovering, et al, *Sunbelt City: A Study of Economic Change in Britain's M4 Growth Corridor*, Oxford: Clarendon Press, 1986.

Bottles, S L, *Los Angeles and the Automobile: The Making of the Modern City*, Berkeley: University of California Press, 1987.

Boyd, Andrew, *Chinese Architecture and Town Planning*, Chicago: University of Chicago Press, 1962.

Briggs, Asa, *Victorian Cities*, London: Oldhams Press, 1963.

Brilliant, Ashleigh, *The Great Car Craze: How Southern California Collided with the Automobile in the 1920s*, Santa Barbara: Woodbridge Press, 1989.

Brotchie, John, Mike Batty, et al, eds., *Cities in Competition: Productive and Sustainable Cities for the Twenty-First Century*, Melbourne: Longman Australia, 1995.

Brotchie, John, Mike Batty, et al, eds., *Cities of the Twenty-First Century: New Technologies and Spatial Systems*, Melbourne: Longman Cheshire, 1991.

Brotchie, John, Peter Newton, et al, eds., *The Future of Urban Form: The Impact of New Technology*, London: Croom Helm, 1985.

Brownill, Sue, *Developing London's Docklands: Another Great Planning Disaster?*, London: Paul Chapman, 1990.

Bunin, AV, *History of the Art of Urban Planning*, Moscow, 1953.

Burke, Gerald L, *The Making of Dutch Towns,* London: Cleaver-Hulme Press, 1956.

Cairncross, Frances, *The Death of Distance: How the Communications Revolution will Change our Lives*, London: Orion, 1997.

Calthorpe, Peter, *The Next American Metropolis: Ecology, Community and the American Dream*, Princeton: Princeton Architectural Press, 1993.

Calvino, Italo, *Invisible Cities*, Picador, London: 1980.

Castells, Manuel and Peter Hall, *Technopoles of the World: The Making of Twenty-First Century Industrial Complexes*, London: Routledge, 1994.

Castells, Manuel, *The Information Age: Economy, Society, and Culture, 1: The Rise of the Network Society*, Oxford: Blackwell, 1996.

Castells, Manuel, *The Information Age: Economy, Society, and Culture, 2: The Power of Identity*, Oxford: Blackwell, 1997.

Castells, Manuel, *The Information Age: Economy, Society, and Culture, 3: End of Millennium*, Oxford: Blackwell, 1998.

Castells, Manuel, *The Informational City: Information Technology, Economic Restructuring and the Urban-Regional Process*, Oxford: Blackwell, 1989.

Choay, Francoise, *The Modern City: Planning in the Nineteenth Century*, New York: George Braziller, 1969.

Chung, Chuihua, Rem Koolhaas et al, eds., *Great Leap Forward*, Cambridge, MA: Harvard Design School, 2001.

Coleman, Alice, *Utopia on Trial: Vision and Reality in Planned Housing*, London: Hilary Shipman, 1985.

Condit, Carl W, *The Rise of the Skyscraper*, Chigago: University of Chicago Press, 1952.

Conzen, Michael P, ed., *The Making of the American Landscape*, Boston: Unwin Hyman, 1990.

Cooke, Philip, *Back to the Future: Modernity, Postmodernity and Locality*, London: Unwin Hyman, 1990.

Curtis, William, *Modern Architecture since 1900*, Oxford: Phaidon, 1987.

Davis, Mike, *City of Quartz: Excavating the Future in Los Angeles*, London: Verso, 1990.

Davis, Mike, *Ecology of Fear: LA and the Imagination of Disaster*, New York: Metropolitan Books, Henry Holt, 1998.

Davis, Mike, *Planet of Slums*, London: Verso, 2007.

de Certeau, Michel, *The Practice of Everyday Life*, Berkeley: University of California Press, 2002.

Debord, Guy, *Society of the Spectacle*, Detroit: Black and Red, 1970.

Dick, Philip K, *Do Androids Dream of Electric Sheep?*, New York: Doubleday, 1968.

Douglass, Harlan P, *The Suburban Trend*, New York: Century, 1925.

Doxiadis, Constantinos A, *Ekistics, An Introduction to the Science of Human Settlements*, London: Hutchinson, 1968.

Estrangement, Albany, NY: State University of New York Press, 2003.

Fainstein, Susan S, *The City Builders: Property, Politics and Planning in London and New York*, Oxford: Blackwell, 1994.

Flink, James J, *The Automobile Age*, Cambridge, MA: MIT Press, 1988.

Flink, James J, *The Car Culture*, Cambridge, MA: MIT Press, 1975.

Flink, James J, *America Adopts the Automobile*, 1895–1910, Cambridge, MA: MIT Press, 1970.

Fulton, William, *The Reluctant Metropolis: The Politics of Urban Growth in Los Angeles*, Baltimore: Johns Hopkins University Press, 2001.

Garreau, Joel, *Edge City: Life on the New Frontier*, New York: Doubleday, 1991.

Gibson, William, *Neuromancer*, New York: Ace Books, 1984.

Giedion, Sigfried, *Space, Time and Architecture*, Cambridge, MA: Harvard University Press, 1941.

Girouard, Mark, *Cities and People: A Social and Architectural History*, New Haven: Yale University Press, 1985.

Goddard, JB, *Electronic Highways, Cities and Regions: Winners and Losers*. Paper presented to Section E (Geography), British Association for the Advancement of Science, Newcastle-upon-Tyne, September 1995.

Gosling, Nigel, *Leningrad*, New York: EP Dutton & Co. Inc., 1965.

Graham, Loren, *Science, Philosophy and Human Behaviour in the Soviet Union*, New York: Columbia University Press, 1987.

Graham, Stephen, and Simon Marvin, *Splintering Urbanism: Networked Infrastructure*s, Technological Mobilities and the Urban Condition, London: Routledge, 2001.

Gregotti, Vittorio, *Inside Architecture*, Cambridge, MA: MIT Press, 1996.

Hall, Peter, and Colin Ward, *Sociable Cities: The Legacy of Ebenezer Howard*, London: Routledge, 1998.

Hall, Peter, *Cities of Tomorrow: An Intellectual History of Urban Planning and Design in the Twentieth Century*, Oxford: Blackwell, 1996.

Hall, Thomas, ed., *Planning and Urban Growth in the Nordic Countries*, London: Spon, 1991.

Hall, Thomas, *Planning Europe's Capital Cities*, London: Spon, 1997.

Harvey, David, *The Condition of Postmodernity*, Oxford: Blackwell, 1990.

Haverfield, Francis, *Ancient Town Planning*, Oxford: Oxford University Press, 1913.

Hiorns, Frederick R, *Town Building in History: An Outline Review of Conditions, Influences, Ideas, and Methods affecting 'Planned' Towns through Five Thousand Years,* London: Harrap, 1956.

Hiorns, Frederick R, *Town-Building in History*, New York: Criterion, 1958.

Howard, Ebenezer, *Garden Cities of To-Morrow*, London: Faber & Faber, 1946.

Hughes, TH, and EAG Lamborn, *Towns and Town Planning: Ancient and Modern*, Oxford: Oxford Clarendon Press, 1923.

Jameson, Fredric, *Archaeologies of the Future: The Desire Called Utopia and Other Science Fictions*, London: Verso, 2007.

Jameson, Fredric, *Postmodernism, or The Cultural Logic of Late Capitalism*, London, Verso, 1992.

Jencks, Charles, *The Iconic Building*, London: Frances Lincoln Ltd., 2005.

Josephson, Paul, *New Atlantis Revisited*, New Jersey: Princeton University Press, 1997.

Kelbaugh, Doug ed., *The Pedestrian Pocket Book: A New Suburban Design Strategy*, New York: Princeton Architectural, 1989.

King, Anthony, *Global Cities: Post-Imperialism and the Internationalisation of London*, London: Routledge, 1990.

Knabb, Ken, *Situationist International Anthology*, Berkely, CA: Bureau of Public Secrets, 2002.

Koolhaas, Rem, and Bruce Mau, *S, M, L, XL*, New York: Monacelli Press, 2002.

Koolhaas, Rem, *Delirious New York*, New York: Monacelli Press, 1994.

Koolhaas, Rem, et al, *Mutations*, Barcelona: Actar, 2001.

Krause, Linda and Patrice Petro, *Global Cities: Cinema, Architecture and Urbanism in a Digital Age*, New Brunswick, NJ: Rutgers University Press, 2003.

Lawton, Richard ed., *The Rise and Fall of Great Cities: Aspects of Urbanisation in the Western World*, London: Belhaven, 1989.

Le Corbusier and Jeanneret, Pierre, *Oeuvre Complète, Zurich: Les Editions d'Architecture*, 1937.

Le Corbusier, *Concerning Town Planning*, Clive Entwistle trans., New Haven: Yale University Press, 1948.

Le Corbusier, *The Radiant City*, London: The Architectural Press, 1933.

Le Corbusier, *Concerning Town Planning*, London: The Architectural Press, 1946.

Le Corbusier, *Vers une architecture*, Paris: G Cres, 1923.

Leach, Neil, *Rethinking Architecture: A Reader in Cultural Theory*, London: Routledge, 1997.

Lefebvre, Henri, *The Production of Space*, Donald Nicholson-Smith trans., Oxford: Blackwell, 1991.

Lefebvre, Henri, *The Urban Revolution*, Minneapolis, MN: University of Minnesota Press, 2003.

Lefebvre, Henri, *Writing on Cities*, Oxford: Blackwell, 1995.

LeGates, Richard T ed., *The Cities Reader*, London: Routledge, 1996.

Lenin, Vladimir Ilyich, *Collected Works 1917–1923*, Moscow: Progress Publishers, 1969.

Lynch, Kevin, *Image of the City*, Cambridge, MA: MIT Press, 1960.

MacDonald, William L, *The Architecture of the Roman Empire*, New Haven: Yale University Press, 1965.

Mann, Eric et al., *A New Vision for Urban Transportation*, Los Angeles: Strategy Center Publications, 1996.

Mann, Eric et al., *LA's Lethal Air: New Strategies for Policy, Organising, and Action*, LCSC publication, 1991.

Martines, Lauro, *Power and Imagination: City States in Renaissance Italy*, London: Allen Lane, 1980.

Marx, Karl and Friedrich Engels, *The Communist Manifesto*, London: Penguin, 1848–2002.

Massey, Doreen, *World City*, Cambridge: Polity Press, 2007.

McLuhan, Marshall, *Understanding Media: The Extensions of Man*, New York: McGraw-Hill Book Company, 1964.

Mercer, *2007 Worldwide Quality of Living Survey*, Mercer Human Resource Consulting, 2007.

Mike Davis, "*LA After the Storm: The Dialectic of Ordinary Disaster*", Antipode, No. 27, 1995.

Miles, Malcolm, *Art, Space and the City*, New York: Routledge, 1997.

Miles, Malcolm, Tim Hall et al eds., *The City Cultures Reader*, London: Routledge, 2000.

Mitchel, William J, *City of Bits: Space, Place, and the Infobahn*, Cambridge, MA: MIT Press, 1995.

Morris, AEJ, *History of Urban Form: Before the Industrial Revolutions*, London: George Godwin, 1979.

Mumford, Lewis, *Technics and Civilisation*, New York: Harcourt Brace, 1934.

Mumford, Lewis, *The City in History: Its Origins, its Transformations, and its Prospects*, New York: Harcourt Brace, 1961.

Mumford, Lewis, *The Culture of Cities*, New York: Harcourt Brace, 1938.

Mumford, Lewis, *The Myth of the Machine, 1: Technics and Human Development*, London: Secker & Warburg, 1967.

Mumford, Lews, *The Highway and the City*, London: Secker & Warburg, 1964.

Negroponte, Nicholas, *Being Digital*, London: Hodder & Stoughton, 1995.

Neuwirth, Robert, *Shadow Cities: A Billion Squatters*, A New Urban World,

Newman, Oscar, *Creating Defensible Space*, Institute for Community Design Analysis, Rutgers: Diane Publishing Company, 1996.

Nicholas, David, *The Growth of the Medieval City: From Late Antiquity to the Early Fourteenth Century*, London: Longman, 1997.

Nicholas, David, *The Later Medieval City 1300–1500*, London: Longman, 1997.

Olsen, Donald J, *Town Planning in London*, New Haven: Yale University Press, 1964.

Oxford: Blackwell, 2006.

Pallot, Judith and Denis JB Shaw, *Planning in the Soviet Union*, London: Croom Helm, 1981.

Papadakaes, Andreas, Catherine Cooke, et al, *Deconstruction: Omnibus Volume*, New York: Rizzoli International, 1990.

Raban, Jonathan, *Soft City*, London: Fontana, 1972.

Rasmussen, Steen Eiler, *Experiencing Architecture*, Cambridge, MA: MIT Press, 1962.

Rasmussen, Steen Eiler, *London, The Unique City*, London: Jonathan Cape, 1937.

Rasmussen, Steen Eiler, *Towns and Buildings*, Cambridge, MA: Harvard University Press, 1951.

Regional Plan Association, *Urban Design: Manhattan*, New York: The Viking Press Inc., 1969.

Reps, John W, *The Making of Urban America*, Princeton: Princeton University Press, 1965.

Rogers, Richard, *Cities for a Small Planet*, London: Faber and Faber, 1997

Rosneau, Helen, *The Ideal City: Its Architectural Evolution in Europe*, London: Methuen, 1983.

Rowe, Colin, and Fred Koetter, *Collage City*, Cambridge, MA: MIT Press, 1978.

Rykwert, Joseph, *The Idea of a Town: The Anthropology of Urban Form in Rome*, Italy and the Ancient World, London: Faber & Faber, 1976.

Saarinen, Eliel, *The City*, New York: Reinhold Publishing Corporation, 1943.

Sadler, Simon, *The Situationist City*, Cambridge, MA: MIT Press, 1998.

Sansone, Vittorio, *Siberia: Epic of the Century*, Moscow: Progress Publishers, 1980.

Sassen, Saskia, *The Global City: New York, London, Tokyo*, Princeton: Princeton University Press, 2001.

Schultz, Stanley K, *Constructing Urban Culture: American Cities and City Planning*, 1800–1920, Philadelphia: Temple University Press, 1989.

Scott, Allen J, and Edward Soja eds., *The City: LA and Urban Theory at the End of the Twentieth Century*, Berkeley and Los Angeles: University of California Press, 1996.

Scully, Vincent, *The Earth, the Temple and the Gods*, New Haven: Yale University Press, 1962.

Sennett, Richard, *Classic Essays on the Culture of Cities*, Oxford: Oxford University Press, 1969.

Sitte, Camillo, *The Art of Building Cities*, New York: Reinhold Publishing Corporation, 1945.

Soja, Edward, *Postmetropolis: Critical Studies of Cities and Regions*, Oxford: Blackwell, 2000.

Soja, Edward, *Postmodern Geographies: The Reassertion of Space in Critical Social Theory*, London: Verso, 1989.

Soja, Edward, *Thirdspace: Journeys to Los Angeles and Other Real-and-Imagined Places,* Oxford: Blackwell, 1996.

Soleri, Paolo, *Arcology: The City in the Image of Man*, Cambridge, MA: MIT Press, 1969.

Spreiregen, Paul D, *Urban Design: The Architecture of Towns and Cities*, New York: McGraw-Hill, 1965.

Stave, Bruce M ed., *Modern Industrial Cities: History, Policy and Survival*, Beverly Hills: Sage, 1981.

Sudjic, Deyan, The 100 Mile City, New York: Harcourt, 1993.

Tafuri, Manfredo, *Architecture and Utopia*, Cambridge, MA: MIT Press, 1979.

Tafuri, Manfredo, *Modern Architecture*, New York: Harry N Abrams, 1980.

Tunnard, Christopher, *The City of Man*, New York: Charles Scribner's Sons, 1953.

United Nations Human Settlements Programme, *The Challenge of Slums: Global Report on Human Settlements 2003*, London: Earthscan Publications Ltd., 2003.

Venturi, Robert and Denise Scott Brown, *Learning From Las Vegas*, Cambridge, MA: MIT Press, 1972.

Vergara, Camilo, *The New American Ghetto*, New Brunswick, NJ: Rutgers University Press, 1995.

Vidler, Anthony, *Warped Space: Art, Architecture and Anxiety in Modern Culture*, Cambridge, MA: MIT Press, 2002.

Virilio, Paul, *Ground Zero*, London: Verso, 2002.

Wachs, Martin, *The Car and the City: The Automobile, the Built Environment, and Daily Urban Life*, Ann Arbor: University of Michigan Press, 1992.

Wigley, Mark, *Constant's New Babylon: The Hyper-architecture of Desire*, Rotterdam, 010 Publishers, 1998.

Wigley, Mark, *The Architecture of Desire: Derrida's Haunt*, Cambridge, MA: MIT Press, 1993.

Wittkower, Rudolf, *Architectural Principles in the Age of Humanism*, London: Alec Tiranti Ltd., 1952.

Yutang, Lin, *Imperial Peking*, New York: Crown Publishers Inc., 1961.

Zevi, Bruno, *Architecture as Space*, New York: Horizon Press, 1964.

The editor wishes to thank Aimee Selby and Nikolaos Kotsopoulos for their invaluable help with picture research, William McBean, Raven Smith and Diana Craig for stepping in at the last minute and Nadine Monem for her continual support and advice throughout the project. Special thanks must go to Maria Crossan for her eloquent and insightful texts and to Julia Trudeau-Rivest for her undivided commitment to the project and for creating such a beautifully designed volume.

Editor: Blanche Craig at Black Dog Publishing.
Assistant Editors: Nadine Kathë Monem and Nikolaos Kotsopoulos at Black Dog Publishing.
Designer: Julia Trudeau Rivest at Black Dog Publishing.

Black Dog Publishing Limited
10A Acton Street
London WC1X 9NG
United Kingdom

Tel: +44 (0) 20 7713 5097
Fax: +44 (0) 20 7713 8682
info@blackdogonline.com
www.blackdogonline.com

British Library Cataloguing-in-Publication Data.

A CIP record for this book is available from the
British Library.

ISBN: 978 1 906155 34 6

Black Dog Publishing Limited, London, UK, is an environmentally responsible company.
Instant Cities is printed on Sappi Magno Satin, a chlorine-free paper, FSC certified.

architecture art design
fashion history photography
theory and things

black dog
publishing

www.blackdogonline.com london uk